CATCH UP WITH
TOP
ACHIEVERS
2020 HSC
and Beyond

Edited by Adam Ma and Fionn Parker

Copyright © 2020 by Adam Ma

The moral rights of the author have been asserted

All rights reserved.

Except as permitted under the Australian Copyright Act 1968 (for example, a fair dealing for the purposes of study, research, criticism or review), no part of this book may be reproduced or used in any manner without written permission of the copyright owner except for the use of quotations in a book review.

For more information, email: info@top-achievers.com.au

 A catalogue record for this book is available from the National Library of Australia

Book design by Grzegorz Japoł (www.book-cover.design)

Editing by Fionn Parker and Jesse Caminer

Illustrations by Grace Hue @xxakanebloomxx, and Jenny Tan

Cover image: iStock

ISBN 978-0-6485633-4-1 (paperback)

ISBN 978-0-6485633-5-8 (epub)

ISBN 978-0-6485633-6-5 (mobi)

Disclaimer

The material in this publication is of the nature of general comment only, and does not represent professional advice. It is not intended to provide specific guidance for particular circumstances and it should not be relied on as the basis for any decision to take action or not take action on any matter which it covers. Readers should obtain professional advice where appropriate, before making any such decision. To the maximum extent permitted by law, the author and publisher disclaim all responsibility and liability to any person, arising directly or indirectly from any person taking or not taking action based on the information in this publication.

NESA does not endorse and is not affiliated with Catch Up With Top Achievers. NESA provides the only official, up-to-date versions of NESA publications and information about courses including HSC. HSC® is a registered trademark of NESA.

Top-Achievers.com.au

TO MUM AND DAD, FOR FEEDING ME.

YEET 2.0.

Welcome

G'day, and welcome back to another edition of Catch Up With Top Achievers. We are extremely excited to have you on board with us in this brand new edition: **2020 HSC and Beyond.**

In this project, we have an exclusive insight into the daily lives of successful HSC Top Achievers:

WHAT were their strategies for success?

HOW did they cope with the stress?

WHY did they work so hard?

It is easy to fall into the trap of thinking that all a Top Achiever does during Year 12 is studying. While this is true for some students, it is not the case for the majority, and definitely not those in this book! Don't get me wrong, in order to achieve great results, you must still put in a significant amount of work to perfect your craft. However, the methods used to approach that work can lead to completely different results. Study both smart and hard, not one or the other!

There is no doubt about it - Year 12 will be a tough year, perhaps the hardest of your life. In the following chapters, you will be given lots of practical advice as to how to study for your HSC exams whilst simultaneously maintaining a balanced, healthy lifestyle.

The contributors of this manuscript have all achieved the best possible results in their area of expertise. It is our hope that, after reading this book, you will too.

Now is your time to shine.

Adam Ma

Founder of Catch Up With Top Achievers

Acknowledgement

Every revolution requires a spark and this one is no different.

As I reflect on last year's journey, I couldn't help myself but to start giggling. Last year did not turn out to be what I had imagined. It was filled with lots of emotions, opportunities, head-spinning news, and newly formed friendships.

But as much as I want to cherish those undeniably enriching moments, I must also admit that there were moments when I felt the most vulnerable. The moments when I doubted myself, and the moments when I thought of leaving. If I could give you one tip, it would be to fail. Fail more and fail harder. Fail so much that you start crying you heart out. Because after all, you have just discovered what not to do, so you became another step closer to the final destination.

Fortunately, with the help of my friends and family, I was able to push through the hardships and continue to grow.

I want to start by thanking mum and dad, Guifang and Zhiping, for always being there for me no matter how agitated I can become. I truly wish time could go slower.

Next, I want to thank Fionn Parker, my editor-in-chief. With b**d**k69@gmail.com being his initial response to my ideas at the end of 2018, all I can say is that we have come a long way since the beginning and there is so much more ahead of us.

For making this year's project into reality, I am thankful to this year's contributors (last name in alphabetical order), Joel Aaron, Tallulah-Rose Adams, Zair Ahmed, Jesse Caminer, Matthew Drielsma, Nicholas Fakira, Christopher Marc Farag, Adam Gottschalk, Lara Hather, Sophie Catherine Howard, Sarah Kaunk, Seohyeong Lim, Julia Lo Russo, Wenquan Lu, Daniel Ross Monteiro, Patrick Nah, Adam Robey, Emma Cate Scroope, Lachlan Tran, Finn Spencer Vercoe, and John Wang. Needless to say, they are the cornerstones of this project.

For help with preparing the manuscript, I want especially to show my artistic appreciation to Fionn Parker and Jesse Caminer for editing and collaborating as a team.

For priceless guidance and assistance, I am thankful for Scott Yung, Helen Sham Ho, and Nathalie Rafeh of UNSW Founders. I am especially thankful to the Parkers, for their unlimited support since the beginning.

For media coverage, I am thankful to the producer at Channel 7's Sunday Sunrise, the State Library of NSW, Dan Cox of the ABC Radio, Cranbrook School, Jingliang Wu of Sydney Today, Donnay Torr of Skills Road, and Southern Media. I'm especially thankful to Jordan Barker, the education editor of the Sydney Morning Herald, for allowing me to showcase this incredible resource to the world.

For last year's book launch, I am thankful to Richard Zhou, Yuhao Chen, Benjamin Luong, Dora Wang, Dwyane Chen, Han Zhang, Haowei Du, John Jiang, and Max Whillias for volunteering.

For help with illustrations, I am thankful to Jenny Tan, and Grace Xue.

My sincere apologies to everybody else who ought to have been remembered here.

As always, the best is yet to come.

February 2020

Adam Ma

Contents

Welcome	VII
Acknowledgement	IX
"They Were Born Smart" - An Introduction of Misconceptions	1
About Us	5
English: To Memorise or Not to Memorise and Mastering the New Syllabus *Jesse Caminer*	7
Ancient History: Staying in my own lane *Sophie Howard*	43
Biology: it's in your DNA *Adam Gottschalk*	63
Economics: Studying Economics economically *John Wang*	81
Economics: Attaining Maximum Output in Economics *Patrick Nah*	97
Earth and Environmental Science: The Hidden Gem of Sciences *Matthew Drielsma*	115
Engineering StuDIES: How to not die *Adam Robey*	125
Geography: How I achieved stress-free HSC success by eating SUBWAY® sandwiches (and studying) *Lachlan Tran*	149
The Rules of Law - Getting through HSC Legal Studies *Zair Ahmed*	167
Hacking Modern History *Seohyeong Lim*	183
PDHPE: How to make studying your new favourite sport *Emma Scroope*	201

Physics: The High School Uncertainty Principle *Daniel Monteiro and Wenquan Lu*	219
Science Extension: How to get ahead of the pack *Nicholas Fakira*	225
Society and Culture: It's So-WHY-ity and Culture *Lara Hather*	245
Taking Standard Maths Seriously *Finn Vercoe and Tallulah-Rose Adams*	259
Studies of religion: How to become a practising adherent *Julia Lo Russo and Christopher Farag*	277
Bonus International Baccalaureate Chapter: Keep it interesting *Sarah Kanuk*	301
Small Worlds: A Conclusion	317
End Note	321

"They Were Born Smart" - An Introduction of Misconceptions

There is an innumerable number of misconceptions that surround the Higher School Certificate. In the pages of this book, many of these will be dispelled by the people who know and understand the process the best – the students themselves who have just come out the other side. However, there is one misconception in particular that I believe needs to be addressed before you dive into the gold-mine that is 'Top Achievers: 2020 HSC Edition' - the concept that these 'Top-Achievers' were born smart. Believing such a statement can be detrimental to one's academic performance as well as one's long term mental health, for it perpetuates a feeling of constant inadequacy – "I will never be good enough."

In truth, many (if not all) of these students suffered significant setbacks throughout their scholastic careers. Indeed, the nature of the HSC journey is that it rewards all types of students for their performance. To believe that there is a genetic predisposition that will automatically guarantee success is misguided at best, and downright ignorant at worst. Having collated and edited this entire manuscript, I have realised that there are only three things that these top achieving students all have in common:

1. They are *not* perfect.
2. They worked smart.
3. They worked hard.

Now, I can guarantee that you, dear reader, have the first of these criteria already down pat. If you believe that you do not, then there is no point in continuing to read this book. Either you are perfect, in which case an HSC study guide such as 'Top Achievers' is of no use to you. Alternatively, you possess an arrogance of perfection that will never allow you to grow and learn from your mistakes, a mindset which is integral to success in the HSC as well as life beyond. (I feel that this paragraph is a bit severe)

The second criterion is one that you should soon also be able to fulfil. After reading this book, it is our firm belief that you will be armed with the strategies to maximise your time and effort, and ultimately emerge from your final year of school having achieved all you ever wanted.

However, this will not be possible without the application of the third principle - hard work. As my Year 9 Mathematics teacher used to say, "hard work beats talent when talent doesn't work hard." It is up to you, and only you, to ensure the realisation of this. Without hard work and application, the rest of this book will be of no meaningful use. If you have bought this text for a 'shortcut' to success, you are mistaken and you may as well put it down now. However, since you have taken the time to both purchase this copy and start reading it, then I imagine you are willing to commit to success in the HSC. In this case, I am sure that you will succeed.

Please do not be disparaged by any preconception of natural capability. Having good genetics helps, but they are a minor piece of the puzzle that can easily be overcome, namely by adopting the strategies in the following 250-odd pages! It is never too late to make the most of your ability.

So, realise that you aren't perfect. Work smart and work hard. If you do so, then neither NESA nor anyone else in this big world that we live in could even hope to contain you.

Best of luck for this year and the future beyond,

Fionn Parker

Editor-in-Chief of Catch Up with Top Achievers.

About Us

Founded by Adam Ma in January 2019, the team of "Catch Up with Top Achievers" consists of a group of passionate students from Sydney, Australia. We all agree that knowing how to learn is far more important than knowing what to learn.

Our mission is to inspire, mentor, and educate students to become well-rounded lifelong learners.

"Catch Up with Top Achievers" also promotes diversity. Our team consists of talents from all different faculties - music, sport, drama, philosophy, you name it. We are not afraid to address and discuss our weaknesses. We do not censor our opinions.

We are grateful to have the opportunity to give back to the community and are excited to continue to do so!

Our Editors

Adam Ma

Adam is a student entrepreneur, speaker, and Computer Science student at UNSW. He is the founder of Top Achievers Education; and founder of Tree Niu Bee Pty. Ltd, an EduTech Start-Up, which aims to combine technology and education. Adam graduated from Cranbrook School in 2018 and won multiple academic/sport awards throughout his time studying there. His first-ever publication, Catch Up With Top Achievers: 2019 HSC Edition, is a bestseller under multiple education categories both online and in-store.

Fionn Parker

Fionn graduated as Dux of Cranbrook School in 2018 with an ATAR of 99.95, subsequently winning a scholarship to the Australian National University to study PPE/Law. He has since worked as a private family tutor in Austria, as well as travelled to over 20 countries in 2019. He is the Editor-in-Chief of Catch Up with Top Achievers, and is also currently working on his own creative projects.

Jesse Caminer

Jesse graduated in 2019 as Dux of Cranbrook School with an ATAR of 99.95, ranking 1st in NSW for English Advanced, English Extension 2 and Chinese Continuers, as well as 3rd in NSW for English Extension 1. He is currently travelling the world on his gap year before going to Cambridge University in the UK to read Modern and Medieval Languages, furthering his passion for language, linguistics and literature. Jesse is a private tutor and an editor of Catch Up with Top Achievers.

English:
To Memorise or Not to Memorise and Mastering the New Syllabus

By Jesse Caminer

"Perfection can kill." —*Anonymous*

English is perhaps the most mysterious beast of the HSC. Everyone does it and, let's be honest, not everyone is a fan. It is also without a doubt the most competitive course the HSC offers and the only compulsory course you will have to do.

My name is Jesse Caminer and I was part of the class of 2019 at Cranbrook School. I graduated as the Dux of Cranbrook with an ATAR of 99.95, placing 1st in the state in English Advanced, English Extension 2 and Chinese Continuers, 3rd in the state for English Extension 1 as well as band 6s/E4s in all my other subjects—French Continuers, French Extension, Latin Continuers and Latin Extension. This year, I have been accepted to attend Cambridge University in the UK and will continue my education overseas.

I can assure you that these results may be just as surprising to me as they are for you. I had never even fathomed the possibility of state ranking in English, let alone two first places and a third. In fact, I was quite the unconventional English student. Not once did I write a practice essay or complete a single pass paper at home. I didn't read all my texts back to front, and you can bet SparkNotes was a frequent guest on my search history. From my highest mark being a 14/20 at the end of Year 9 to achieving a first in course at the end of Year 12, I hope to show you that you don't need to be born a genius or a book-worm to succeed at HSC English...

You've probably already heard your fair share of metaphors describing the HSC – from *'it's a marathon, not a sprint'* to *'it's only a drop in the ocean, your ATAR doesn't define you.'* While these statements are true, I will spare you the cliché advice which you all probably know well by now. I figure that you would rather appreciate an honest and detailed overview of HSC English, as well as the essential tips and tricks that you never learn inside the classroom.

Please note that while I am writing this with English Advanced in mind, most, if not all my advice is applicable to English Standard as well as English Extension 1.

My Experience Surviving HSC English

2019 was the first year of the new syllabus. Thus, no one knew what to expect, including the teachers! Everyone was trying their best to prepare themselves for what was possibly coming. Would NESA call our bluff and give us an easy exam, scaring us out of memorisation only by threat of an impossible question? Or would they instead follow through and produce a challenging exam no one was expecting? For us, it was definitely the latter.

At first glance, my results may indicate that I had everything under control the whole year and never doubted myself. On the contrary, I had my fair share of all-nighters, panic attacks and existential crises, largely with English to blame. I gave up on assignments and studied the night before on a few occasions. I even came out of Paper 2 of the English Advanced HSC exam all but in tears, thinking that I had bombed the final module.

This brings me to a valuable lesson that I learned over my HSC year, "*perfection can kill*". As all perfectionists will understand, our own expectations and pressure can be crushing. I shot myself in the foot many times during the year when I let some vague idea of what I thought was a 'perfect' essay get in the way of actually writing an essay, getting things done on time or preparing healthily and effectively for an exam. 99% of my stress leading up to the English exam was the thought 'what if I didn't produce the perfect essay in the exam?' Naturally, I never did produce a perfect essay. The reason for this is simple: the perfect essay doesn't exist. Each time, regardless of my mark, I sought feedback from teachers and peers to keep bettering my essays and my skills in English.

The HSC isn't demanding perfection, only effort.

A Word of Advice

Perhaps the biggest mistake I observed during my HSC year was the collective stigma that surrounds English, which often prevents students from excelling. People chose to stubbornly fight against the inevitable and end up shooting themselves in the foot. If you don't absolutely LOVE English, like me at the start of Year 12, your best bet is to accept the fact that you will have to dedicate time and energy in order to succeed and try to make it interesting for yourself. Don't make the mistake of wasting as much effort despising English as you could use to get it done and move on.

It is my belief that English is what you make of it. If you are bored and uninterested in English, you will mostly likely produce an uninspired and uninteresting essay. You get what you give. Do yourself a favour and don't give up before its even started. If you allow yourself to get over the collective stigma around English (that it's boring, useless and doesn't deserve your time), and instead endeavour to find and develop ideas that interest you and that you are passionate about, English can be extremely rewarding.

Staying on Top of the New English Syllabus

Before anything, I would like to point out the newest requirement of the syllabus which is perhaps the most overlooked— this is your *own* personal response. See the following statements/requirements plucked verbatim from the Advanced syllabus rubrics:

- formulate a **considered response** to texts (*Common Module*)
- reflect **personally** (*Common Module*)
- express a considered **personal perspective** (*Module A*)
- engage deeply with the text as a **responder** and composer further develops **personal and intellectual connections with the text**, enabling them to express **their considered perspective of its value and meaning** (*Module B*)

For example, let's take the 2019 Advanced Common Module Essay question for Arthur Miller's 'The Crucible':

> To what extent does the exploration of human experience in The Crucible *invite you to reconsider your understanding of love?*

Here, in order to thoroughly satisfy all the requirements of the question, you will have to link the text's exploration of a human experience with how your understanding of a certain human experience—here, love—has changed. It is often difficult for students to reflect upon their own understanding within an essay which is usually thought to be 'academic' or 'intellectual', but here are a few nice ways to include your own point of view in an essay:

- Considering the audience's perspective as a way of highlighting your perspective as a viewer/responder. For example: *"….alienates the audience and thus challenges **our** understanding of…"*
- phrases such as *"I, as the responder"* or *"as a responder, I am challenged/invited to…"*
- definitely do not be afraid to say *"I"*—the question is inviting you to do so.

Further, with the implementation of the new syllabus, the question of whether or not to **memorise responses** has become the hottest topic. Previously, English Advanced questions were either rather predictable or broad, allowing for students to succeed with a generic memorised response. However, the new syllabus gives NESA scope to write much more challenging exams as far as memorisation is concerned. This means questions may be:

- character-specific.
- theme-specific.
- a response to a certain line of your text (as stimulus).
- a response to a piece of critical theory (as stimulus).

This all means that pre-memorised responses have taken a big hit, and Advanced now requires a more holistic yet detailed understanding of each of your texts and their respective modular rubrics. This also means that markers will be looking for specific considered responses to the question on the day more than ever.

This does not mean you cannot memorise an essay per se. Fortunately, the question won't be impossible—NESA wants to give all students state-wide the best opportunity to produce their best work. This means that you can often twist the question in your favour, or get creative with it, as many questions will be abstract or conceptual, rather than concrete. The most important thing to remember is that if you are going to memorise an essay, you need to learn how to be fast on your feet and a creative critical thinker.

So, Should You Memorise?

Frankly, I think it's ridiculous and even naive to expect a great essay on the spot with nothing at all prepared, just an understanding of the text and a long list of quotes memorised. So, the question remains, did I memorise? Yes. Can you succeed by memorising? Yes. Do I think you should memorise? Only for the right reasons.

It is a well-known fact that many students have tutors/external writers compose essays for them, essays that later regurgitated on the spot regardless of the question's specifications. Of course, this is completely the wrong thing to do and will not earn you any marks. I think NESA has, rightfully so, attempted to discourage this tendency by demanding a higher understanding of the text through much more specific questions. If you are memorising an essay to not have to think on the spot or for an easy way out, this is the wrong approach.

For me, memorising an essay alleviated a lot of stress as I always knew I had something to write. It also helped immensely with structure—if you have the skeleton of a well-structured essay already learnt, it's one less thing to think about. I was also able to write much more than if I had to make everything up on the spot, and was much more concise doing so. In short, the reason I memorised an essay was to have a structured essay full of well-analysed quotes and a flexible and versatile thesis that I could tailor to a question, not one that I regurgitated word for word no matter what was asked.

Naturally, I had a deep and considered understanding of each text. Most of what I had 'memorised' I did not end up using word for word, but instead as a guide. I did, however, use almost every quote in my essay. Indeed, I mostly memorised evidence, however, the evidence just happened to be in the form of an essay. Thus, if you are memorising, it is also important to understand what you have memorised and understand the significance of each of your quotes so that you can manipulate your theses easily.

The trick to memorising is having malleable theses as well as versatile quotes from a range of different characters. Generally speaking, a memorised introduction can also pass, as much of the information will stay the same. However, you should of course adapt your opening and closing sentences, as well as your introduction of the texts to the question. For example, here is the generic first sentence of my introduction for module B:

> *William Shakespeare's revisionist history play Henry IV: Part 1 (1600) spearheaded a new political contract by broadcasting new modes of leadership, critiquing Elizabethan England's feudal hierarchy of the old-elite.*

If I had written this word for word, I would already be in the B or even high C bracket of the marking criteria as nothing is answering the question (*"Comedy steps into the path of history and is crushed"*). However, I was able to use my sentence as a base to guide a thesis I made up on the spot:

> *William Shakespeare's revisionist history play Henry IV: Part 1 (1600) harnesses the power of <u>comedy</u>, irony and satire, and applies them to stories of <u>history</u>, broadcasting new modes of leadership and critiquing Elizabethan England's feudal hierarchy of the old-elite.*

For the final HSC exam, I wrote three body paragraphs for each essay (as well as an introduction and conclusion). However, I had prepared roughly 4-6 paragraphs in total for each module, meaning that I had more than enough quotes from an array of characters to choose from, as well as a wide variety of theses to manipulate. In many cases, I was able to substitute in quotes from another paragraph and reorder them to tailor my argument to the question. Before my exams, I wouldn't practice writing out essays in full, but rather test myself in my head on how I would mould my thesis to any given character, rubric point, concept or theme. That way, I was confident going into the exam knowing that I had something to work with for whatever they threw at me.

Thinking Ahead

I would like to point out that with the new syllabus, NESA has also restructured what internal examinations for Year 12 English will look like. Where previously students would have written essays for internal assessments as they would in the external exam, this year is the first year that you may only write one or two essays out of the four internal assessments. For example, you may instead be asked to compose a multimodal presentation or a speech. While it is important you focus on these assessments, it is most important to keep in mind that on the day of the HSC, you will be asked to write essays. Therefore, you should target your study from the very beginning of Year 12 to composing essays. Writing essays will also still greatly help you in your internals, as the structure of an essay is highly translatable to these tasks.

Putting the Read in Ready

Before you read your texts, I would advise that you go online and find a summary of your specific text as well as its key theme. Yes, this is an indirect invitation to consult SparkNotes. I often found that when I would go into a text and read it cold, I would not understand it or take out what I could have if I was already familiar with the story and the key themes to look out for.

Then, as I read the text, I would have a highlighter and a notebook/word document open beside me. I would highlight any quote I thought was interesting or might be useful as evidence for a future essay. Although it takes longer to read like this, once you have finished the book you will have a bank of evidence at your fingertips that you know you have read. Indeed, you would spend just as much extra time in the future combing the internet and fumbling through online resources for a list of generic quotes than if you completed this process from the outset. This is also very important for your essays as HSC markers look for original pieces of evidence and are bored by the same Schmoop quotes every student who hasn't read the text has at their disposal.

Hopefully, once you have read the text and have pages of quotes, you should understand more intimately the themes of the book, as well as be able to come up with your own interpretations. Now, you should put your quotes into a table with three columns (this is much easier on a word document). One column for the quote and one for the analysis of the quote. You should then organise the paired quotes and analysis by theme and concept, making it easier for you in the future to draft coherent paragraphs. For example:

Concept/ Theme	Quote	Analysis
Othering (collective oppressing individual)	[Act I] Abigail (about Tituba): *"She spoke Barbados."*	The use of the detached 3rd person pronoun isolates Tituba as "speaking Barbados" and affirms her position of servitude—the legacy of the Trans-Atlantic Slave Trade.

You can also see in the next example that for Module A (comparative study), I paired pieces of evidence from both texts and commented on their similarity/difference to make the composition of a comparative essay in the future much easier:

Concept/ Theme	Text 1 (Camus)	Text 2 (Daoud)
Landscape/Man and the Natural World	*"I often thought I lived in the trunk of a dead tree"* Meursault's nonchalant assertion harnesses the forefronted "I" pronoun to typify his privilege as a 'pied-noir' in Algeria who was afforded an easeful lifestyle while the colonised suffered.	*"My ear was glued to the ground of the tree's struggle"* Daoud anthropomorphises the tree and its "struggle" as distinctly human, speaking of the tree as if it is telling a story. Thus, Daoud animates the landscape and draws a difference between an authentic African culture where

	Camus dissects and thus objectifies the landscape by emphasising the "trunk of a dead tree", seeing the landscape as merely an object.	the soul is connected to the landscape, a far cry from the western culture which objectified the landscape namely through Scorched Earth Policies.
Comparison: Daoud reveals that the "tree", symbolically routed in the landscape, represents the shell of a pillaged Algerian culture whose "dead trunk" Meursault physically seeks to inhabit. Thus, Daoud alludes to the cultural pillaging of the Algerian culture not only by colonialism but the legacy of violence and othering it left behind.		

It is important in your analysis to write in full sentences rather than in indecipherable abbreviations. In this way, you have fully fleshed out sentences and ideas up your sleeve for whenever you need them.

Note-Taking

For many people, note-taking for English is difficult, useless and for the most part unclear. As I said earlier, the final exams you will sit will mostly be essays. While this may not correspond to your upcoming internal assessments, you should target your notes to serve this purpose (essay composition).

Over the term, you should continue to make the same style of notes as I suggested you make by reading the text—quotes paired with techniques and analysis, organised by theme or concept. Again, remember to write full sentences of analysis, this way you will become familiar with the 'formula' and will be able to make up your own analysis on the spot in the exam to better suit the requirements of the question.

Another important point is communicating the notes you take in class with your essay. My biggest tip is to pair the ideas and concepts you discuss in class with evidence in your own time. Hopefully, after reading the text, you should already have a nice bank of evidence, so try adding any new points you discuss in class to existing quotes you have jotted down, or even search up quotes online to support new concepts. Ultimately, you should aim to synthesise notes taken in class and transform them into full sentences with analysis which can later be used as building blocks when you are drafting essays.

This system of note-taking allows you to compose an essay quickly. This also allowed me to stay motivated and not be intimidated by the upcoming exam. I would take notes in class as normal and complete any set tasks, whilst compiling a big table of quotes paired with full sentences analysis, but wouldn't think about the exam until two weeks before the date. Once these two weeks had begun, I would then begin to draft paragraphs and eventually an essay based on ideas I had.

Another big tip I have is for when you get your internal marks back each term. This is when you most want to lie around while everyone else does nothing, but it is a crucial time for applying feedback as everything is still fresh in your head. If you can seek and apply feedback received from your internal assessments, you won't have to worry about doing it before the external HSC exam; everything will be ready.

Handwriting

Another thing to keep in mind, considering that on the day you are asked to write essays, is handwriting. The two vitally important things for HSC English that you should keep in mind for handwriting are speed and legibility. In terms of speed, while quality beats quantity, the reality is quality AS WELL AS quantity beats just quality. This means you have to write meaningfully whilst also trying to keep the length up.

Secondly, if the marker cannot read your handwriting clearly, not only is it frustrating for the marker who will inevitably become uninterested in having to decipher every third word, but you may not be awarded all the marks that you DESERVE. One of the biggest favours you can do yourself is to practice writing as much as you can. Writing fast for long periods of time throughout the year is great preparation for your Trials and the final exam. I am not saying that you should hand write every word of your notes, but make sure you practice your handwriting and speed. After all, the final exam is with a pen, not a keyboard.

There are many helpful tricks you can find online, such as attaching a weight to your pen, but all I can recommend is finding the right pen for you and trying to write 10 minutes every day to train your hand for what is coming. I went from writing 800-900 words in 40 minutes to 1300 in the final exam.

Approaching Essays

What is an essay? An essay is an argument. This means the HOW of your essay—how you argue (i.e. thesis)—is just as important if not more important than WHAT you argue (i.e. content). For the final HSC exam(s), you will be required to write 3 essays or 'extended critical responses', as well as complete a reading comprehension task that requires much the same analytical skills as an essay. With this said, essay responses will make up roughly 80% of your overall marks, so knowing how to approach, draft and produce an essay is the most important component of HSC English.

Answering the Question!

You'll be hearing this throughout the whole year, but it is the most important component of an essay. As I said earlier, with the introduction of the new syllabus, answering the question is perhaps the first and biggest thing a marker is looking for.

The first step to answering the question is understanding it. As soon as you read the question, you should already be making links to how it applies to the module rubric and your specific text, especially if the question is not text specific. You should also be identifying the key terms and components of the question and drafting in your head how you will cover each element directly and how you can link all the elements together.

Making connections and conclusions about multiple terms of the question is key to elevating your essay to a cohesive and sophisticated response. You should also consider how you can extend key points of the question, and how these points may challenge and collide with your ideas about the text. As before, let's take the Module B question for Shakespeare's Henry IV: Part I for example:

> *Comedy steps into the path of history and is crushed. To what extent does this view align with your understanding of* King Henry IV: Part 1?

Many students are stumped by off-kilter questions as they feel obliged to agree with the statement and force their view to align with it. On the contrary, it is impressive to be able to confidently disagree with the statement and create a sophisticated and elevated response to support how your view **doesn't** align. For this question, I completely disagreed and was able to extend the statement to form a thesis. I argued that Shakespeare in fact uses comedy to revolutionise stories of history in order to package it to his modern audience and, rather than being crushed, it becomes a device that operates alongside history to reimagine, reshape and reconstruct it. See how instead of just disagreeing with the question and explaining how comedy is not crushed by history, I have created my own thesis of what comedy does instead, extending the terms of the question and linking it to key concepts that I studied in class such as socio-political agenda and metatheatre.

Finally, the last point I will make is about letting the marker know explicitly in your response that you are answering the question. This is known as 'signposting.' Signposting includes using the exact terms of the question in your response to indicate that you are, in fact, directly responding to the question. This means that in your response, in the context of this question, you should constantly be referring back to the role of **comedy** in terms of **history** and whether it is **crushed** and, if not, how so. You should also be extrapolating the key terms of the question in terms of your text. For example, **comedy** in King Henry is manifested most strongly in the character of Falstaff, and

history in the historical narrative of the War of the Roses and the Welsh Rebellion that Shakespeare seeks to retell. In each of your thesis statements of your body paragraphs and all throughout your conclusion and introduction, you should be using the exact terms of the question as well as synonyms.

Introductions:
Where the Battle Can Be Lost and Won

I would argue that introductions are equally as important, if not more so, than body paragraphs. This is the first impression you make on the marker. From the introduction alone the marker is already deciding what band to put you in. It sets the tone for your essay and is the first and best opportunity you have to jump straight onto the question and all its requirements/key terms. If you set down an air tight thesis and argument, the introduction also becomes a point of reference for YOU, the writer, to make sure that you don't get lost on the garden path and diverge from the question.

My introductions ended up being towards 250 words. However, depending on style, texts and the question, this can easily change. In the introduction, you MUST mention the following:

- Key terms of the question – your first line should be your thesis explicitly interweaving the words of the **question.**

- Introduction of texts (with dates) as well as their contexts and how they are relevant to the **question.**

- Brief and general extrapolation of the question in terms of your texts (and for comparative studies an extrapolation of the links between both texts). Again, this should be expressed in terms of the **question.**

- A comment on the function of the text (in terms of the **question**!). For example, does the text warn us, expose blind spots overlooked by society, or hold a mirror up to injustice?

Notice that in all of these elements, I have mentioned the word question. The first call of business for an essay is—you guessed it—answering the question! In the first sentence, you should avoid broad, non-specific statements. This screams 'pre-rehearsed response' and doesn't add anything to your argument. Aim to be as specific as possible.

Quick note: although for English Advanced, you won't have a related text for the final exam, in your internal assessments, context and information regarding a text (that isn't prescribed—i.e. a related text) should be only given on a NEED TO KNOW BASIS. Only include the things that are necessary for the reader to understand your argument. Not enough explanation will leave the marker confused. Equally, too much information gets boring and recount-y.

The 5-step Recipe to Good Analysis

This is the big question and one of the most important skills to hone if you want to succeed in composing a sophisticated, air-tight essay. More often than not, we are never taught how to analyse evidence in the context of an essay. Luckily, there is a simple formula that you can master which will make analysis much easier and more understandable. It goes as follows:

CONTEXT of EVIDENCE – **E**VIDENCE – **T**ECHNIQUE – **E**FFECT of TECHNIQUE – LINK

The "context of evidence" refers to the information needed to make sense of a quote or piece of evidence. This often includes an act (or sometimes chapter) number, an explanation of the events occurring and of the character who says the quote as well as their delivery. Try to express this in as few words as possible.

The "evidence" is simple enough; it refers to a quote or piece of evidence from your text. This can also include mention of form. It is also important to not include 50 word quotes, you can often paraphrase a quote or include ellipsis (…) to make the evidence shorter and sweeter.

The "technique" and "effect of the technique" is where the real analysis happens. You should always attach a (substantial and meaningful) technique to the evidence and explain the technique's effect in its context. The "link" then follows on from the effect and is an extrapolation of how the effect pertains to the question and your thesis. Here is a quick example taken from an essay I wrote:

> *Finally, Miller reveals how theocracy implodes in response to its own construction as Tituba affirms,* **"the devil have white people belong to him.***" The subversion of the traditional master-slave power dynamic in the "devil's" possession of "white people" that conjured it reflects the emergence of the civil rights movement in America, <u>as the witch becomes a metaphor for minority oppression in America, ironically undermining the longheld Christian platitude—'love thy neighbour'</u>.*
>
> (Common Module, Arthur Miller's "The Crucible.")

Notice here too that I haven't necessarily attached a fancy technique with an extremely complicated name, but rather just explained the quote—*"the subversion of the traditional master-slave power dynamic in the "devil's" possession of "white people."* Also observe the underlined clause at the end. While this is not strictly necessary, it adds another layer of analysis as I analyse the function of the witch archetype in the text as a whole and link this to context as well as the question (centred around 'love.')

For those who wish to take it further or demonstrate a more sophisticated manipulation of analysis, you can try to integrate evidence into your prose. While this is not necessary, it can be a quick and convenient way to pack in as much evidence as you can. For example:

Anomalous within Salem's polarised spectrum of good and evil in which individuals are either **"with the church"** *or* **"counted against it,"** *Miller describes Proctor in an aside as* **"not belonging to any faction,"** *humanising him as the entry-point through which audiences can interact with the play.*

(Common Module, Arthur Miller's "The Crucible.")

See how I have integrated into my sentence the quotes *"with the church"* and *"counted against it"* without analysing them, rather just giving more evidence to contextualise my main piece of evidence and analysis that comes later in the sentence.

Body Paragraphs: The Meat of the Sandwich

Hopefully your teachers will have already explained how to structure and execute a solid body paragraph, so I won't blabber on about what everyone knows. Instead, I shall endeavour give some life saving tips that you probably haven't heard before.

Firstly, every thesis statement of a body paragraph needs the words of the question—signpost!

A body paragraph should be a progression where each sentence builds upon the sentence before it. There should be a conclusion made at the end of each body paragraph which contributes to the argumentation of your thesis. A good way to test whether there is a progression in your argument is to see if you can take a whole sentence (or sentences—more like a whole quote and analysis) out and the paragraph still makes logical sense. If you can then, either you are repeating yourself or that specific sentence is dispensable. Let me break down an example of a paragraph (taken from Common Module Crucible essay) in terms of progressing towards a conclusion:

Thesis for paragraph:

Miller critiques the construction of women as polarised to the binary human experiences of either a hyper-religious Christian love as the 'Madonna' or an overtly sexual love as the 'whore.'

Progression:

1. Miller portrays Abigail as overtly sexual and promiscuous—the "whore" archetype.
2. Miller portrays Elizabeth as portrayed as chaste and hyper-religious—the "Madonna."
3. Miller inhabits Elizabeth as to highlight her unnuanced construction.
4. Miller then warns of the dangers of restraining the human experience as the girls rebel against theocracy in the court house scene.
5. They are briefly liberated as theocracy implodes, critiquing the reductive binaries thrust upon an irrepressible and subjective human experience.

You can see how each point relies on the development of the previous one to operate properly. If you take out one point, the flow and logic of the argument starts to crumble. Another point you may notice is that I always speak in terms of Miller, rather than the characters themselves. You should always write in terms of how the author/composer has purposefully constructed a character to serve a certain purpose. For example I say, "Miller portrays Abigail/Elizabeth as..", thus with an *active* voice, rather than "Abigail/Elizabeth is portrayed as...", with a *passive* voice. You should always treat the text as a 'construction to serve a purpose' in an essay.

Another nasty habit to avoid in a body paragraph is recount of plot. You should only outline parts of the plot that are absolutely necessary for the reader in order to understand your argument. We have a tendency to mindlessly recount events in an essay when we are underprepared. If you are ready with evidence and ideas, this should be easy enough to avoid.

While there is no magic number of quotes to have in one paragraph or number of paragraphs to have in an essay, all my essays contained 3 paragraphs. I found that this was the perfect number that gave me the space to go deeper into my argument, as opposed to 4 paragraphs, which I personally felt only allowed me to explore ideas superficially. Each of my paragraphs included about 4-5 quotes with in depth analysis, as well as a few more sprinkled throughout which were integrated as I demonstrated before.

Conclusions: Ending with a BANG!

Contrary to introductions, nothing is really lost or won in the conclusion. This is only to say there are no 'home runs'—you aren't really going to jump up or down a band. The conclusion is, however, your last chance to hammer home your point and leave your marker with no choice but to put you in the highest band. Suffice to say, a weak conclusion can leave doubt in the markers mind.

One of the biggest mistakes you can make is to neglect a conclusion, or even leave it out completely. You can lose up to 3 marks (15% of your total marks out of 20) for 'poor structure' if you don't have a conclusion. Leave a good 2 to 3 minutes for a conclusion. This is more than enough time, as they shouldn't be longer than 100 words—roughly 3 sentences. Conclusions also cannot usually be memorised as they are almost completely dependent on the question.

The conclusion is not a place to introduce new evidence (definitely not) nor a place to make up a new point. It is a place to firstly extrapolate how your thesis has answered the question (mentioning your texts and using words of the question) and, for those who are gunning for band sixes, to add a comment on the value and pertinence of the module in contemporary society.

For example, taking the 2019's English Advanced question for Arthur Miller's 'The Crucible' (1953) *love* question, one may write:

> *In a time of transactional love and online dating in which traditional notions of love are being questioned and subverted, an analysis of love in Miller's 'The Crucible' in all its forms reveals…*

Showing the marker that you not only understand the question and its nuances but can also extrapolate the relevance of the study you have conducted is a nice touch to your essay. With this said, veer away from statements that are controversial or inflammatory—you never know who your marker will be!

Hippopotomonstrosesquippedaliophobia

This is the fear of long words. It is also what 9 out of 10 Advanced markers undoubtedly have. Please don't use big words just for the sake of it! Also on this note, avoid long sentences. Don't try and squeeze massive quotes with techniques and the analysis AS WELL AS the link into one sentence. Take two sentences and let the marker breath. Your train of thought will be much clearer, as well as both easier to follow and digest.

Marker takes about 5 minutes to mark an advanced essay. You are shooting yourself in the foot if your argument is hard to follow. They are looking for CLEAR, SUCCINCT sentences.

QUICK TIPS FOR EACH MODULE.

BIGGEST TIP: Keep in mind the underlying purpose/aim of each module! It's all in the titles—focus on specific human **experiences**, the textual **conversation** and dialogue between two texts, or the **critical** study and analysis of literature depending on the unit.

Common Module: Texts and Human Experiences

- This is not a close analysis of literature, but rather an examination of how a given text REPRESENTS the human experience.
- Focus not only on individual and collective experiences but the inherent link between the two. Don't ignore important aspects of the rubric such as 'paradoxes, inconsistencies and anomalies' or 'emotions.'
- Consider strongly the function of the text—what is its purpose? To warn? To shine a torch onto society? To predict? To expose a certain aspect of our society and relationships? A discussion of a text's function in society as a piece of literature to illuminate the human experience should be discussed all throughout your essay.

Module A: Textual Conversations

- Focus on the 'conversation' between the texts, rather than texts in isolation that have similarities and differences. How do they grow from each other and how are they in some cases even dependent? Be sure to use the language of the rubric: 'resonance,' 'dissonance,' 'mirror,' 'collide,' and so on.
- I would recommend integrated paragraphs, meaning a discussion of both texts in each paragraph, rather than in separate paragraphs.
- You should treat each text equally, which means a (roughly) equal amount of evidence from each text.

Module B: Critical Study of Literature

- Engage in some critical reading which can be mentioned in an essay to show you are making an informed and unique personal interpretation of the text.

- Make sure to highlight your own reading or interpretation of the text, as this shows that you are an independent thinker.
- Make links between your text and contemporary society.
- A discussion of textual integrity in each paragraph is extremely important! How do all the separate parts of a text make it whole/balanced? What makes the text timeless? Why are its concepts and themes still relevant today?

Module C

Module C is the newest and, to many, the trickiest module of the new English HSC. It is the first time NESA has introduced a module of this kind where you may have the opportunity to explain your creative choices and are free to your form: persuasive, imaginary or discursive. You normally study two prescribed texts at school and use them as a basis to inform and challenge your own writing.

Unfortunately (or fortunately, depending on how you look at it), there is no one size fits all instruction manual to acing module C,. However, I will try my best to share what I think is the most useful advice to succeed.

Preparing for All the Possibilities

There are many different formats for a Module C question that may be thrown at you, both internally and externally. You may be given a 20-mark response, a 10 mark part A and 10 mark part B response, or a 12 mark part A and 8 mark part B response. Furthermore, all of these question types may either be open to all texts from all modules (A, B and C) or to either one or both(!) of your module C texts. Further, some questions or stimuli may favour a discursive over a creative, for example, or vice versa. With this said, it is daunting to contemplate being completely prepared for the exam with so many combinations…

I think the most effective way to prepare yourself for module C is to have at least one story or discursive composition that is long enough to pass for a 20 mark question—roughly 800-900 words—which can also be easily cut down to suit either a 10 or 12 mark part a response, as well as a part B response to go with it (roughly 350-450 words). I feel that this is the smartest way to prepare. Ultimately though, no matter what, there will always be an element of surprise for module C. All you can do is best equip yourself with the tools to deal with any curve ball.

Composing a Part A Response

The greatest irony of 'the craft of writing' is that NESA expects you to 'craft' something in 40 minutes. It is my belief that you should most definitely have something prepared before you go in. Unfortunately, there is no trick here. Personally, coming up with and perfecting a story/discursive was the most painful process for me. However, I do have a few tips that might help:

- Think of setting your story (if you opt for an imaginary response) somewhere relevant or even topical. For example, I set a creative amidst the Hong Kong riots. However, do avoid being too controversial/political as you may upset your faceless marker!

- Be inspired by your module C prescribed texts—borrow ideas, then challenge them. Markers love to see an engagement with the texts (not too explicitly) and to see how they have shaped your writing.

- Play with the form—you can consider what is called 'hybridity', meaning that you combine imaginary with discursive. This can mean, for example, a creative story or extended metaphor used to illustrate a point weaved throughout a discursive piece

- I would avoid writing persuasive pieces—it seems a bit year 5 NAPLAN to me and is hard to make truly 'innovative.'

Approaching Part B

Part B or the reflection component is the newest aspect of any part of the new syllabus. While this may have you shaking in your boots, it is actually big advantage. Previously, when students were expected to write a 15-mark creative composition, they were not given the chance to explain themselves or their creative decisions. In part B, you can easily elevate your part A response by explaining and in some cases exaggerating exactly what you did. This means that if a marker hadn't picked a crucial part of your story up or an underlying subtle metaphor or motif, you have the opportunity to fill them in and collect the marks you deserve, without risk of something being misunderstood, misinterpreted or completely overlooked.

In a part B response, you need to get used to saying "I" a lot and adopting a reflective tone. To achieve this, you should familiarise yourself with what NESA calls "evaluative language." Here are some examples:

- "I deployed the metaphor of…"
- "I attempted to channel the narrative voice of…"
- "I sought to replicate the style/tone of…""
- "I transferred the motif of…in order to…"

I would also suggest trying to make substantial links between your writing and your prescribed text's form and content. Substantial techniques such as narrative voice, metaphor, perspective, tone and even setting are very effective. The underlying concept of your piece should also link some way or another to your prescribed text without plagiarising it completely.

Responding to a Stimulus and the Requirements of the Question

While you most likely will have the opportunity to explain how you answered the question in your part A response with your part B response, signposting is still very necessary. Picking out techniques and key pieces of information from a stimulus you are asked to 'continue' or 'be inspired by' for example, and weaving them through your own composition shows the marker that you are answering the question. Let's break the 2019 module C question down:

> "**Twice before**, *a book had turned him inside out and* **altered who he was**, *had blasted apart his* **assumptions about the world** *and thrust him onto a new ground where everything in the* **world suddenly looked different** — *and would remain different for the rest of time, for as long as he himself went on living in time and occupied space in the world."*

a. Continue this extract as a piece of imaginative, discursive or persuasive writing that evokes a particular emotional response in the reader.

b. Compare how you have used language in part (a) to evoke emotion with the way writing has been crafted in at least ONE prescribed text from Module C.

This question was about the link between reading, re-reading, identity and emotion. The key in these questions is being specific and identifying exactly what emotion you are trying to evoke. Picking up details such as "twice before" which you may include in your story is a great way not only to show the marker that you have read and are engaging with the stimulus, but also to give your work layers and specificity. This detail is also very important as it implies the process of not just reading but re-reading and how, upon each experiencing of a text, your assumptions and interpretations fluctuate and challenge your previously held ideas.

Lastly, the luxury of part B here is that if you didn't manage to 'evoke a particular emotion' in the marker with your part A response, you can point out how you attempted to in order to earn a few extra marks. Personally, I think I was able to save my part A text with part B as I realised I hadn't considered an emotion in my text. I stretched the word 'emotion' and said that in my text I *"critiqued modern media and invited the reader to* **emotionally** *respond and engage in their own role in either supporting or decrying the modern age of pop culture and fake news".* See how I am not just naming an emotion such as sad or happy, but extending it to incorporate "emotionally" and thus further signposting how I attempted to answer the question. This is the key to module C, and at that, the entire exam—constructing a nuanced point of view and argument to, again, **answer the question!**

The Reading Comprehension Task

The reading comprehension task comprises section 1 of the common module. You have roughly 45 minutes to complete it as well as 10 minutes reading time. However, this reading time is also shared with your common module essay in section 2 of paper 1. The questions can be anywhere between 3 marks all the way up to 7 marks in some cases, adding up to a total of 20 marks. This section is equally as important as any other section, holding the exact same weighting, yet it is often completely neglected…

Why Is It So Dangerous?

The reading comprehension task of paper 1 of the common module is the most dangerous section for a number of reasons. Not only is it often completely neglected up until Trials, but it is the easiest section to lose marks in.

Firstly, reading comprehension questions are, to an extent, much less subjective than an essay. Marks are much more prescriptively awarded, meaning that the marking criteria will have specific expectations for you to meet otherwise you won't be awarded all the marks.

Secondly, it is also dangerous for advanced students, particularly those who take up English beyond two units (extension 1 and extension 2). Statistically, standard students do better in this section, as advanced students tend to overthink and overcomplicate.

Thirdly, the reading comprehension task can be very tricky to time well. You must take into account how much time you will need for each question and plan how you will tackle the reading of the texts. Will you start writing when the writing time starts even if you haven't finished reading everything? Do you skim the text or read every word? What order will you tackle the questions in? These are a lot of things to be considering on the spot, so I suggest you plan this all (as best as you can) before the exam.

How To Answer the Question?

The most important element of answering the question is signposting. As I explained above, this means using the language of the question in your response to make explicit to the marker that you are answering it. Your first sentence should be a rephrasing of the question. However, you should aim to add more specific information and detail. For example:

> **Q: Explain how Text 1 represents an intense moment. (3 marks)**
>
> *This poem depicts a lively and vivacious experience in the weather to represent an intense moment.*

While I have restated the exact words of the question, I have given detail and linked my response already to the rubric (human experiences) by specifying that it is "a lively and vivacious experience in the weather" that is used to represent an intense moment. Note that for questions with higher mark values (4+), you might want to also have a concluding sentence that functions in a similar way as your opening one—again answering the question just to be sure.

While reading and understanding the question is important (and extremely obvious), you should also pay close attention to the question words of the question. For example "explain how" and "analyse how" are two different things. More often than not, the word "how" will appear somewhere in the question. This is an invitation to use analysis of language to respond.

The second most important thing to do is to pay extremely close attention to the mark value of each individual question. This will guide the length, depth and amount of evidence of your response. As a general rule of thumb, you should aim for one point per mark. One point means a piece of evidence, analysis of said evidence and finally a link of the analysis back to the question. 3 simple steps. This may seem like a lot, but it is quick and simple if you don't overcomplicate your answer/thesis.

Many students are afraid of being too 'obvious' or 'simple' with their answers, but the more succinct, straightforward and easy to follow your answer is, the better. Unlike the other sections, this section is a game of ticking boxes, rather than skill. Techniques such as imagery, tone, word choice, alliteration, auditory imagery, while they may be looked down upon as elementary in the essay sections, are very much acceptable in the reading comprehension.

Q: Explain how Text 1 represents an intense moment. (3 marks)

In the truncated sentence "Thunder cracking.", the forceful and vivid present tense verb "cracking" represents an explosive moment in the weather, concentrated to only a few words.

It is also a great idea to spend one point on discussing form. The discussion of form is sophisticated and will elevate your response, not to mention that it is always easy to link to the question—it's a freebie! This may include:

- **Poem**— Is it free verse, or does it have metre/rhyme? Free verse form evokes a vivacious and irrepressible human experience, while metre may imply a measured or even repressed experience.

- **Photo/picture**—Consider the composition (foreground, background, middle ground). Where does the picture draw your attention to and why?
- **Article**—The informative nature coupled often with quotes and statistics supports the argument and persuades the reader.
- **Anecdote (story)**—This evokes a highly personal tone and connects intimately with the reader. It can also inspire empathy and other intense emotions.

...just to name a few. Here is a complete response, incorporating all the above points—a clear and detailed opening sentence, three pieces of evidence and analysis (including form) to correspond to three marks:

Q: Explain how Text 1 represents an intense moment. (3 marks)

This poem depicts a lively and vivacious experience in the weather to represent an intense moment. In the <u>truncated sentence</u> "Thunder cracking.", the forceful and <u>vivid present tense verb</u> "cracking" represents an explosive moment in the weather, concentrated to only a few words. Further, the poet <u>humanises</u> the weather, thus giving the moment life and intensity in "the cloud...a puffy hand...sending the boomerang off course." Finally, The <u>poet's free verse form</u> enhances the emotional intensity ascribed to the weather in "rain disguised tears," depicting the intense moment of an irrepressible human experience as the speaker's human "tears" merge with the weather ("rain").

Note that it is fine to 'paraphrase' quotes as I have done by using an ellipsis (...) in order to pick out the most important and relevant parts of the text. It is also a good idea to underline the techniques like I have done so when the marker is reading for example a three-mark question, they can see three techniques already jumping off the page.

What Is the Most Effective Technique?

While everyone's way of tackling the reading task may be different, I came up with a great method to maximise time and thus gain marks. As soon as the reading time starts, you should firstly read the common module essay question once so you have some sort of idea what is to come after the reading. This should not take more than 20 seconds.

Then, you start reading the texts in order of each question, reading the respective question before each text so you know what you are looking for. You shouldn't skim the texts too fast, but you shouldn't spend too much time either. It is most likely going to take more than 10 minutes to read all the texts so do not panic when they announce the end of reading time and the start of writing time. While it is tempting to get into it, it is important to finish all the texts. It shouldn't take more than 12-13 minutes. Once you have finished reading, you should complete the questions backwards. Generally, the later questions are worth more marks. Since it would have been the final text you would have read, you can complete the most amount of marks first whilst also having it fresh in your memory.

Also, be prepared for the mark value of each question to not follow a pattern. You may have an ascending mark value, or, like in my exam, we had the second question at 5 marks, where we were normally used to such a highly-weighted question towards the end. Finally, don't get caught up on a question. If you are struggling, just move on. Use the time you have on answering questions you know you can ace and try to come back to it at the end. I advise you to use the whole 45 minutes on the reading task. Also, do not switch to your essay half way through and hope to come back to the reading questions at the end. You probably won't.

The Actual Exam

Exam Technique:
everything you need to know before 'pens down'

I'll be honest, I rolled my eyes when my English teacher said we should take 5 minutes to plan before we start writing our essays. English is a game of time, and you can't afford five whole minutes of the forty short ones that you have to produce an essay. Instead, I took no more than 30 seconds to annotate the question and jot down and order my thoughts. I also used the reading time to plan in my head what paragraphs I was going to write and what my overarching thesis would be.

In the reading time, you may also want to consider what order you would like to complete the exam in. I advise leaving module C to the end, as you can get away with a shorter creative if need be. Personally, I completed my module B essay before moving onto module A, as it was the harder question and I wanted to just get it out of the way. If you leave the harder question until later, you risk fatiguing after the first essay and not being able to put in all your effort and focus to get as many marks as you can.

For Paper 2, be strict with yourself in terms of timing. Take no more than 40 minutes per section. If 40 minutes is up and you are still writing a body paragraph, wrap it up and write a quick conclusion and move on. In the case of a mental block, I found the best thing to do was not to sit there until the train of thought came back to me, but to instead keep writing. It will come back soon enough—you can't afford to waste time not writing.

Most importantly, do not fluster yourself or panic if you are unhappy with the essay you wrote or the question you received. Don't let it spoil the rest of the exam. Take a deep breath and start the next section anew. Lucky for you, 2 hours fly by. I envy you all who will have the feeling of putting your pens down for the last time for English. Savour the moment!

In conclusion, it is to a great extent that...

On an endnote, make sure that you help others. This is a great way to consolidate your learning and to boost your external marks. I had a running Google Doc for each module with a friend of mine and we would give feedback on essays we wrote.

Finally, take my advice and experience with a grain of salt. For the most part, I was making it up as I went along and I most definitely did not follow every piece of advice that I am giving. It's okay not to succeed the first time. Perfecting English is not an overnight job, nor, in my opinion, can you succeed to the best of your ability by studying last minute. Draft early, draft often and good luck!

Jesse's English Cheat Sheet

- Pay attention to the newest requirement of syllabus: your own personal response (see specific extracts from modular rubrics)—include comments that relate to the responder.

- You shouldn't memorise as an easy way out of having to think, but rather so that you have a basic essay structure, an array of quotes and a malleable thesis, which can then be tailored with specificity to any given question.

- You should tailor your study and notetaking towards the final goal of essay composition, regardless of your internal assessments, as ultimately, you will be asked to write an essay.

- Before you read your texts, read a summary of the plot and an outline of the main themes online so you have an idea of what the text will entail before you read it.

- As you read the text, jot down any and all quotes you think may be useful and interesting in a word document. Once you have read the text and, hopefully, have a nice list of quotes, transfer them into a table and analyse each quote, grouping them by theme/concept.

- Once you have a full bank of quotes and fully fleshed out analysis you can begin to draft paragraphs and eventually a full essay.

- Once you receive marks back from internal assessments, seek out feedback to apply to your notes and essay while it is fresh in your head. Do not leave it until just before the external exam.

- Quality beats quantity, the reality is quality AS WELL AS quantity beats just quality.

- ANSWER THE QUESTION!

- Don't feel obliged to agree with a stimulus statement—you are free to disagree and explain why you disagree if you can back up your argument with sufficient evidence, reasoning and logic.

- Learn to signpost—how to make it explicit to the marker that you are engaging and answering the question.

- In an introduction, you must: set down a thesis in response to the question, introduce the texts (with dates) as well as their contexts and show how they are relevant to the question, extrapolate the terms of the question in terms of your text and its ideas and comment on the function of the text in terms of the question.

- Be specific as possible. Avoid broad, general, sweeping statements—this screams pre-rehearsed response

- Master the five-step formula to analysis: Content of evidence, evidence, technique, effect of technique, link.

- The thesis statement of each body paragraph should include the terms of the question (signpost).

- A body paragraph should be a progression, whereby each sentence both relies upon and builds on the sentence that came before it.

- Speak in terms of the composer constructing the text in the active voice, rather than the passive voice (i.e. "Miller portrays Abigail as…" rather than "Abigail is portrayed as…").

- In your conclusion, do not introduce any new evidence or points but rather restate your thesis and add a comment of the value and pertinence of the module or question on contemporary society (without being controversial or inflammatory).

- Avoid overly long and technical words, and incomprehensible sentences—don't be afraid to split your sentences up as the ultimate goal is clarity and succinctness.

- Keep in mind the underlying purpose/aim of each module! It's all in the titles—focus on specific human **experiences**, the textual **conversation** and dialogue between two texts, the **critical** study and analysis of literature.

- Consider strongly the function of the text—What is its purpose? A discussion of a text's function in society as a piece of literature designed to illuminate the human experience should be discussed all throughout your essay.

- Make sure to highlight your own reading or interpretation of the text—show you are an independent thinker and make links between your text and contemporary society.

- For module C, I recommend having at least one story or discursive composition that is long enough to pass for a 20 mark question—roughly 800-900 words—which can be easily cut down to suit either a 10 or 12 mark part a response, as well as a part B response to go with it (roughly 350-450 words).

- Be inspired by your module C prescribed texts—borrow ideas, then challenge them. Markers love to see an engagement with the texts (not too explicitly) and to see how they have shaped your writing.

- Play with the form—you can consider what is called 'hybridity,' meaning you combine imaginary with discursive.

- In the short answer section, pay attention to mark value as a guide to length and amount of points for your answer.

- For the reading task, do not be afraid to be simple or obvious—the more clear and straightforward the answer the better as the reading comprehension is less about skill and more about ticking boxes.

- As a general rule of thumb, one mark corresponds to one point of evidence and analysis linked back to the question.

- It is a good idea to discuss the form of a text as a piece of evidence. For example poetry, photo/picture, article or anecdote.

- Do not start writing until you have finished reading the texts. When you have finished, complete the questions in inverse order so that the text you have just read is fresh and you can knock out what is usually the highest weighted question.
- For paper 2, take no more than 40 minutes per section.
- Help others.
- Draft early, draft often!

Ancient History: Staying in My Own Lane

By Sophie Howard

"Comparison is the thief of joy" - Teddy Roosevelt

Introduction

My name is Sophie Howard and I completed the HSC in 2019. My HSC and broader high school experience was definitely both academically and socially rewarding, but it was also extremely stressful and slightly traumatizing. I received an ATAR of 99.9 and placed 4th in the state in Ancient History.

One may look at my grades and be led to believe that I am some genius who consistently achieved perfect marks throughout my scholastic career. However, this couldn't be further from the truth. This iceberg mentality fails to recognise a lot of the self-inflicted stress, self-doubt and a truck load of (metaphorical, but close to literal) failure.

I was highly anxious, with a really unhealthy mindset of comparing myself to others and the unrealistic image that I felt others possessed of me. I had an obsessive attitude towards grades which meant that when I fell short of my impossibly high expectations I would fall into an, again metaphorical, pit of misery. 'Highlights' of this include my

50% Chemistry mark and 54% English Extension mark in various exams throughout the year.

However, these experiences of failure and stress were also highly valuable in kick starting a long journey of changing my mindset surrounding grades and academics (which I will hopefully develop further in university). I was able to develop techniques to improving my grades, and, more importantly, mental health, which I hope may prove useful for you.

Part 1: My top studying tips

1. <u>Consistent note taking</u>

    Notes must be both aesthetically pleasing (at least for me), as well as understandable, in order to lessen study stress. I would complete my typed study notes organised under syllabus headings as a progression from the practically illegible written notes that I made in class. This meant consistent consolidation of thinking, and it helped me identify areas that confused me and give me time to manage them before it was too late.

2. <u>Motivation</u>

    I would always keep in mind what motivated me long term to power through procrastination. Having a set goal for yourself (a dream ATAR, a dream course you want to get into etc.) is more sustainable than just studying because everyone else wants you to.

    If you can't find a good reason to feel motivated, it is okay to re-evaluate your priorities. The HSC isn't a direct measurement of intelligence or a crystal ball into your later success in life. If your mark doesn't concern you and your future, and you don't see yourself regretting your decision to not work and want to devote your time to other priorities then that is 150% valid (although I'm sorry that you may have wasted your money on this study guide...).

For short term motivation, I found having set breaks throughout the day and an attainable plan of what I wanted to achieve each day helped me circumnavigate the guilt of procrastination.

In hindsight, I wish that I had given myself even more of these breaks, since I'd be doing approximately 10 hours of work a day in the lead up to the HSC, but it wouldn't be completely productive.

Being kind to yourself should be one of your priorities - if you take a proper break when you need it (and don't label it as procrastination and feel guilty), then you will be more likely to have the energy to do what you need to do later.

The same applies for the entire HSC - it's better to pace yourself throughout the year rather than go hard at the start and burn yourself out and completely lose motivation later. Consistent study is also better than the alternative of taking it easy until the actual exams before pulling all-nighters.

Remember the HSC is not a sprint - it's a marathon.

3. <u>Stress!</u>

    I have a lot of it, so I really had to develop techniques to calm my farm and stave off any major breakdowns. These really paid off towards the end of the year. Identifying the source of your stress - for me it was feeling like things were out of control (which is pretty common) - can help you to handle it. Some specific things that helped were:

    Lists/ counting hours

    Counting my study hours as a quantitative measure of how much I had achieved and still had to do helped me feel a lot better.

    Music

    The general scientific consensus is that it isn't good for focus unless it's classical, but I did approximately 90% of my work to music. It both helped to drown out the noise of my house and distracted me from stressing about what I had to do instead of focusing on the moment. Even if having music or watching TV means you aren't 100% productive - that is still better than not working at all. It is important to develop strategies that work for you, and I am sure that listening to music was a great help in alleviating many of the stresses and distractions that came with studying.

Advanced preparation

I would always try to keep ahead in my subjects. This made it easier to immediately start studying as soon as I got a notification about the upcoming assessment. It also made me feel a lot calmer, since I was comparatively more prepared than a lot of people. This obviously isn't feasible for everyone given extra curriculars and the resources available, but if possible try to stay a bit ahead without affecting your higher priorities (and giving yourself enough down time). This can be done by simply reading ahead in the textbook, as well as the use of private tutoring or extra resources from your teacher.

Generally taking care of yourself

I have been guilty of sacrificing self-care for studying and marks, but it was not worth it. You will feel less stress if you have some semblance of a healthy routine.

1. Always eat - do not skip meals to study, or because you feel you haven't exercised etc. You need fuel.

2. Sleep - every time I studied past 9 - 10 it usually wasn't productive (even with caffeine) and I regretted it when I crashed the next day. Throughout the HSC, I learnt to stop working at around 9 because I needed time to destress and sleep, and the lost hours clearly did not affect my results. Just because everyone else is pulling all-nighters and downing energy drinks doesn't mean that you should too!

3. Balance - don't quit all your extracurriculars (unless you have truly over committed yourself). Not only can they be helpful for university applications - but they can maintain a sense of sanity in your life.

4. Support systems - keep your friends around you, and try not to be too competitive. Talk to your parents and teachers, who hopefully want the best for you extraneous of your results. Also, please don't be afraid to seek extra support through counselling. I was fortunate enough to have these support networks in place which definitely helped me, something I am eternally grateful for.

Part 2: Ancient History Advice

I came 4th in the state for Ancient History. However, this did not come naturally to me at all, and I really had to work hard for it. I also can attribute a large part of my result to my phenomenal teacher, who gave me and my classmates amazing resources and support.

I only received a mark of 77% in my trial exam, and I had to really re-evaluate what I was doing wrong and how to fix it. So, take it from me, you can totally turn around your average marks and surprise yourself. The Trials (even if they don't feel like it in the moment), can definitely be a springboard to doing better next time.

A dangerous misconception about Ancient History is that it is just memorising content. It's not. While you do need to memorise a considerable amount of content, you also need to possess the thinking and writing skills to evaluate the information you have memorised and use it to structure a variety of lengths and types of responses.

I am going to focus more on these than the memorising component because I feel knowing the content is the baseline for strong performance. This should be done as early as possible to allow you to focus on developing the higher order thinking skills required for top marks.

I will organise my advice into four components:

1. Notes
2. Memorisation
3. Answering questions
4. General exam technique

Start with the right tools (i.e. great notes):

Having amazing notes can greatly improve both how quickly and how much you can memorise in order to maximise your marks for assessments.

1. Make great use of the syllabus
   - Organise notes under syllabus dot points (distinguishing between major dot points and the minor ones so you know which are related).
   - The syllabus will be your primary structure for answering questions (especially for the short answer section), so it's essential that you cover **everything**.
2. Have overdetailed notes as your basis for each topic - this is where people talk about having 60 or something pages per topic. I made these on the computer so I could constantly add to them. While I didn't memorise every single detail of these notes, it was a great reference point for when I needed more clarification. Making them also helped me to familiarise myself with the content, making memorisation easier later.
   - Resources - I used as many resources as possible and was overly ambitious in terms of content. This is because if you want top marks, it is essential that you deepen your learning to differentiate yourself from everyone else in exams.
     - I used the textbook first as a basis. **However, the textbook is never detailed enough to be your only source of information.**

- I would then develop my notes by using in-class resources provided to me (websites, videos, slides etc.).
- Finally, I would evaluate what areas are lacking and use other resources to deepen my research further e.g. books in the library or online papers through websites such as JStor.
- Structuring - my structure consisted of the main dot point, followed by sub dot points with corresponding content (which included dates, information and definitions) and corresponding sources to support the content. I personally had a secondary document with colour coded Ancient and Modern sources that included images to help me remember.
- See below: notes for the core, and corresponding source notes.

Local political life
Pompeii had constitution, city divided into vici (wards, voting districts). Politicians expected to pay for buildings.
Comitium (people's assembly) - included all adult male citizens over 25, including freedmen (lower classes). Elected magistrates and voted honours. Dealt with matters of city finance, religious authority and other public business. Place were the people of Rome would vote, have the electorate. Although private parties would also conduct major commercial and financial transaction there.
Basilica - is the centre of the administration of justice. Large rectangular building located on the south-western side of the forum. Housed the law courts→ at the back was a structure reached by stairs which has been interpreted as a tribunal where the magistrates sat when hearing cases
Curia - a place where the town council could come and meet and could directly speak to government. Controlled aspects of public life. Drawn from a census of prominent citizens. Council building.
Forum - Large open area of Roman town where the main public buildings were located and where there was space for public meetings. Main forum→ located south-western section of Pompeii. Buildings around the forum was a mixture of religious, commercial and political buildings. Where aediles and duumvir would have met, at the comitium.

Magistracy/ executive (comprised board of four quattuor viri) - needed to be male, freeborn, over 25, of the required wealth and unblemished character.
    Duumviri/ duovori (two) - senior magistrates for 1 year. Administered electoral rolls, Administration of justice Responsible for criminal and civil cases murder, robberies, making judgements about electoral candidates. Elected quinquennial duoviri every 5 years to take **census and control morality**. Occurs in Basilica, in forum - local courts.
    Aediles (two) - junior magistrates for 1 year, responsible for judicial system, public works (sacred and public buildings), roads, sewerage system, administration, municipal cults, games and public entertainment, the markets. Maintained public order, quelling public brawls. Look after buildings, responsible for gladiatorial functions. Pathway up to duumviri.
    Quinquennial duumviri - responsible for revising ordo decurionum every 5 years. Take census.
Ordo decurionum - made laws, carried out by magistrates, members called decuriones, new members admitted every 5 years, lifetime membership, usually 100 members.
*These positions only held by freeborn, honourable men.

Political life	Epigraphic sources - *programmata*/ election slogans which indicate people participated enthusiastically in elections. Building inscriptions show wealthy people paying for political favour, doing their political duty. Duumviri Valgus and Porcius built small theatre in Pompeii. "Lucius Sepunius Sandilianus the son of Lucius and Marcus Herrenius Epidianus the son of Aulus, duumviri with judicial authority, caused [this sundial] to be erected at their own expense" R. Laurence ii: Space and Society, Routledge, London 1996, p. 33. Patron client relationship: Eumachia and guild of fullers, erected statue in her honour. ' the fuller (dedicated this statue) to Eumachia, daughter of Lucius, public priestess. 'Eumachia, daughter of Lucius, (built this) for herself and her household' → source indicates her wealth, status and family. Electoral graffiti - Graffiti, mostly electoral posters from AD 79, on the façade of Asellina's tavern in Pompeii - More than 2500 electorial posters "I beg you to elect Marcus Epidius Sabinus senior magistrate with judicial power, a most worthy young man" from Bradley: Cities of Vesuvius: Pompeii and Herculaneum 2013 'Vesonius Primus urges the election of Gnaeus Helvius as aedile, a man worthy of public office' 'Vote for Lucius Popidius Sabinus, his grandmother worked hard for his last election and it pleased with the results' ' I ask you to elect Aulus Vettius Firmus aedile. He is worthy and the municipality. I ask you to elect him playballers. Elect him' Transcript of graffiti in Herculaneum. "The bakers proposed Julius Trebius for aedile" "The millers ask for and desire Cn Helvius Sabinus as aedile, together with all his neighbours" "I beg you to make Gaius Julius Polybius aedile. He brings good bread." "Almost 3,000 election notices have survived on the walls of Pompeii, and more than half of them are for the election in the last year of the town's existence..... The vibrancy and number of election notices show a town alive and well, coping with the earthquake disaster of AD 62 future." (Paul Wilkinson, Pompeii, the Last Day)

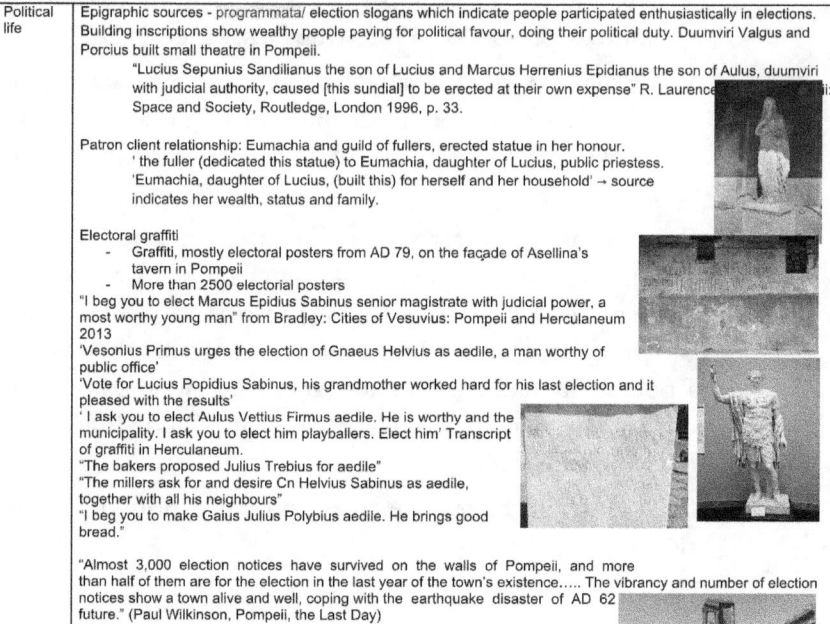

3. Have condensed and refined notes for the actual exams.

    - The second set of notes that I made was more realistic in what I could memorise.
    - I would pick the best source per dot point from my extensive notes to remember (and try to overlap as much as possible to lessen my workload.
    - In these notes, I cut all unnecessary parts and the things that I already knew in order to make memorisation easier.

4. Have condensed and refined notes for the actual exams.

    - The second set of notes that I made was more realistic in what I could memorise.
    - I would pick the best source per dot point from my extensive notes to remember (and try to overlap as much as possible to lessen my workload.

- In these notes, I cut all unnecessary parts and the things that I already knew in order to make memorisation easier.

5. Make use of extra studying resources for memorisation/ familiarisation with content:

    - Palm cards
        - Were helpful especially for sources and concepts
    - QUIZLET (or other study apps)
        - I religiously used this on the bus etc. These helped me to learn the content/ concepts (not just for Ancient but for other subjects).
    - Quote sheets
        - I made sheets for quotes memorisation so I could ensure that I had them word for word memorised for exams. Try and make quotes as short as possible, editing out any unnecessary parts.

6. Additional notes for the essay:

    - Since Historical Period is tested with one essay which can be on a specific tiny dot point, or on a trend that runs across numerous dot points, it makes sense that your notes might change slightly for this topic.
    - I made enormous tables with all the information and sources for every trend, as well as additional tables for the obscure dot points.
    - I essentially memorised these (without the quotes which I memorised separately) for this section, which meant I had information for an entire essay on a specific person with prepared paragraphs, as well as essays prepared including information on each significant person of that period.

See below notes on historical periods:

Person	Religious

AIII	- Solar theology - increased emphasis on solar theology and deities Aten, Nekhbet and Thoth. Deification as the sun disk, Introduced epithets - "Dazzling Sun Disk". Daughter Bekataten. Malkaata called the dazzling sun disk.
	    ○ Architect twins Suti and Hor recorded a hymn to the sun on a stele, acknowledges sun disk as the god "who created everyone and made their life".
	- Amun - continued amalgamation of Amun and Re (before Amunhotep III), maintained development of Amun as Chief God of state (temple of Amun at Luxor). Removed title of "Overseer of all prophets of all the gods" to limit power of First Prophet of Amun.
	    ○ Merymose temple stela records AIII's building in honour of Amun "I made another monument for him who begat me, Amun Re lord of Thebes, who established me upon his throne"
	- However, promoted minor gods and less Amun e.g. Ptah (built temple at Memphis Nebmaatre), Thoth (temple at Hermopolis) and Hathor, Sekhmet (600 statues to in Karnak).
	- Continues Divine Birth Scene at Luxor Temple - to perpetuate power, as mother not royalty.
	    ○ Divine birth scene (ankh, mother impregnated by Amun, depicted as crafted on potter's wheel, the usual). "His father, Amun-re"
	- Deification at Nubia - Worshipped as god (with Tiy) at Nubian temples Sedinga and Soleb. Unusual within life time, usually done posthumously.
	    ○ Soleb temple - seb/ opet festival, shows Tiy's involvement, crook and flail, double crown. Shows Amun delivering oracles to Amunhotep III. Wall inscription sees him bow to himself, also conquering others.
	- Festivals - 3 Heb seb festivals (after 30 years then every 3 at Malqata palace). Festival of Opet and beautiful festival of valley at Luxor, rites celebrating kings divine birth and dedication.
	    ○ In his tomb references Heb Seb "It was His Majesty who did this in accordance with writings of old. [Past] generations [of] people since the time of ancestors had never celebrated [such] rites of the jubilee" - Kheruef (Tiy's official).
	Modern historians
	- W.R. Johnson said solar temples were added to almost everything he constructed. (Amunhotep 111: The Living Sun Disk? published in KMT (1991))
	- "Amenhotep, ruler of Thebes, is the name of this child... he shall exercise the beneficent kingship in this whole land... he shall rule the Two lands like Ra forever." (Berman 1998)
	- Angela Thomas said he lessened Amun's cult which he perceived as a threat, part of a "wider political struggle" (Akhenaten's Egypt)

Ak	- Changes to worship - from polytheistic to monotheistic, gradual exclusion of other gods, plural 'gods' not used, persecution and eradication of Amun from monuments, other god's names removed. Maat spelt phonetically without female hieroglyph. Only Akhenaten has an intimate relationship, focus of religion is on royal family not personal piety (divergence from NK and back to OK separation of Pharaoh). Aten in coregency with king, triad of royal family. ○ Shrines to royal family of all classes of citizens.

	- Aten - creator, sustainer of life, universal, eternal, absolute. Aten is father, Aten is love, beauty, light. Maat is Aten and doing what the king wishes. New version during Akhenaten "Living disc, Ruler of the Two Horizons, rejoicing in the horizon".
	    ○ Hymn to Aten - found in Ay's tomb, speaks of danger of night, a time of death. "Aten, creator of life... beauteous, great, radiant... O Sole God... no other who knows you, only your son, Neferkheprure... the great Queen, Nefernefruaten Nefertiti, living forever" (M. Lichtheim, Ancient Egyptian Literature, Vol. II)
	    ○ Aten existed before Akhenaten but not nearly to the same degree: e.g. Hat had suncourt for Aten at Deir el-Bahri, Thut IV "Sun disk" scarab "with the Aten before him", AIII "the dazzling sun disk".
	    ○ Re name still used (evident in throne name and references to "son of Re")
	- Changes to afterlife -
	    ○ No afterlife (only present) "here and now" (Jan Assman)
	    ○ Elimination of Osirian afterlife and funerary customs, practices considered forbidden and were persecuted

Women Trends
Role and contribution of women

Person	Women

Pre Period	**MK and OK**
	• Provide many children, ensure the smooth running of the palace, act as regent if king died before his son was old enough to rule on his own.
	• Give silent support to king; a passive, but visible, complement to the king.
	
	NK
	• Traditional: Emotional and physical partner of king (producing male heirs to continue dynastic line)
	• Religious: Religious counterpart of King
	    ○ Manifestation of Hathor
	    ○ Associated with Maat
	    ○ Identified with Nekhbet – one of the "Two Ladies" (protective vulture goddesses) of royal uraeus crown
	    ○ Amun feathers or Hathor sun disk
	    ○ Ahmose-Nefertari (wife of Ahmose founder of Dyn XVIII) to role of divine patroness of Theban necropolis. She was associated with her son Amunhotep I rather than her husband – divinisation of this queen unparalleled in En hist.
	• Political: acquired secular and religious titles – with jobs, and estates with land, servants and administrators to provide independence and income (eg Gods Wife of Amun)
	• Diplomatic: engagement in foreign relations
	• Tites: "King's Great Wife" (as more wives, needed to differentiate) "King's Wife" and "King's Mother"
	• See roles across generations

AIII	• Tiy -
	    ○ General - consort, companion, counsellor, strength of character, striking, prominent, venerated, multigenerational influence, as a mother, wife and grandmother.
	    ○ History: daughter of Yuya and Thuya (commoners, but later courtiers from Akmim). Referred to as commoner Queen. Established changing role of the queen over this period.
	    ○ May have been coregent during last years of AIII.
	    ○ Representation
	        ■ Wears solarised crown of Hathor (first to do so), bust with two feathers on top (Amun)
	        ■ Had lake dedicated to her - Marriage Scarab (Yr 11) -
	            • Dedication of lake "Great Queen Tiy, may she live".
	            • Djaruka (Yr 11): "11 His majesty commanded the making of a lake for the great royal wife Tiye, may she live, in her town Djarukha...His majesty was rowed in the royal barge Aten-nefru in it."

	• Pleasure Lake at Shrine stela of AIII and Tiye from the house Panehesy, Amarna she is seated behind her husband and shown as Mistress of the Two Lands.
	    ■ Deified in temple at Sedinga (as a form of Hathor)
	    ■ Statue found in the Cairo museum shows the two of equal stature and linking arms (surrounded by small children).
	    ■ Colossal statue of both from Medinet Habu both same imposing size.
	    ■ Tomb of her Steward Kheruef
	        • Depicted as sphinx trampling enemies → (formerly reserved for kings).
	        • The God's Mother and King's Chief Wife Tiye, may she live and be young.
	    ■ Lock of her hair found in Tut's tomb - indicates intergenerational aspect.
	    ■ Statues carved in the image of gods: Tawret, Hathor, Isis/Nephthys/Selket/Neith
	    ■ Shown at the heb sed festival of Soleb wearing the Maya headdress and participating

Memorisation:

- I would only deliberately memorise quotes and dates word for word - everything else I would memorise loosely and most came naturally through long term familiarisation.

- I didn't memorise quotes until I actually had an assessment.

- I tried to be aware of the significance of sources and their relationship to syllabus dot points so I knew where to apply them. There is no point knowing things without having anywhere to use them.

- When memorising concepts/ actual content, ensure that you are not wasting time on inessential parts (use your own judgement as to whether some content is relevant or not). This will lessen your workload.

- There isn't a shortcut! Sitting with your notes and repeating them back to yourself, writing them down (I would create mind maps from memory), and having someone to test you (mum/ sibling/ class mates) are all helpful strategies. Ultimately, you have to put the work in if you want to succeed.

Answering questions:

I will look at breaking down questions into their key components in order to best answer them, a strategy which I think works for all questions with slight adjustments based on topic.

The three main things to look at are:

- Verb/NESA term
- Course words mentioned
- Mark value

1. NESA terms: the verbs in questions will affect how you answer the question, so you should be familiar with which ones appear in what topics and their subtle differences.

    - The Core and Society having lower mark value will often use lower order terms (though not always in the new syllabus). These terms include words such as outline or explain.

    - Personality and Historical Period will usually use higher order verbs asking for judgement and personal interpretation such as assess or evaluate.

- The new syllabus emphasises assessing the validity of sources. This is where higher order verbs and mark values can come into previously lower mark sections like Pompeii and Society.
- Tips for using verbs:
  - Evaluate and assess ask for a judgement (which you should include in your opening sentence).
    - Assess, however, means quantifying. I.e. if your judgement is that something is valid, how valid is it? It is important to give an extent. On the other hand, evaluate means creating your own criteria and then judging based off that.
    - Make sure that you **sustain your argument** and do not contradict your judgement. If you said that something is significant, don't later judge it to be insignificant, as this shows lack of planning and cohension in your response.

2. Course/ syllabus terms: questions will 100% of the time be derived from the syllabus, and the key words/ concepts will direct you. This is why it is essential that you know syllabus words and concepts and have your notes structured according to them to easily recall the appropriate information.
   - Often questions will have a macro topic which will demand the inclusion of its corresponding sub dot points to achieve full marks.
   - It can be really easy to include information/ content outside of that topic as it can seem relevant, but you need to prioritise relevant information and include the essentials first. *Not putting essential information from the syllabus dot point is mostly what got me in the 70s in Trials.

- Pepper the course terms throughout your response, as this is a clear indication of engagement with the question.

3. Mark value is also essential for evaluating the **structure** and the **amount** required for your response. However, you should also consider the topic when assessing these factors. For example, The Core and Society section emphasises content to answer the question, whereas Personality and Historical Period emphasises personal judgement and structure more (in line with the different NESA verbs used).

- For lower mark questions (1 - 5 marks approx.) → **include one relevant piece of information, backed by a source per mark.** Structure is not essential for full marks, and as such no introduction or concluding sentence is required.

- For mid mark questions (5 - 8), structure tends to matter a bit more. Therefore, you should treat the response as a mini essay. Include the following:
    - Introduction – A short introductory sentence including the key words of the question (to show you are responding directly to the question).
    - 'Body' – Use one mark per one idea and a source
    - Mini conclusion - one short sentence.
    - It is important to keep in mind that if you must pick between content and an intro/conclusion due to time constraints, ns you should **always** pick content. This is especially true in the Core and Society sections as per above.

- Higher marks (10 - 15). Again, this depends on the topic. You should still have enough points and sources to cover mark value and ensure points cover all syllabus areas asked for in the question.

- For Personality → structure really matters with mini intro and conclusion as well as a logical ordering of points.
- However, introduction for points/ body paragraphs are not needed.
- Essay (25 marks). This is often considered the hardest section to attain high marks in (for good reason). Similar to the Personality section, it is not just what information you include, but how you include it (using an essay structure and the logical organisation of paragraphs) and how you evaluate/ justify it.
  - Introduction: this should be approximately 4 - 5 sentences long. Look at the verb and answer that in your introduction (i.e. give judgement/opinion in your first sentence). The second sentence might provide a bit of context on the subject of your essay (if it is about a person, then when/ where they lived and what they did). Last sentences might briefly introduce points and then restate your position/ judgement to conclude.
  - Body paragraphs - this will vary on your topic. The following structures apply to my Egyptian topic, which isn't necessarily compatible with others.
    - For essays on a person I would dedicate a paragraph to their building, as well as one each on their religious and foreign policy.
    - For an essay on a trend (e.g. building or women) I would group several rulers across the period chronologically on what they did similarly and have those as the basis for three paragraphs.
    - My paragraph structure followed PEEL -
      - My topic sentence or 'P' would introduce the person/ idea, what I was to talk about in relation to this idea and why this proved my position.

- My 'EE', would include a bit of knowledge dump on what I knew about the topic sentence and why this supported my point. I would always make sure to evaluate Ancient sources (if possible, with a Modern Historians opinion) as this really shows sophistication.
- Conclusion - would essentially be 3 sentences, summarizing and more confidently stating my case.

Sample questions and how I would answer:

Q1: **Assess** the **validity of sources** in understanding the **status of women** in **Pompeii and Herculaneum.** (8 marks).

- Assess - I might judge that the evidence is <u>somewhat valid</u> given that much of what we know is interpretive, however <u>majorly useful</u> in the absence of other methods to understand women in this society.
  - Note how I included two assessments, which I weighted with adjectives.
- Status of women - this falls under the social structure dot point in the Core Unit, and there is no other mention of women in the syllabus.
- I might then organise my response (considering it's a longer one) across other sub dot points in social structure and other relevant main dot points - women as slaves (i.e. low status), as businesswomen (both freed and elite), as wives, as public or religious figures (higher status).
  - In explaining and supporting these ideas, I would provide one relevant source for each (e.g. "seize your slave girl..." graffiti for low status, Praedia of Julia Felix for high status). I would then assess these source's validity as I introduced them (arguing them as useful but flawed to sustain my judgement).

- Pompeii and Herculaneum - this indicates that both sites should be considered rather than one (Don't forget Herculaneum!).
- 8 marks - a longer response required with mini intro and mini conclusion if possible.

Q2: **Explain** the **ethical issues of conservation and reconstruction** of **Pompeii or Herculaneum**. (15 marks)

- Explain means relate cause and effect. Therefore, I would provide details on what caused the issue, the issue as it stands and its effects going forward to cover myself.
- Ethical issues of conservation and reconstruction -
  - Ethical issues concerning conservation - This could include whether we should conserve or excavate, tourism (which provides money but damages sites), how to conserve/ treat human remains and display them.
  - Ethical issues of reconstruction - artistic interpretation when conserving, as well as how we reconstruct the past by reinterpreting evidence (particularly important for human remains).
  - I would try to discuss most of these issues for a 15 marker, explaining the history of the issue, the impacts and methods of addressing it as well.
- Pompeii **or** Herculaneum means choose only one site (sometimes they might also specify either site). Pompeii being larger generally has more content to work with, but using Herculaneum can set you apart.

General exam technique:

The only way to improve this is by doing papers under timed conditions. No matter how prepared you are, if you are not good at finishing responses in the given time period, you can never achieve really high marks.

Timing

Typically, Personality and Society are meant to take less time than Personality and Historical Period. I was advised to spending approximately 40 minutes on the first two to provide more time for the other sections. I advise working out the time to spend on each section before the exam begins. It is important to do exams before the real thing to work this out for yourself. This does not necessarily have to be in three-hour blocks as this can be quite taxing. It is alright, and in some cases even more preferable, to do your past papers in 45-minute sections.

Always plan your responses in the exam

This will help you to immediately answer the question in less words for more marks. Furthermore, a physical plan will be a great aid if you lose track while writing, for you can always refer back to it.

Conclusion

I hope these tips and tricks will prove helpful for tackling the Ancient History course.

Before I wrap up, I just want to wish you the best of luck in your HSC year and to remain optimistic. As per my quote in the opening line, be kind to yourself and be content with your own best, staying in your own lane rather than focusing on someone else's.

I am now studying a high-pressure academic degree (Actuarial science). This time around, I hope that I can take my own advice and focus on my own health and happiness and not compare myself to others. If I can do it, then you definitely can too!

Sophie's Ancient History Cheat Sheet

Notes/ study materials

- Use the syllabus to structure notes → relate main dot points to sub dot points to help in answering questions (use syllabus as a framework, especially in short answer).
- Make detailed notes → good reference point for more detail when studying.
- Resources → use textbook as basis, then class resources, library books, documentaries etc.
- Refined notes → only relevant information, use colour and no big blocks.
- Palm cards/ quizlet → make use of otherwise wasted time (e.g. on the bus).

Memorisation

- Familiarise yourself with content (definitions and information) throughout the term (not memorising).
- Only memorise dates/ quotes days before exams (you probably will not retain these long term).
- Make quotes count (make them short and know how to apply them) to lessen the workload.

Answering questions

- Look at the NESA term/ verb → this directs how to answer the question.
- Look at course words → which direct you to corresponding dot points you MUST refer to.
- Use keywords to show the marker you are engaging with the question.

- Mark value → indicate length (1 idea and source per mark usually) and structure (higher marks require an intro and conclusion, especially in the Personality topic.
- Plan responses → in your margin/even at the top of your page to ensure all relevant information is included. This also helps you to have a logical structure and avoid waffling.

Exam technique

- Timing → Approximately 45 minutes for each section (plan timing before exam). Know that Personality and Historical Period might need more time, so you may want to do other sections quicker to make these sections less stressful.
- Practice papers → Use past HSC Papers and available Trials for new syllabus. Do not necessarily always prepare in three-hour blocks, rather timed 45 minutes of one section. Try to improve writing speed and write concisely.

Again, good luck!

Biology: it's in your DNA

By Adam Gottschalk

> *Biology, wow*
> *What a wonderful subject*
> *Here is some advice* – Haiku, Anonymous

Introduction

My name is Adam Gottschalk and I graduated from Sydney Grammar School in 2019. I achieved an ATAR of 99.95 and placed 1st in the state in Biology, French Extension and Visual Arts. This year, I'm going to Canberra to study a Bachelor of Arts and a PPE. These are both degrees that are broad and allow me to do things I'm interested in and passionate about.

When it came to studying and exams, however, they didn't mess around at Grammar. From Year 7 we had study strategies drilled into us, and the exams were always looming on the horizon. Although that aspect of school wasn't exactly enjoyable, it did help us when it came to Year 12, because a lot of people had already developed fairly good study systems.

It's these study systems that I'd like to talk to you about. I'll tell you what worked for me, and hopefully you can use at least some strategies to succeed in your HSC studies. Just remember, this isn't a one-size-fits-all kind of thing. Different things will work better for different people, so I'd encourage you to try various methods out, and see what works for you.

In all honesty, the HSC is a slog. As I'm sure you're aware, you're unlikely to waltz effortlessly through the year. You're more likely to totter along with a tall pile of books in your arms, and an even taller to-do list. I certainly did.

But that doesn't mean that the HSC has to be all pain and no gain. Hopefully, by sharing my experiences and giving you some advice, I'll help make the process of studying more effective and more efficient. Before I begin though, a quick caveat: no advice I give, no matter how good or how original, is going to change the fact that working as hard as you can is the best way to do as well as possible. There is no way around it.

That being said, I hope that in this article I can give you some tips that will help you both maximise your potential and allow you to enjoy the year, despite all the work.

General Study Tips
Plan in advance:

If you're already considering flicking over to the next article, please postpone your departure until after you've read this paragraph because if there's one thing that I want you to take away, it's this:

You need to plan in advance.

When you wake up in the morning, you need to know exactly what you have to do that day. This will be so much more effective than juggling a haphazard list at the back of your mind. Instead, you'll be able to tick tasks off one by one efficiently.

Even though it doesn't sound special, I found this to be the most useful study strategy for me during the HSC.

This is how I went about actually doing my planning: I would draw up a timetable, dividing each day into 'morning', 'afternoon' and 'evening.' I would then cross out all the times I knew that I would be busy (sports training, music practice, social activities etc.) and then fill in all the work I had to do. Simple, right? If you lay out your timetable like this, you'll be able to visualise your workload far more easily and assuage any stress simply because you have a clear game-plan.

Some other important points:

- Use pencil to fill in the timetable so you can be flexible. If you wake up one morning and really don't feel like writing an English essay, then just rub it out and swap it with the biology notes you'd planned for the next day. Don't forget about the English essay though!
- Always make sure you've got at least 1-2 weeks of work planned out ahead of you, so that you stay on track.
- Plan your work by **task NOT time.** This is a crucial point. A lot of people will say to themselves: "Right, on Monday morning, I'm going to sit down and do 3 hours of maths," and then proceed to twiddle their thumbs and watch the minute-hand until 3 hours are up. Not ideal. Instead, what you need to do is write in your timetable: "Monday morning: 1 maths past paper." If it takes you 45 minutes, that's great (and you're a Maths whiz). If it takes you 3 hours, that's also great. The timing doesn't matter. What's important is that you've actually done the *work*, rather than the hours.

Keeping a balance:

I'll keep this short and sweet:

1. Don't give up your hobbies. Keep playing piano. Keep playing soccer. Keep reading for leisure. I didn't give up my hobbies,

and it helped a lot. Yes, it'll feel like you're giving up an hour that could be spent studying. But you need to stop feeling guilty, and realise that having a break will make you so much more efficient during the time you *are* actually studying.

2. <u>Get some exercise.</u> After a run or a game of basketball, your mind will be much clearer and you'll get so much more work done.

3. <u>See your friends.</u> You can't become a hermit just because you've got exams. You need time to relax and have fun to offset the time you spend studying.

Again, these are simple, but they work. Don't disregard the things that everyone says, just because everyone is saying them. (what does this mean?)

Step back:

At many points during the HSC, I found it difficult to step back and put things in perspective. I got tunnel vision, caught up in the stress and the exam frenzy. As is to be expected, this got worse and worse as the HSC exams approached, until one afternoon, a few days before English Paper One, I was just sitting in front of my computer, immobilised, exhausted and overloaded.

If you find yourself in a situation like this, go outside. Go for a walk, even if it's not something you like to do normally.

I found going for a walk to be one of the best ways to clear my head. And without wanting to sound too much like an aspiring Zen guru, clearing your head and stepping back is essential, especially during the HSC.

I know you don't feel like hearing this for the millionth time, but they *are* only exams, after all. They're important – that's why you're reading this – but in the greater scheme of things, they're not everything. Taking a break will make you realise this.

And if you *do* remember this, then you'll be able to enjoy Year 12 a lot more. Indeed, in Year 12 there is a lot to enjoy! Remember when you were in Year 7 and looked up at the giants wandering around the school in their final year? This is you, now. Studying and exams are only a part of school, so try and make the most of the whole experience before it's finished.

Motivation:

Find something that motivates you. It doesn't matter what it is. Maybe you want to get into a specific course, with a specific ATAR? Good. Think of that while you're studying. Or maybe you don't want to look back on the HSC and think to yourself, "Wow, if only I'd worked a bit harder." Also good. Think of that while you're studying. The key part is that *you're* motivated. If the only reason that you're working is because your parents are telling you to, you're probably not going to get as much done.

In my case, I don't like the idea of approaching something half-heartedly. When it came to studying, I wanted to do it as well as I could, and to know that I had genuinely tried my best.

So find a reason to work – something that *you* care about – and use that to spur yourself on. And if you really can't think of a *single* reason to work, well, that's fine too, but I guess the rest of this article isn't going to be particularly interesting to you.

Work first, play later:

The best way to reduce distraction and stay on task is to get your work done *early* in the day. You work better if you study hard for an hour or two in the morning and take the rest of the day off. I found I was spurred on by the thought that in a couple of hours I could relax and do what I wanted. And then, while I was relaxing later in the day, I didn't have that guilty "I'm procrastinating" sensation hanging shamefully around my neck, because I'd already done my work.

On that note, I think that working consistently and doing a little bit every day is better than taking large chunks of time off and then trying to cram everything into a small period.

Talk to your teachers:

Our teachers are a fantastic resource, but I only really realised this towards the end of my time at school. Ask your teachers questions, arrange to meet them, send them emails with practice questions to be marked. They'll be happy to help. This is especially useful for biology, when there's so much content to learn and when practice questions are essential.

Liking your subjects:

I did Advanced and Extension 1 English, Advanced Maths, French Continuers and Extension, Biology and Visual Arts. The reason why I mention this is because I actually liked my subjects. I think that this is one of the most important things to consider during the HSC.

Whilst I'd be lying if I said I was enthralled for every second of every class, on the whole I really enjoyed learning about my various subjects. This meant that sitting down to study was a lot easier.

Even though most of you have probably already picked your subjects, I would suggest reconsidering your choices if you find yourself driven to subjects that supposedly "scale well" over subjects that you enjoy.

The advice I was given was that one will do better in the subjects one likes, irrespective of scaling, because one will spend more time working on them. From my experience, this held true.

In my case, art was an especially good example of this. When I would head up to the art department to paint, I was doing something that was both enjoyable *and* productive. Subjects with a major work component, like art, although stressful at times, can be a real pleasure, so I would highly encourage you to think about doing one.

Moving onto Biology

I was fascinated by most of Biology. I loved learning about the processes and structures that facilitate life, and about the hidden complexity of the world around us. I loved the idea that there is so much going on that we are completely unaware of, and how biology and science can open our minds to these things. I loved learning about the seemingly limitless possibilities presented by new biological technologies, how these developments can shape society as a whole, and how they can solve far-reaching problems.

Studying for biology, though, takes a lot of time. The course is jam-packed with info, and there are always areas to extend one's understanding. They can never fit all of it into an exam, which puts one in the slightly awkward position of not knowing how much to study.

Follow the syllabus

My main suggestion would be to follow the syllabus tightly. Even though some parts of it might be a little bit vague, scrutinising it carefully is the best way to determine what they can test you on. The syllabus dot points should serve as a framework to base your study off and keep you focused. Think of them as histone proteins, around which the DNA strands of your knowledge are coiled.

This is how I suggest you do this:

- I'd encourage you to set out your notes according to the syllabus dot points, like so:

    6.1 How does mutation introduce new alleles into a population?

    a. explain a range of mutagens, including but not limited to:
        - physical – eg electromagnetic radiation sources
        ...

- chemicals

  ...

- naturally occurring mutagens

  ...

Making notes according to the syllabus will mean that you start to think in terms of the syllabus, and what types of questions they could potentially ask you.

- Examine the syllabus dot points closely. The question verbs will tell you what you need to be focusing on. I'll talk about this in more detail later on.

- You'll notice that the main sections are phrased as inquiry questions – for example, "5.1 How does reproduction ensure continuity of a species?" This should guide the way you think about the content grouped under the question. In this example, the syllabus lists 5.1 a) "mechanisms of reproduction" and 5.1 b) "fertilisation, implantation and hormonal control of pregnancy and birth in mammals" under the broad 5.1 enquiry question. Therefore, you should think about how "mechanisms of reproduction" and "fertilisation, implantation…" ensure continuity of a species. Even though they're probably not going to give you the enquiry question word for word in the exam, the questions you get might require you to link your understanding of the specifics (e.g. "mechanisms of reproduction") to the more general enquiry question.

Essentials first

Focus on the essentials first. The course can sometimes seem like a giant pedigree diagram, with each topic branch leading into another topic branch, and ample opportunities for getting sidetracked with extra information. My advice is to first focus on the basics (be guided in this respect by the syllabus dot points). Once you're comfortable with the fundamentals, branch out and extend your understanding. In other words, be sensible about how you allocate your time.

Answering exam questions:

Get to the point

Two of the most important things to keep in my mind when answering questions in any subject, but particularly in biology, is to be **clear** and **concise**. I struggled with this for a long time. At the beginning of the year, my answers to any question above 3 marks would trail on way past the allocated lines, and I would take ages to get to the point. As my teacher told us again and again, in Biology you don't get marks for correct but irrelevant information, and you don't get marks for beautifully formed sentences. You get them for *correct, relevant* information. So, stick to the point, and do it in as few words as possible. Dot points work well, as long as you're writing in full sentences.

Here's a practice question to show you what I mean:

> **Question**: *"Evaluate the effectiveness of different methods used to prevent and control the spread of malaria."*
>
> **(Beginning of) answer 1:**
> *Malaria is an infectious disease spread via the Anopheles mosquito, which serves as a vector for the malaria pathogen - the Plasmodium protozoan. This disease affects millions of people worldwide and causes hundreds of thousands of deaths each year. There are numerous methods that can be employed to prevent the spread of malaria at the local, regional and global levels, all of which have varied degrees of effectiveness. One method of growing importance at a regional level is gene driving, where genetically engineered genes that code for infertility are 'driven' through a mosquito population by biasing the typical laws of inheritance, with the ultimate goal of preventing vector proliferation. Whilst this method presents an effective way of preventing disease spread by removing the vector, it is still in testing and is not ready for widespread use...*

Whilst this information is correct, a lot of it simply isn't relevant to the question. The first three sentences are a wordy preamble that don't add anything to the answer. We have been asked to "evaluate" the methods used to control malaria, not to give a precis of what malaria is. The fourth sentence finally begins to answer the question by describing a method (gene driving) and evaluating it. However, it still doesn't do this in a particularly clear way.

To make sure that you're *really* answering the question, and that you're being as **clear** and **concise** as possible, I suggest you go about doing something along these lines:

(Beginning of) answer 2:

One preventative method of growing importance on a regional scale is gene driving:

- *This entails biasing the laws of inheritance so as to ensure that a genetically modified gene that codes for infertility is passed on through a mosquito population.*
- *Positive: This method enables the eradication of the malaria vector population, thus preventing disease spread.*
- *Negative:*
  - *The method is still in testing and is not ready for widespread use.*
  - *Genetic modification is opposed by numerous sectors of society, and so the implementation of gene drives may be difficult.*
  - *Eliminating mosquitoes may upset ecosystemic equilibrium and lead to damaging environmental impacts.*
  - *Judgement: Although the exact effects of gene drives are uncertain, it is likely to be an effective control method if implemented on a wide scale.*

> *Another method used to control malaria on a global scale is the use of antimalarials…*

This answer responds to the question more directly. It eliminates the preamble and gets stuck into the meat of the question. Because the question asks us to "evaluate", I organised the answer around the key sections of my response – the method, the positives, the negatives, and the judgement – and labelled each of them. I used dot points, but still used full sentences. The judgement acknowledges that the situation is not clear-cut, but it still makes a firm judgement (I was told that it's better to be black and white when making evaluations in biology, as unrealistic as that is).

These are all techniques my teacher recommended to us, and the key idea is clarity. Remember, the marker is going to be marking hundreds of answers. If yours is clear and concise, they'll understand it better and there's a good chance you'll get more marks.

Key words

Another essential part of answering questions is familiarising yourself with the key words and with what each one demands of you. Use the NESA glossary of key words (it's on their website) and learn the prescribed definitions of each one. Then, when you get an "analyse" question in the exam, you'll know exactly what they're asking you to do, and you'll know how it's different to an "explain", an "examine" or a "discuss". In the above example, the key word is "evaluate," which as you saw, means I had to give positives, negatives, and a judgement. If you know these key words really well, you'll be able to stick to the point more tightly.

Note-making:

I found that the majority of my study was dedicated to making notes. There's a good chance that I spent *too* much time making notes, meddling around with the layout and finer points, so be wary of that.

The way that I approached note-making involved several stages. In my opinion, this technique works best for content heavy subjects like biology.

Stage 1: "Melting pot"

>These are the notes you'll make in class. When people are throwing around ideas and the teacher is listing information, this is what you'll be scribbling down. It'll probably be a bit messy and disorganised, but that's okay, because you'll fix it up in the next stage…

Stage 2: "Broad notes"

>Read through your "melting pot" notes in your own time, and take out all the important, relevant information and ideas. Lay them out neatly, and organise them according to syllabus dot points. During this stage, you would read the relevant pages of the textbook and combine textbook information with your other notes.

Stages 3+: "Condensed notes"

>Take the main points from your "broad notes" and focus on learning them (I'll come to some memorisation strategies in a second). Gradually whittle down your notes until you're left with brief summaries, mind-maps and key words that will trigger a whole cascade of associations in your memory. When you've got to this point, there's a good chance that you'll be comfortable with the topic, and ready for the exam.

Memorisation:

Do you remember that scene in Harry Potter, where Professor Umbridge makes Harry write lines as punishment, and the lines get etched into his skin at the same time? If you've read it as many times as I have, you probably do.

Many people see memorisation as the final stage of studying – something to be done just before exams start. The thing is, the actual process of note-making is a process of learning and memorisation as well. This is especially true of a content-heavy subject like biology. Because of this, buying a study guide or someone else's notes is a good idea if you're going to use them as a reference, *not* as your primary study material. So, make your own notes. As you write out line after line of notes, they'll be imprinted into your brain at the same time, subconsciously, just like Harry and the pen. Although it'll probably (*probably*) be a bit less painful.

A side note (about...notes): Writing them, rather than typing them, is meant to be even better in this regard, but for subjects like biology that simply isn't practical, so I wouldn't stress about it.

However, there's a lot more to memorising notes than simply making them. This is especially true for a subject like biology, where memorisation seems to be such a big part of the course (I say 'seems', because with the new syllabus, this might not be the case anymore, but I'll get to that in a bit). So, how on earth do you memorise a large stack of notes that are filled with more information than the human genome?

Start early

If it's three days before the exam and you look at your notes for the first time since making them...well, good luck. If you start several weeks, or even several months beforehand, then you will be in a much stronger position.

Use colour

Brightly coloured notes are so much easier to memorise. When you're chewing your nails in anxiety an hour into the bio exam because you can't remember which enzyme synthesises the mRNA in transcription, the colour of your highlighter will trigger your memory and you'll think "Yellow! RNA polymerase!" Buy a pack of coloured pens, so you can underline and circle to your heart's content.

I would suggest making notes in monotone, and then going back over them with colour while you're revising. Memorising is always easier when you're actually doing something (like highlighting), as opposed to just staring blankly at a page.

Read aloud

Explain the difference between the humoral and cell-mediated immune responses to your parents. Teach the principles of population genetics to your baby sister. Describe the menstrual cycle to your dog. This works best when you're talking to someone who knows nothing about the subject. Then you'll be thinking on the spot, trying to explain things as **clearly** and **concisely** as possible.

Create your own 'shorthand' vocabulary

I substituted symbols for common words to speed up the process of writing and reading my notes. ☆ means 'because', Θ means 'however', and so on (plus the usual ones, like arrows). It might seem silly, but I found it useful. Eliminate long sentences by using symbols and shortening words.

Keep summarizing

Condense your notes until the memory of whole concepts is triggered by key words, mind maps, and short lists. This will make your process of memorisation *active* (in a similar way that highlighting will) rather than a passive process of reading and yawning.

Talk to your friends

Discuss parts of the course you're struggling with. Test each other. Work through practice questions together. Having a sounding-board to bounce ideas off is great.

Flashcards

Good for (testing yourself on) biological processes and definitions.

Don't try and memorise your notes word-for-word

That's not useful, and you'll waste time. What's important is that you actually *understand* them.

Focus on what you don't know

Don't waste time with what you're super comfortable with. Get stuck into the parts you find challenging, until you don't.

Practice questions

They're useful if you check the answers, or even better, get them marked by your teachers. Time yourself closer to the exam to see if you're staying on track.

Memorise while you're doing other things

When you're ironing your clothes or having a shower, go through your notes in your head. Just be wary that you can't do this *all* the time. Otherwise the biology will just start clogging up your mind, like some kind of mental plaque. You'll just get more and more stressed. Sometimes, I had to consciously stop thinking about biology because it (and the stress) was preventing me from falling asleep. If this happens to you, take a step back.

New Syllabus Exam:

The main thing that struck me and a lot of people I know, was just how little content we were actually tested on in the 2019 HSC exam. It seems somewhat counter-productive to create a syllabus jam-packed with content, and then write an exam that doesn't really test you on it. However, I think that's the flavour of the new course. It's more interested in you solving problems *using* your biological understanding, rather than getting you to spew out memorised info.

So, do practice questions that get you to solve problems, process data, and use evidence to come to conclusions, rather than purely doing ones that require you to regurgitate information. This should prepare you well for the exam. The thing is, you do have to actually understand the biology as well. There's a fine balance between focusing too much on memorising information, and not doing enough. I would advise you to err on the side of caution, and make sure that you understand the whole course well, even though they might not test you on all of it.

SUMMARY

Now we're nearing the pointy end of my article, here's a short summary of the main ideas (a "condensed" version!). To get my ideas across, I've developed a delightful, encouraging *and* informative acrostic poem for you to enjoy:

Ensure you keep your hobbies and see your friends.

Need to clear your head? Go outside.

Just talk to your teachers.

Only do subjects that you actually like.

You must be motivated for *yourself*.

Be **clear** and **concise**.

It's important to focus on what you don't understand, until you do.

Old syllabus is more facts-based, new syllabus (seems to be) more interested in *applying* your understanding.

Learn what the key question words mean, and how to answer questions for each of them.

OMG notes work way better in colour! And when you condense them! And acrostics are harder than they seem!

Good to make your own notes.

You need to use the syllabus.

!Plan your work in advance!

I hope that some of this has been useful for you. I just want to reiterate — stay organised, stay focused, and work hard, but keep your wits about you and don't lose perspective. Good luck!

Economics: Studying economically

By John Wang

> "However true something may be, if it is not fully, frequently, and fearlessly discussed, it will be held as a dead dogma, not a living truth." - John Stuart Mill's on Liberty

Hello! My name is John Wang, I graduated from Sydney Grammar School in 2019 and placed 8th in the state for Economics. The path of the dreaded High School Certificate may seem thorny and stressful now. However, it doesn't have to be, especially when you recognise that it is a path well-trodden (by pretty much everyone before you). Have faith, relax but stay firm, and enjoy the ride!

General Advice for Year 12

1. Think about the post-HSC Life

> After rain there's a rainbow. After a storm there's calm. After the night there's a morning and after an end there's a new beginning.

This was always my attitude towards the HSC. During assessment periods, I drew motivation and strength from optimistic prospects about the freedom of the post-HSC life. Things such as being able to return to my past-time of swimming at the beach every second day gave me great motivation to get to the end. The current time period which you are in - the HSC marathon - may seem painfully perennial. However, like all things, it is only transitory; something you will retrospectively look back on with bittersweet laughter. Seeing those in the year above me continuing to prosper - with a good ATAR or not - really helped bring clarity to my vision of what was in store after the HSC journey if I put in the hard work. I now know that this could not have been truer, having reached the other side.

2. Don't sweat the small stuff

Dropped 10 ranks because of one mark? Broke your laptop a week before exams? Forgot to bring some books home to study? Haven't even started your art major work after an entire term and a half into the HSC? Yep, all of this happened to me throughout my HSC year. Did it matter at all in the end? At all? Nope.

At the moment, things might seem catastrophic, disastrous, or like "THE WORLD IS GOING TO END" in the myopic bubble of the HSC, but these trivial issues really do not matter as much as you think! I spent most of the year biting my nails over minute mark differences and calculating assessment weightings. However, in the end, the HSC mark calculations are so blunt that often a 10 or even 20-rank difference in a subject means you will still get the same internal mark as the other person! Cut-throat competitiveness is way too overblown!

Remember too that the HSC external exams make up 50% of your entire ATAR. This means that you should never feel like stuffing up an internal assessment cluster or a few exams cannot be turned around later!

3. Spend time on your weaker subjects

Even though you may love spending time on stuff that you're good at or enjoy, this isn't the best strategy to cracking the HSC. The ATAR counts 10 whole units and your best bet is to spend more time on the weaker subjects. From an Economics point of view, according to the law of diminishing marginal returns, you will get less back for extra time spent on a subject that you are good at, as opposed to spending that time on a subject you are worse at. You might improve by one or two marks in the good subject, whereas if you spent time on the bad one you'd improve by five or six. More bang for your buck, so to speak. In my experience, I adhered to this rule by making Economics one of the subjects I spent the least time on, as it was probably my best subject.

4. The "It's Now or Never" Mentality

This was my best defence against the fiendish goblin known as procrastination.

"It's ok I will just do my homework tomorrow; I have tons of time."

"I don't need to write notes for this until Term Two."

Don't listen to the "Procrastination Goblin". These are lies. Pure lies. I know because throughout my high school career I was somewhat of a master procrastinator. I definitely improved during the HSC year, however even during Trials there were points where I said, "It's all right, I will just study harder for the actual HSC."

Take it from me, "saving brain power for later" is not a legitimate strategy. In fact, you get even more worn out in studying for the external HSC exams because it's after the emotional rollercoaster of graduating school. Moral of the story: put in your all throughout the year because you won't be able to "magically put in more effort" down the line. Cold showers, morning swims, drawing and becoming a meditative early bird helped me stay focused and disciplined.

HSC Study Tips

1. Cover your wallpaper with homework assignments and exam notices
   - This keeps you on track and cognisant of deadlines.
2. Teach others and make study-buddies
   - Having placed first in my school for Economics, I was often asked by peers for help. I was always open to helping others do their work - it didn't hurt. However, only when I started helping teaching content to others did I realise this action actually BENEFITED ME TOO, as it brought clarity to my knowledge of the subject. Counter-intuitively, teaching is one of the best ways to memorise and learn things for yourself.
   - I also collaborated with my friends who placed second and third in my grade for Economics. We shared notes/essays, explained material and asked challenging questions to each other. **All three of us ended up state-ranking!**
3. Write neatly
   - I can't stress how much good handwriting can affect your mark.
   - It makes it so much easier to read for the marker and puts them in a good mood.
   - If you are looking to state-rank, the markers can sometimes actually differentiate the top few ranks based on things like handwriting and concision alone!
   - So, you should practise handwriting, or at least try to write really big and neatly in normal class time!
   - I watched YouTube tutorials, purchased a kindergarten handwriting book and literally started tracing out my ABCs again.
4. Note-making

Most of my study time was dedicated to making notes. Without a doubt, structuring your syllabus knowledge and writing these notes out in dot points is the absolute best study tool. I personally never used flashcards as I found them tedious to make and with little space to write on - but that's just me! Due to the way I made my notes, I personally didn't even start doing past papers until a week before the exam block. I also didn't memorise my notes until the exam was very soon, as the process of refining and deepening my notes over and over again allowed me to basically commit them to memory whilst making them anyway. My alternative memorisation technique is to write out my notes three or four times, moving on to the next section slowly after memorising a previous section.

Although this worked for me, it may not work for you - everyone has their own study style and mine is slightly odd! Give it a try and see if it works for you. If not, there are definitely many others in this book!

Economics

HSC Economics was challenging, dense and complex but that's part of the reason why I liked it! Learning to balance and trace the dozens of factors affecting the exchange rate at one time or understanding the real-world impacts of the Sino-US Trade War were really intriguing. Economics is beautiful because it is a subject which operates not on a restrictive, archaic syllabus but instead has deep relevance to the contemporary real-world.

Noting this, Economics is one of the most content-heavy subjects of the HSC. If you want to excel, you need to be stretching yourself beyond the classroom by reading news articles casually.

How I made my Economics notes

I had syllabus topic notes (for Multiple Choice and Short Answers) and an essay theory/statistic bank (specifically for the Essay section).

Topic Notes

In terms of formatting, this is what a standard page of my notes would look like.

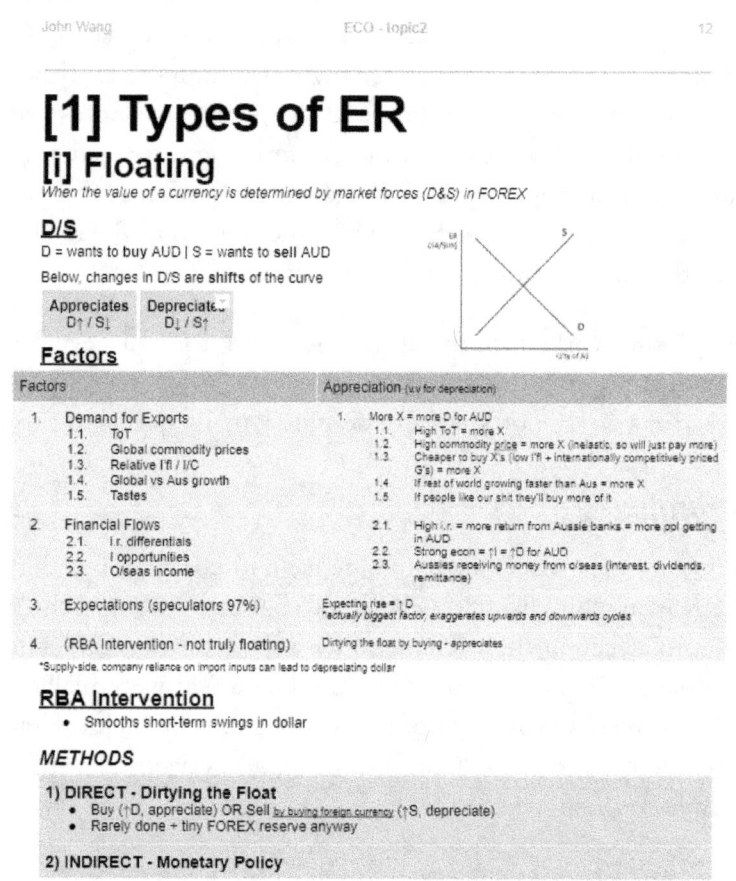

- In my syllabus topic notes I basically summarised the Dixon/O'Mahony textbook into a SUPER CONCISE form, making sure to remove all statistics and extraneous information.

- Both my notes and in my essays, I used abbreviations to increase concision - especially since Economics is filled with so much jargon. Economic growth became "EG", international competitiveness became "I/C" and distribution of income and wealth became "D'n of I + W".

- Writing your notes in tables and dot points is extremely beneficial for aligning yourself with the "correct mental approach" one should take to learning a subject like Economics. Heuristics for Economics basically comes down to learning lists and processes: numbered dot points really assist with digesting this sort of information.

Essay Plans

1. **Why you shouldn't memorise full essays**

   Rather than memorising full essays word-for-word, I wrote essay plans and loosely memorised specific parts of these plans. This gives you an immense amount of flexibility and reduces the stress of rote-memorising 30 essays only for the examiner to ask a question you haven't prepared for. For example, in Topic Three, I would know how to explain the links between economic growth, unemployment and inflation, and have memorised certain statistics for each period. Memorising them as components allowed me to interchange them in my mind depending on what combination of economic factors the question was asking for.

2. **Learning theory**

   I also made super concise explanations of "theory" for each topic which I could basically say word-for-word in the examination. For example, I would have half a page diagrammatically explaining the process through which a cash rate is set and its subsequent impacts on the economy through the transmission mechanism.

3. Statistics

Alongside the statistics embedded in my essay plans, I also made a statistics-table of all the significant statistics in the past few years for convenience. This included numbers like: growth, unemployment, inflation, interest rates, nominal Trade Weighted Index, Current Account changes, Net Foreign Liabilities, Iron Ore price, Terms of Trade, Budget Stances and wage growth. But remember, Economics is a highly dynamic subject, so make sure you are keeping up with the latest statistics in the news or online.

Exam Techniques

- *Try to answer questions to the best of your ability before moving on:* otherwise it wastes time to go back to the question and reread/rethink everything.

- Use Reading Time to skim-read the short answers and essay stimuli and then carefully read the Multiple-Choice section to gain an initial boost in the exam.

- Stay disciplined timing-wise. For a Band 6 student completing the external HSC exam: multiple choice can be completed in 10-20 minutes, short answers in 45-60 minutes and essays can take up to an hour each.

- *Plan the essay*: Use 5-10 minutes to write up a framework before diving in. This will help you immeasurably!

Multiple Choice Section

1. Re-read every question.
2. Do not overthink it. Think about what the marker wants (most of the time Economics is pretty straightforward, it's probably not a trick question).
3. Eliminate clearly wrong answers.

4. Go back to check your answers with a fresh mind after you have completed the Short Answers section as there could be trick questions or little nuances that you did not initially recognise.

5. Don't trace back too far in causes. This is an extremely common mistake. Most often, the correct answers is the most direct one.

Some trick questions that I have seen come up a few times:

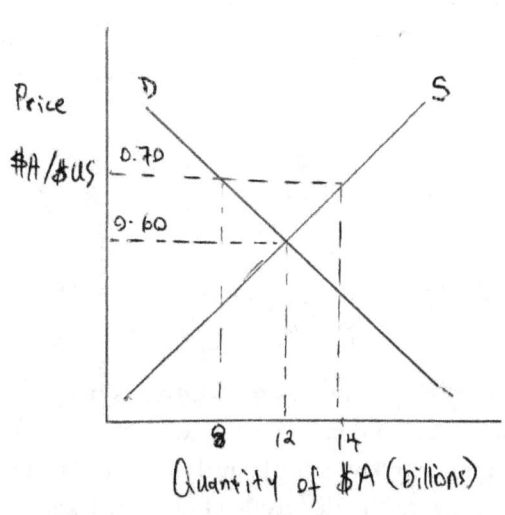

1. If the Reserve bank of Australia wishes to raise the exchange rate from $A1 = $US0.60 to $A1 = 0.70, then it must:

   (A)   Buy $A2 billion
   (B)   Sell $A2 billion
   (C)   Sell $A6 billion
   (D)   Buy $A6 billion

2. Which of the following is an example of reducing protection?:

   (A)   Increasing tariff levels on imports

(B)	Increasing local content rules
(C)	Increasing quota levels
(D)	Decreasing the cash rate

Year	National Income ($)	Savings ($)
1	1000	400
2	1500	500
3	2000	600

3. If the govt wishes to raise the level of national income by $1000 in Year 4, by how much will it have to increase investment?:

(A)	$100
(B)	$200
(C)	$600
(D)	$1000

1. The answer is **D**. The reason for this is because if you want to artificially raise the exchange rate to $0.70 you must make up for the gap between supply and demand at the price point of $0.70 by buying the difference between 14 and 8 billion. Many people confuse themselves by thinking that all you need to do is to buy the difference between 12 and 14 billion to bump it up there but that would only move your exchange rate up a couple of cents.

2. The answer is **C**. This one catches so many students out in Economics past papers. Increasing quota levels means increasing the allowance of import volume, thus reducing the amount of protection you are providing for domestic producers.

3. The answer is **B**. Marginal Propensity to Save is calculated as. The formula for the multiplier is . The answer is calculated by the formula . Therefore, . Change in investment = $200.

Short Answer Questions

My main tips can be summarised as follows:

1. Have a clear stance.
2. Be concise.
3. Don't waste time restating the question.
4. Thoroughly flesh out every logical step
5. Use connecting terms like "Naturally" and "Indeed".
6. *Don't be afraid to dot-point your response*: Make the marker's life easy. Full sentences or paragraph responses which lose structure is exactly what you should NOT be doing for short answers.
7. *Name-drop key syllabus terms*: For example, in questions regarding the Environmental topic you should be name-dropping at least a few of the following terms where relevant: free-rider, tragedy of the commons, Kuznets Curve, externalities, market failure, non-excludable/non-rival public goods.
8. *Statistics:* You will hardly ever need statistics for short answers, however they are necessary in certain questions which most often occur as relating to: specific international organisations/trade agreements, specific microeconomic/macroeconomic policies, or the country case study
9. *Mark Allocation:* This is not a hard-and-fast rule; however, a good framework is that if the question has:
    a. Even marks:
        - For every 2 marks: Identify ONE idea (1) and explain that idea (2)
    b. Odd marks:
        - Round up and use the same logic for even marks (treat 5 marks like a 6 marker, i.e. 3 ideas)

Writing Essays

Introduction

1. *Make your introduction short and sweet:* It should be half a page at MAXIMUM. Don't be afraid to split this into two paragraphs just to relieve the eyes of the marker.

2. *Define the key terms of the question:* A good trick I use is to slot in definitions WHILST conveniently answering the question.

    - E.g.: **"Discuss the relationship between economic growth and unemployment:** Economic growth, [definition], is inversely linked to unemployment..."

3. Unlike English, you SHOULD NOT list the points that will be addressed in the body of an essay.

4. Include a general stat glossing over a recent trend in the last line of the introduction.

Theory

1. Theory should take up around 30% of the essay content.

2. *Diagrams:* Make sure to label and reference diagrams correctly. Remember, however, that diagrams are supposed to help propel your argument by elucidating a mechanism, not just sit there to tick the marker's boxes.

Here is an example of effectively using a diagram to explain demand-pull inflation:

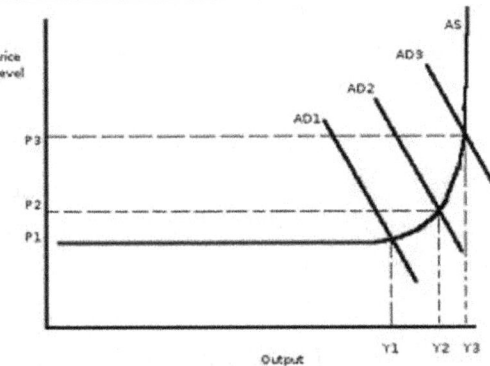

Fig.1 "When aggregate demand exceeds aggregate supply, demand pulls inflation results. In the short run, an economy cannot increase its productive capacity, and prices rise as consumers are forced to bid against each other for the limited goods and services. This is shown in the diagram below, where increases in aggregate demand from AD1 to AD3 has caused price levels to soar from OP1 to OP3. Aggregate supply becomes highly inelastic in the short term as output approaches Y3, and hence, further increases in AD would result in significant levels of demand-pull inflation rather than increases in output."

Body Paragraphs

1. *Stimulus:* If there is a stimulus, make sure to make specific references to it in every paragraph. This means taking out quotation extracts if it is a passage or referencing specific statistics if it is a graph.

2. *Constantly name-drop the question's key terms:* This signals to the marker that you are answering the question and staying on track.

3. *Slip in bits of theory throughout:* This helps ground your assertions and streamline your logic.

    i. For example, a nice insertion of theory can be: "Household investment rose by 10% in Q3 2019, resulting in a 0.5% uplift in growth **(AD = C + I + G + X-M)**."

4. *Paragraphing:* Split up paragraphs into sub-paragraphs just to relieve the marker's eyes from facing a page-long block of text. A strong response can have anywhere from 6-10 paragraphs.

5. *Statistics*

    i. *Form links between your statistics:* Everything is about building a cohesive argument and you do that by tracing a chain of cause and effect.

        - For example: *"Being our main trading partner, the fall in Australian GDP between 2012-15 was catalysed by China's deceleration in growth from 12.2% (2010) to 7.6% (Q3, 2012). As Chinese demand dwindled and global supply increased due to Mark II mines coming on-stream, iron ore prices fell from the $US 187/tonne peak to just $39.60 USD/tonne by 2015. A devastating loss in export revenue caused economic growth to fall from a 4.8% peak (2012) to 1.9% (2015)."*

    ii. Remember, stats are used to **back up** your argument, not spearhead it. Thus, you need to **evaluate** by outlining the positives and negatives of something, then making a judgement.

    iii. *Get extremely up-to-date statistics:* Economics is a constantly changing game and sometimes you could be completely wrong saying that growth is skyrocketing when in fact the week before the exam quarterly growth plummeted. For my monetary policy essay, 60% of the statistics I used were from the last month.

    iv. Don't just give the statistic in its isolation, make sure to give the change and compare it to its long term figure.

    v. *Researching statistics:*

        - What I like to do is start to write a sentence, see what I am talking about, and then spend about 2-5 mins looking up a few stats for that specific sentence. This process is extremely laborious but ultimately worth it as your statistical knowledge will directly impact your success in the exam.

6. *Standing out:* Although not necessary, you can slide in bits of extra economic knowledge to show you are a student who goes above and beyond the syllabus - this will help you to stand out.

   i. *Extra Economic Theory:* I was often name-dropping economic theories in my essays from seminal economists. Some commonly useful ones include Ricardo's Principle of Comparative Advantage, Lewis Turning Point, and Okun's Law.

   ii. *Quotations:* common economists to quote include: Ross Gittins, John Kehoe, Phillip Lowe and Guy Debelle. If you want to use quotations, you must **reference** them in the correct format. For example, "It would be so much less risky just to have some fiscal stimulus" (Gittins, 2019).

Conclusion

1. It should be a concise one-two sentence summary of your line of argument and clear statement of your stance if it is a judgement question (*Assess, Evaluate* etc).
2. Do NOT introduce new concepts in the conclusion.

Good Luck!

Purchasing this book and bothering to hear from students who have completed the HSC means you're already on the right path! Stay relaxed, good luck and all the best for your HSC journey!

John's Economics Cheat Sheet

Multiple Choice Questions:
- Read the question. Read it again.
- Don't overthink it
- Don't trace back too far in terms of the "causes"

Short Answer Questions:
- Dot-point your response
- Don't repeat the question
- Thoroughly step out your logic
- Name-drop key syllabus terms

Essays:
- Constantly name-drop the question's key terms
- Split up your paragraphs to relieve the marker's eyes
- Form links between your statistics

Economics: Attaining Maximum Output

By Patrick Nah

> *"The will to win, the desire to succeed, the urge to reach your full potential... These are the keys that will unlock the door to personal excellence."* — *Confucius*

Introduction

My name is Patrick Nah, and I graduated from Baulkham Hills High School in 2019 with an ATAR of 99.95. I achieved a state rank of 3rd in HSC Economics with a mark of 99. At UNSW, I intend to study a double degree comprising a Bachelor of Economics (Honours) with a major in Econometrics, plus a Bachelor of Science.

Throughout high school, I possessed a mentality to be the very best that I could be and strived to achieve an ATAR of 99.95. In doing so, I developed strict study habits, which I have summarised into 5 key pieces of advice.

General Advice
1. Prepare a Study Timetable

In order to remain focussed on my academic goals, I produced a weekly study timetable. However, I did not strictly follow the timetable, because it is very difficult to estimate exactly how long a task would take to complete. Instead, I used the timetable as a rough indication of the level of work I needed to complete in one day.

It is crucial that you allocate adequate study time to all your subjects. You should not excessively focus on your strongest subject at the neglect of your weakest subject. This is a common pitfall for many students, as they prefer to study the subjects which they enjoy most. Instead, you should prioritise your weakest subject(s), and devote less time to your strongest subject(s). For example, my weakest subject was English, so I dedicated approximately 30 hours weekly towards studying English in the holidays before the HSC, compared to around 20 hours for each of Economics and Chemistry, my strongest subjects.

The reasoning behind this is that the ATAR is based off your HSC aggregate. If you devote more time to your strongest subject, you may only be able to boost your mark by a few percent. However, if you use this same time studying your weakest subject, you can improve your mark by a much larger margin – say 10 or 20 percent. As such, your aggregate, and hence your ATAR, will benefit more.

Below is my timetable for October the 7th to 13th – just before the start of the HSC.

As you can see, despite the hectic study regime, I was still able to enjoy hobbies such as playing the piano, weights training and cross country running. It is crucial to maintain extra-curricular activities throughout Year 12, because they provide an opportunity for you to take your mind off your studies, and ultimately retain your mental sanity.

	Monday	Tuesday	Wednesday	Thursday	Friday	Saturday	Sunday
06:00	Weights training	Cross Country	Weights training	Cross Country	Weights training	Cross Country	Cross Country
07:00	Chemistry HSC 2008	Chemistry HSC 2007	Chemistry HSC 2006	Chemistry Notes	Chemistry HSC 2005	Chemistry Notes	Chemistry Notes
08:00	Breakfast	Breakfast	Breakfast	Breakfast	Breakfast	Breakfast	Breakfast
09:00	English Trial JRAHS 1	Mod C Practice – 2 questions	Module A Quotes and Essay	English Trial HAHS 1	English Trial HGHS 1	Common Module Quotes and Essay	English Trial NBHS 1
10:00	English Trial JRAHS 2	Module C Techniques	Module B Quotes and Essay	English Trial HAHS 2	English Trial HGHS 2	Module A and B Context	English Trial NBHS 2
11:00							
12:00							
13:00	Lunch	Lunch	Lunch	Lunch	Lunch	Lunch	Lunch
14:00	Economics HSC 2012 Essays	Economics HSC 2011 Essays	Economics HSC 2012, 2011 SA and MC	Economics HSC 2010 Essays	Economics HSC 2009 Essays	Economics HSC 2010, 2009 SA and MC	Economics HSC 2008 Complete
15:00							
16:00	JRAHS 4U 2010	JRAHS 4U 2009	JRAHS 3U 2008	JRAHS 4U 2008	JRAHS 4U 2007		
17:00							
18:00						Economics Notes	Economics Notes
19:00						Break/dinner	Break/dinner
20:00	Break/dinner	Break/dinner	Break/dinner	Break/dinner	Break/dinner	Piano	Piano
21:00	JRAHS 3U 2010	JRAHS 3U 2009	JRAHS 3U 2007	JRAHS 3U 2006	JRAHS 3U 2005	Economics/ Chemistry Notes	Economics/ Chemistry Notes
22:00							

When people complain about not having enough time, it is often due to the presence of distractions. Perhaps the most widespread distraction is social media, although this is one which can easily be foregone. I would only check Facebook for 10 minutes just after waking up, and just before going to bed. Therefore, it did not interfere with my productivity. Additionally, I ensured that my study was productive and was able to focus by minimising the presence of distractions. While I did study at the library, I often studied by myself. I mention this because many students fall into the trap of visiting the library to socialise and will waste countless precious hours in the process.

Overall, I would recommend that you plan a study schedule that suits you and your academic goals. My timetable was very ambitious as I was aiming to achieve an ATAR of 99.95, but if your academic goals are different, then feel free to allocate more or less free time.

2. Self-accelerated Study

In order to maximise my understanding of the content, I would learn the content three times prior to the HSC.

1. I would first study the content on my own at least 1 year before it would be taught at school. For example, I started studying preliminary Economics and Chemistry at the beginning of Year 10 and finished my self-study of the HSC course for these subjects at the end of Year 11. In this stage, it doesn't matter if you can't understand everything – even if you can only understand half the content, you already have a head start over everyone else.

2. Secondly, I would learn the content at school, already having familiarised myself with it.

3. Thirdly, after the trial examination, I would read over the textbook and any other resources supplied by my teachers in order to cover any gaps in my knowledge. This follows a principle

known as spaced learning (also discussed below). By learning the content several times over, you will progressively retain more of the knowledge required. It is impossible to retain 100% of the content which you learn. However, if you progressively re-learn this content, then you will attain a greater understanding of the subject over time.

Even if you have such a high level of dedication, you must ensure that you continuously revise the content so that you do not forget it. In order to do this, I would complete one past paper every week throughout Year 11 and 12.

However, many subjects have had their syllabuses updated, and some questions in older exams may no longer be relevant – if this is the case, only attempt the questions which are relevant to the new syllabus.

3. Making Notes Effectively

After each lesson at school, I would complete my notes for the content covered that day. This would allow me to complete my notes at a reasonable pace, instead of cramming and writing large amounts of notes just prior to exam periods. Additionally, I would not have to re-learn content that had not been revised across an entire term and would naturally have been forgotten.

After completing a rough draft of your notes (ideally 2 to 3 weeks before your exam), you should begin condensing your notes by removing any extraneous information. This is where the syllabus comes in. By referring to the syllabus, ask yourself the following question when reading over each section of your notes:

> *Is this information relevant to the syllabus?*

While it is perfectly acceptable (and actually encouraged) to extend beyond the syllabus, you should ensure that you do not stray from the key ideas presented by the syllabus.

If you are not sure whether some information is useful for your exam, don't hesitate to ask your teacher. Their job is not to make your life miserable by devising harsh and unreasonable exams. They are there to assist you in maximising your HSC mark.

By reading over your notes and removing excess information, you should have a concise copy of the theory you require for your exam. I followed a rule in which the length of my notes would be no more than one-fifth that of the textbook. For example, if the textbook was 400 pages long, then my notes would be at most 80 pages (excluding any case studies or additional information not found within the textbook).

This ensured that my notes covered the content tested by the syllabus, plus some extension content, but no more. Some students fall into the trap of thinking that they must memorise every little detail in the textbook. Remember, the textbook authors are experts on the subject matter, and would have extensively researched the topic prior to writing the textbook. Therefore, there will more than likely be content which is not directly relevant to the syllabus in the textbook.

4. Past Papers

Past papers are your best friend in understanding the style of questions that you will face in your exams. Even if you have a very strong understanding of the content, you may not achieve exceptional marks if you don't understand how to answer questions. The HSC is becoming increasingly focussed on skills and application of knowledge, as opposed to the simple recitation of said knowledge.

Therefore, you must learn how to answer questions effectively. Use the marking criteria and sample answer provided as a benchmark for your answer. However, you should note that the HSC sample answers are by no means exceptional and will not always score full marks. Therefore, you should attempt to extend your response to a level beyond these sample answers.

You should also learn and understand the directive terms. For example, if a question's directive term is *evaluate*, you may only receive half of the available marks if you simply regurgitate information, even if you demonstrate an extensive understanding of the content. This is because, for this directive term, you are required to make a judgement based off of statistics or information.

Another example is for simpler questions, such as those requiring you to *identify* or *outline*. If you provide a comprehensive analysis and evaluation of the content, you will not lose any marks and will most likely attain full marks for that question. However, you will have wasted time that could have been better spent answering harder questions, and you may find yourself short on time later in the exam.

5. Spaced Learning

Like my strategy of learning content three times, I also employed the principle of *"Spaced Learning"* to ensure that I did not forget any theory. This would involve revising content four times by going over my notes and attempting some sample questions. I revised the content according to the following pattern:

- Two days after learning the content
- One week after learning the content
- One month after learning the content
- Three months after learning the content

I spent no more than half an hour for each piece of revision.

A common pitfall for many students is neglecting to revise content after they learn it, and only re-learning it when cramming for their exams. This is inefficient, as more time must be spent re-learning the basic principles behind the theory. On the other hand, by using *Spaced Learning*, I would already have a decent understanding of the content when it was time to revise for exams. This allowed me more time to do practice papers.

Economics

Economics is a subject that is unique because it is extremely applicable to our lives. Our daily decisions are guided by supply, demand, interest rates, wages and opportunity cost to name a few. It was for this reason that I passionately enjoyed studying economics, and I have included five pieces of advice for those of you studying the subject below.

Some General Tips and Advice

1. A common misconception is the need to memorise each and every niche statistic in the textbook. In reality, no marker will expect this from you – they will take your word for a made-up statistic, as long as it is reasonable (although I *do not* recommend doing this).

   Nonetheless, to achieve an exceptional essay mark, you must endeavour to memorise key statistics. These include, but should not be restricted to:

   - Australia's GDP growth rate
   - The inflation rate
   - The cash rate
   - The current account (and its components)
   - The unemployment and underemployment rates, and the NAIRU
   - Effectiveness of microeconomic policies
   - Effectiveness of environmental policies
   - Country case study statistics

   If you don't use statistics in your essays, your mark in the HSC can be restricted to around 17 to 18 out of 20 for an otherwise exceptional response.

To assist in memorising statistics, I devised a revision sheet of the key economic indicators, plus some other useful statistics for essays.

2. Another area of controversy is how much you should write for short-answer questions. In reality, the lines provided are a reflection of how much the *typical student* would write. But *typical* shouldn't be your benchmark! As such, I have devised a method of estimating how much to write, based off the type of short-answer questions:

    - "SHORT" answer questions (1 – 3 marks): Simply write until all the lines are filled. Any more is optional and depends on your answer.
    - "MEDIUM" answer questions (4 – 6 marks): It is much easier to attain full marks if you write beyond the lines for these questions, preferably to the bottom of the page for longer questions.

    Of course, this is just a guide. If you have miniscule, neat writing (I do not recommend writing too small if you can help it, because markers have difficulty reading this and it is often slower), then filling up the lines provided is often sufficient.

3. Time allocation really depends on how you feel after having completed several practice exams. However, I would not recommend adhering to the suggested times provided on the front of the examination paper. These values come from dividing the number of marks by the number of minutes. But some marks (such as the multiple-choice questions) are much easier to gain than others (such as the essays). Consequently, I followed the following time plan:

    - 25 minutes for multiple-choice questions
    - 45 minutes for short-answer questions
    - 55 minutes per essay (including 5 minutes planning time per essay)

4. Keep up with economic trends on the news. Economics is a highly dynamic subject, because statistics which you learn now may no longer be relevant or correct when you sit the HSC exam. By reading the news daily (or even weekly), you will familiarise yourself with changes in both the Australian and Global economies, and you can use more updated information in your exams. A great example is that Australia recorded its first Current Account Surplus in 40 years in the June Quarter of 2019. Had you not read the news, you would simply have learnt the structural and cyclical factors which have led to the persistent Current Account Deficit. While these factors are correct and should be learnt, it is equally important to understand how these factors were overcome, namely due to rising commodity prices and export volumes, low global interest rates and a lack of inward investment leading to a lower Net Primary Income Deficit.

5. Making notes allows you to consolidate your knowledge, because you are required to paraphrase long sections of text into more concise dot-points. While using other people's notes may save you time, it ultimately does not allow you to study effectively. Firstly, you may have a false sense of security because you feel that you have a complete resource which you can use to study for your exams. However, you can never guarantee that another student knows everything! Secondly, everybody has their own way of writing notes, and the formatting and layout of someone else's notes may not suit you.

Keynesian AD Cross

- AD is generally considered for the 3-sector model (C, I and G)

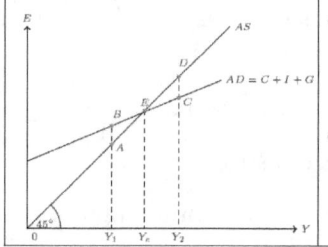

- Inflationary gap occurs if AD exceeds the level of income required for full employment
  - Excess demand causes demand-pull inflation
  - Excess AD is the area between the two curves (area ABE)
  - To close inflationary gap, contractionary FP reduces AD
- Deflationary gap occurs if AD is smaller than the level of income required for full employment
  - Excess AS is area between the two curves (area CDE)
  - To close deflationary gap, expansionary FP stimulates AD

Therefore, you should prepare your own notes. You do not need to make your notes neat, but you should at least make sure that information can be found easily. I found using headings, dot points and abbreviations to be useful in condensing my notes, an example of which is shown on the previous page.

I used LaTeX to write my notes, because I found the need to input lines of code more mentally engaging than simply typing text in Microsoft Word. This allowed me to retain information better, whilst also providing a more aesthetically pleasing appearance.

Some Practice Questions

I have already covered some of the exam techniques and strategies, although it is easier for you to learn these techniques by including examples.

Multiple Choice:

For most multiple-choice questions, the simplest piece of advice I can give is to eliminate any incorrect options, and if necessary, make an educated guess. Questions involving two variables are quite common, and most often require elimination of incorrect options in a *progressive manner*. Consider the following question:

If the national unemployment rate rises from 3% to 4%, how will taxation revenue and welfare expenditures be affected?

	Taxation Revenue	Welfare Expenditure
A	Increase	Increase
B	Increase	Decrease
C	Decrease	Increase
D	Decrease	Decrease

Let us consider the column for taxation revenue first. Because less individuals are contributing to production of goods and services, there are less individuals earning an income and hence paying PAYG income tax. Therefore, taxation revenue falls, so the answer is **C** or **D**. Now, let us consider the welfare expenditure column. Because there are more unemployed individuals, there are higher federal expenditures on social security and unemployment benefits, so the answer is **C**.

Short Answer:

Short-answer questions are relatively straightforward if the question has a lower mark value. However, mid-length questions (such as those worth 5 or 6 marks) do require substantially more effort. I would recommend using the following three tips in answering these mid-length questions:

1. Do not waste time with an introductory statement. Whilst it does not lose you any marks, you certainly won't gain any from it.
2. Include statistics to support your point.
3. Insert key words from the question into your answer. Often, markers do not read an answer in detail and skim through it. If you insert these key words, you will provide a good impression and be more likely to receive a stronger mark.

Let's use the following harder question as an example:

Evaluate the implications of the current fiscal consolidation strategy used by the Australian Government in being able to achieve its economic objectives. [5 marks]

Overall, the Australian Government's fiscal consolidation strategy has had mixed impacts on its economic objectives. The fiscal consolidation that has occurred since roughly 2013 has led to a forecast surplus of $7.1 billion in the 2019-20 Budget. By returning to surplus, the government can begin paying off public sector debt, demonstrating fiscal responsibility that overseas financial markets respond positively to, re-affirmed by Australia's continued AAA credit rating. In doing so, the government ensures external stability by preventing the need for lenders to raise interest rates due to higher perceived risk. This will minimise potential increases in the Net Primary Income Deficit and hence the Current Account Deficit. Such an improvement in investor confidence also leads to increased inflow of investment into Australian firms, such as in the mining industry. This increase in capital can then contribute to an increase in aggregate supply and hence economic growth in the medium term. However, the contractionary stance of fiscal policy has in part contributed to a decrease in economic growth, which was 2.3% in 2018. This has presented a contradiction to monetary policy, which is extremely expansionary with a cash rate of 0.75%. Hence, fiscal consolidation has contributed to a slowdown in economic growth below the sustainable 3-3.5%. In regards to inflation, the lessening of net government expenditure has put downward pressure on demand-pull inflation by reducing aggregate demand (since $AD = C + I + G + (X - M)$), leading to inflation being 1.3% across 2018 – below the 2-3% target range. However, this is not severely detrimental as prices are still rising at a stable rate, and there is no immediate risk of deflation or hyperinflation.

Now let's take a look at my answer. Take note that I:

- Immediately answered the question by providing a judgement
- Included key terms from the question and syllabus
- Included relevant examples and statistics to support my argument

Extended Responses:

Extended responses are perhaps the most difficult questions to achieve full marks in, because they are inherently open to more subjective marking. Nonetheless, there are ways in which you can provide an outstanding response!

In some subjects such as English, it is perfectly fine to have long, bulky paragraphs which stretch over the page. Not in economics. In fact, markers will view this as a lack of planning and structure, which you could lose marks on. You should try to split your argument and examples into as many sub-sections as possible, each one comprising a paragraph. Outstanding essays will aim for 6 – 10 paragraphs.

Let me guide you through an example. Consider the relatively simple question:

Analyse the effects of recent monetary policy on the Australian economy.

Such a broad question will allow you to divulge into multiple areas of discussion, and hence write multiple paragraphs. In order to know what you will write about, I recommend spending 5 minutes writing a brief plan – just a couple of dot points is enough.

For this question, my plan would look something like this:

- Operation of monetary policy, domestic market operations
- Impacts on:
    - GDP growth, consumption and investment
    - Inflation
    - Unemployment
    - External stability and cash rate
    - Exchange rate and trade balance
    - Exchange rate and net primary income
    - Income inequality

As you can see, I have split the core of my essay into around 8 areas of discussion, covering a broad scope of the Australian economy as required by the question. Of course, if you are running short on time, or decide to allocate more time to other sections of the exam, you can have less paragraphs. It is always better to cover fewer points in greater detail than more points in less detail.

Introduction

In your introduction, you should briefly identify or outline the economic areas which you will be discussing. Try to include relevant terminology from the question and the syllabus, so it is obvious to the marker that you are answering the question. It is not necessary to include statistics or significant detail in the introduction. My sample introduction is as follows:

> *Monetary policy refers to the RBA's manipulation of the supply of money in the Australian economy in order to determine the cash rate. The transmission mechanisms of monetary policy describe how changes in the cash rate flow on to impact spending, investment, the exchange rate, and hence exports and imports. Consequently, monetary policy can have far-reaching effects in the areas of economic growth, inflation, unemployment, external stability and income and wealth inequality.*

Notice how I:

- Included areas of subsequent discussion on the impacts of monetary policy
- Included key syllabus terms such as the cash rate and transmission mechanisms
- Ensured the introduction remained concise

Body paragraphs

Your body paragraphs should follow a structure where you systematically argue your point. A common format is the PEEL structure, which I used.

For clarity, I have split up my paragraph into 3 sections: P, EE and L.

Section	Paragraph	Notes
P	*While the expansionary stance of recent monetary policy is designed to stimulate aggregate demand, and hence demand for labour, the effect on unemployment has been varied.*	I have addressed the question (how monetary policy impacts an area of the economy) and provided a judgement.
EE	*Across the period of 2012-2019, the cash rate has fallen from 4.75% to 0.75%, while unemployment has fallen from 6.2% to 5.0%. This trend, however, cannot be solely attributed to expansionary monetary policy (and may be due to correlation rather than causation), because fiscal policy also plays a role in influencing unemployment. For example, the $14 billion NDIS has contributed to adding 200,000 jobs nationally since the program's initiation. Additionally, there was an upwards tick in unemployment from 5.0% to 5.2% in July 2019, indicating the presence of spare capacity in the labour market that can only be reduced by fiscal expenditure, since demand for goods and services is growing very slowly. This excess capacity is further evident in unemployment being above the NAIRU of 4.5%.*	I have provided a balanced argument with both advantages and limitations of monetary policy in addressing unemployment. I have also used extensive statistics to support my answer.
L	*Hence, while monetary policy has contributed to a longer-term reduction in unemployment, it must be supported by fiscal policy in order to further reduce unemployment to the NAIRU level.*	I make a brief summary of my previous analysis and present a judgement based off this analysis.

Conclusion

In the conclusion, simply summarise the key points of your argument, and present a judgement if required by the question. You can refer to your introduction as a starting point for your conclusion, because it should ideally cover much of the same content.

Final Remarks

Wow! Congratulations on getting to the bottom of this article! I know that not every piece of advice may suit you, and that is perfectly fine. Good luck with the HSC! If you work hard, the rest will fall into place.

Patrick's Economic Cheat Sheet

Five General HSC tips:

1. Prepare a study timetable that prioritises your weakest subjects first. However, don't completely neglect studying your strongest subject.
2. Learn and re-learn the content! Accelerated self-learning and *Spaced Learning* are effective methods to achieve this.
3. Prepare concise, summarised notes as you learn, and avoid writing notes as you cram for exams.
4. Past papers, past papers, and more past papers!
5. Minimise distractions during the lead-up to the HSC. Turn off your phone. If you want to study with friends, ensure they remain *focussed*.

Five Economics-specific tips:

1. Memorise the key statistics, plus any statistics which take your interest. Also make a data sheet of key statistics which you can use in exams.
2. Don't be afraid to write beyond the provided lines or use extra paper. To achieve full marks, I actually encourage this.
3. Plan your time allocation however it suits you best. Don't just follow NESA's suggestion, and most definitely do not go into the exam without a time plan.
4. Stay updated! Read the news, and don't restrict your learning to the textbook.
5. Make effective, summarised notes that cover each syllabus dot-point. Make sure all your information is accessible.

Earth and Environmental Science: The Hidden Gem of Sciences

By Matthew Drielsma

My name is Matthew Drielsma and I was a 2019 HSC graduate from Cranbrook School. For my HSC I did 4 Unit Maths, Physics, English Advanced and Earth and Environmental Science. My favourite subject out of these was Earth and Environmental Science, or EES as I'll refer to it as. Having received a state rank of 9th in NSW in the first year of the new syllabus, I'll give insight into why I chose this subject, why I enjoyed it so much, and how I succeeded in it.

A common misconception with HSC science is believing only in what they call the big three: Physics, Chemistry and Biology. There is no doubt that these three are the most common and popular sciences for Year 12 students to study in the HSC, but it doesn't necessarily mean that they are the most interesting, most relevant, and most useful to society.

Before choosing to study Earth and Environmental Science, I had the preconceived idea that it was a course designed for lower achieving students who were not able to grasp the complex concepts of the other sciences. Having previously planned to do biology, a course that

I severely disliked in year 11, undertaking EES allowed me to engage in a course that was not only more interesting personally, but also challenged me and stimulated my study and organisational skills much like the other sciences would have.

1. Why I chose to study Earth and Environmental Science

As I mentioned before, I knew that my HSC studies were going to be paved with science and maths. However, as I only chose to study ten units for the HSC, I was limited by the number of subjects I could undertake. I did not want to just limit my science studies to any single subject of Physics, Chemistry or Biology, so I was faced with a dilemma of which one to choose.

However, luckily before I was due to submit my subject selection, I stumbled across Earth and Environmental Science which completely solved this dilemma. What is unknown about EES is that it involves aspects from Physics, Chemistry and Biology, and provides mixtures and combinations of the three.

This provided me with the perfect storm that catered to all my scientific interests. I highly recommend that if you're facing the same dilemma that I did, you should definitely choose EES. This is because it will constantly offer interesting content that encompasses all the sciences, whilst also avoiding the boring and repetitive concepts that arise. It is a highly diverse and varied course that constantly had me thinking on my feet, and that is why I chose to study it for my HSC.

2. How I succeeded

Enjoyment and success definitely go hand in hand. My enjoyment for the subject propagated my success. However, this would not have happened had I not adopted many study and note taking techniques to prepare me for my EES HSC tasks.

As 2019 was the first year of the new EES syllabus, I was the first cohort to be exposed to this course. This meant that there was very little material available as there were no past papers, former students, or questions and examples online for to refer to. This essentially made our cohort the 'test subjects' for this seemingly daunting new syllabus.

I instantly undertook a planning process to ensure that I was covering all the content of the syllabus so that I was prepared for my exams. I will divide these into three sections:

- Note taking
- Preparing questions
- Planning my answers

Note Taking

Effective note taking played a major role in my success in EES. As the new syllabus is very content-heavy and requires a lot of qualitative answering, it's a course that demands an advanced grasp of extended knowledge and fine details. This was addressed in my detailed note taking which was influenced by the structure of the syllabus.

Below is an example of my notes which I have annotated to explain the different components of it:

By using this structure of breaking down a large concept into its constituent components of inquiry question, syllabus dot point, and subheadings, I was able to easily categorise my content. This made it simpler to digest and specific information easier to find when revising.

Another integral part of my note taking involved using tables and diagrams.

An example of this is shown on the next page:

Fossil Formation and Stratigraphy

Inquiry question: What is the role of fossils in expanding what is known of geological time and past life on Earth?

12.4.1. Investigate and model processes of fossil formation by examining a variety of methods in rock, including: Mould, Cast and Trace fossils.

What is a fossil?

- Fossils are the remains, moulds or traces of organisms that died a long time ago and were preserved in (usually) sedimentary rocks such as sandstone, limestone, shale or siltstone

- Fossils can include shells or other invertebrate parts, skeletons or even plant remains, sometimes footprints can be fossilized.

- Fossils provide evidence of past forms of life.

How are fossils formed?

- For about 3000 million years, life was present only in the oceans. The oldest fossils are therefore marine creatures.
- When these organisms died, their remains accumulated on the sea floor where they were quickly buried by mud, sand or silt.
- Over very long periods, these sediments became sedimentary rock, and the organism's remains became encased in the rock.
- By **430 million years** ago, organisms had colonised the land. Upon death, most of their remains decomposed, but hard parts (bones, shells) could be preserved.
- Through **lithification** of sediment, fossils were able to be preserved.

Fossilisation

- Fossilisation only happens in the **rarest of cases**, when a plant or animal dies in the right circumstances.
- *Why?* This is because animal corpses are usually **eaten** by something, or **bacteria rots them away (decays)** before fossilisation can occur,
- Even hard parts like bones and shells are eventually destroyed through **erosion** and **corrosion**.

Table with multiple columns gives great detail

Tables are a great place to include numerical facts and statistics make them easier to remember

13.1.5 Account for the types of magma in each of the above types of volcanoes, and analyse how this affects the explosivity of their eruptions

Magma feature	Shield volcano	Cinder cone volcano	Stratovolcano (Composite)	Caldera volcano
Silica quantity	Low silica (50%) 42-52%	Low silica	High silica (60%) 55-60%	High silica (74%) -extremely thick, very dense
Viscosity	Low-effusive Runny lava Flows readily	Low-effusive Runny lava Flows readily	High viscosity -traps gas, allowing pressure to build until a **violent explosive eruption** happens.	Very viscous
Gas content/ explosivity	Low (1%) -Gas has been able to escape through openings over time since magma has low viscosity -Not explosive	Contains a lot of dissolved gas Violent eruptions	(3-4%) -Gas bubbles find it harder to rise to the surface since viscosity is higher. -violent eruptions	
Location/ boundary	Divergent boundary in oceans -build up from the sea floor	On slopes, near the edges of larger volcanoes where secondary vents have opened up.	Convergent boundary -ocean-continental subduction zones	
Magma Composition	Mafic (basaltic) High in iron and magnesium	Very little lava Basaltic and andesitic	Magma rising from the deep has time to drop out silica poor components and pick up silica rich ones -Andesite rock	-Rhyolite rock
Shape	Runny lava, travels a long way from the vent before cooling, therefore forms **broad shallow** volcanoes. -Tall and broad with flat rounded shapes	Erupt loose volcanic rock fragments called cinders, which settle and pile in a conical shape -small, steep sides -cylindrical shape	Viscous lava can't travel far from the vent before cooling, forming sharp **steep sided** volcanoes. -Symmetrically shaped with steep sides	Magma erupts quickly, the chamber empties and the unsupported rock then collapses. The resulting depression, a caldera, can be tens of kilometers wide.
Example	Ex. Hot spots- Mauna Loa, Hawaii	Mt Etna, Italy Cerra Negra, Nicaragua Pu'uka Pele Kea, Hawaii	Ex. Mt Pinatubo Mt Krakatoa Mt St. Helens, US Mt. Fuji, Japan Mt Vesuvius	Yellowstone caldera, Utah Kraktatoa, Indonesia

Diagrams give a visual representation of the key concepts to aid understanding

By using tables and diagrams, I saved myself a lot of large blocks of text which are daunting to read and hard to memorise. Condensing your notes is a key skill that will save you a lot of time and ultimately benefit your study.

Preparing Questions

Once I had my notes written and collated, I then needed to test my knowledge with questions to prepare me for what they may ask in my exam. As I was a part of the first cohort to sit the new syllabus, there were not many questions available to me to prepare. Due to the nature of the course, there probably won't be many for the second or third year of the syllabus either.

To solve this, I used the syllabus to develop my own study guide and practice papers. Using the inquiry questions and their dot points, I essentially turned them into exam style questions that I predicted would appear in my exams.

For examples one of the dot points for module 5 is:

> **12.1.2 Investigate the evidence for the development of photosynthetic life, including cyanobacteria and stromatolites.**

I used this dot point, which was in the form of a statement, and turned it into an exam style question:

> **Discuss the evidence for the development of photosynthetic life, including cyanobacteria and stromatolites.**

Both your school EES exams and the EES HSC can only ask questions that are relevant to the syllabus. Therefore, it is logical that one of the best places to build up a question bank is from the syllabus itself.

Another example of where I did this is from one of the dot points for module 6:

> **13.1.5 Account for the types of magma in each of the above types of volcanoes, and analyse how this affects the explosivity of their eruptions**

I used this dot point to predict questions that went beyond what the original dot point was stating, such as:

- How does silica content impact eruption type?
- What determines the nature of magma?
- Compare effusive with explosive eruptions
- Contrast lava typical of convergent boundaries with lava typical of divergent boundaries

By having an in-depth understanding of the syllabus, I was able to extrapolate questions that could be asked based on the relevant content that was associated with it.

Planning my answers

Once I had reviewed all the content of my notes and had tested my knowledge with practice questions, I had to develop a plan for writing my answers within the exam. Exam conditions are a unique experience that are hard to simulate outside of the exam room, as factors such as time pressure and writing space must be taken into account.

Like many students, I faced issues such as either spending too long on a question by writing irrelevant details, or by using up too much writing space which would in turn also waste time. To solve this, I adopted the use of flow charts to plan my long response questions.

Flow charts are a strategic tool that encourage a logical and sequential thought process that summarises and organises the structure of your responses.

An example of a flow chart that I would use in an exam to answer an extended response question is shown below:

Question: Outline the formation of Banded Iron Formations [4 marks]

Planned flow chart answer:

Soluble iron salts are leached from the land into the ocean

↓

Soluble iron reacts with oxygen in the oceans to form insoluble iron oxide

↓

Insoluble iron oxide falls to ocean floor as sediments to form iron rich layer

↓

Iron and/or oxygen is depleted and silica is precipitated over iron oxide layer

↓

Cyanobacteria re-establish and the cycle begins again

↓

Alternating levels of iron-rich and iron-poor sediments are deposited to form banded iron formations

Using this method allowed me to plan out a structured approach on scrap paper before I wrote anything on the exam paper. Now this might seem counterintuitive, as you may suggest that I'm wasting time by writing on another piece of paper. However, I can assure you that the time saved by writing a plan is far more than the time it would take if you wrote a long, irrelevant and over complicated response.

My belief is that when answering extended response questions, you should always aim to achieve the maximum marks in the minimum amount of time. This means that planning is vital to establish what content the question is looking for, and how to answer it in the most concise way.

Conclusion

To conclude this article, it has been a beyond enjoyable and interesting experience undertaking the new Earth and Environmental Science HSC course. My main advice to people considering doing this course for their HSC is summarised below:

- Study what interests you
- Develop an effective and strategic note taking system early on
- Be able to prepare a wide range of questions that covers every aspect of the syllabus
- Adopt an effective, clear, and logical planning strategy to make your answers concise to save time

The EES syllabus is packed with interesting and thought-provoking content which is sure to be an escape from the tedious and repetitive aspects of many other subjects.

If you do decide to do EES for your HSC, following my advice in this article is sure to land you with a high mark and optimise your enjoyment and knowledge gain from the course.

Engineering StuDIES: How to Not Die

By Adam Robey

What do you get when you mix the concepts of Maths and Physics, throw in a sprinkling of trigonometry, and then add an entire dictionary of things to memorise on top? You get the wonderful HSC subject that is *Engineering Studies* — an hotchpotch of theoretical knowledge, practical application, and problem-solving that would challenge even those acing Physics and 4 unit maths!

Don't be too daunted though; passion for Engineering and a bit of effort will make this subject one of the most rewarding experiences you'll have.

An Unorthodox Year 12 Journey – a bit about me

My name's Adam Robey, former Vice-Captain of Sydney Technical High School (2019). I graduated with an ATAR of 98.85 and All Rounders for my 13 units, as well as ending up placing 2nd in the state for Engineering Studies. Listening to that resume, one could assume that I was one of those super organised and disciplined students you hear about in HSC seminars. That couldn't be further from the truth!

While this is an article on Engineering Studies, I'm going to start off with some stuff about myself and general advice and thoughts on HSC. Bear with me if you will!

My Time at Tech and Your Journey into the HSC

If you asked any of my friends, they'd probably tell you I shouldn't have done as well as I did. Harsh, but probably true. Although I had plenty of excellent tips and tricks up my sleeve to do well (which I'm about to share), the reality is that I made plenty of mistakes along the way. I was fortunate enough to select subjects that I ended up having a natural aptitude for, which is what enabled me to do so well.

Your HSC journey is going to be a formidable challenge, and some pitfalls on the way will be inevitable. The best advice I can give you is to expect less than perfection. Of course, you should aim as high as possible, but don't let yourself get too absorbed into what you deem "perfect." The best thing you can do for yourself is be realistic: put in as much effort as you can and do your very best, but don't sacrifice your own physical and mental health for an extra percent on a piece of paper.

Regrets – I've had a few

I absolutely have regrets from my HSC year. I should have studied more, I could have done better in all my subjects, and ultimately should have achieved a higher ATAR. But ultimately what's done is done, and I'm OK with how everything turned out. Even so, timetabling, planning, studying and all should have been more of a priority for me. Learn from my mistakes!

Stress (Not the Kind that's Force/Area)

To be honest, I was never the type of person to get stressed out that much. I tended not to worry too much about exams. Paradoxically, this ended up being a bad thing. Just as much as too much stress is a bad thing, too little is also an issue. The right amount of stress is able to propel you to the great heights you can achieve. However, if you are like me, finding this balance can be hard.

In truth, everybody's capabilities are different. Some will be able to push themselves to the ragged edge without fail and achieve amazing results, while others become incredibly stressed very easily. Everyone is different, and you need to find the balance of pressure, effort, and expectations that works for you. Whilst every mark does add up and you should endeavour to achieve your best in every assessment, one or two fewer marks in an in-school assessment will have a negligible impact on your final HSC results. Ninety-nine percent of the time, you will get to university and achieve everything you have set your mind to even if you flunk a test.

Academic Pressure and All Its Joys

Like many others, I shared an Asian heritage and attended a selective school: academics were ingrained into my time at school. This extreme focus on academics, whilst providing an excellent springboard for growth and development, at times could become toxic and stifling. In my time as not only a student but as Vice-Captain, I saw many of my peers 'burn out', becoming anxious or depressed because of their results and the extreme pressure they put themselves under.

You shouldn't measure your own academics too much by the results of others. However unfair it may be, there will be people who achieve higher than you with more or less effort, and also those you achieve better than with more or less effort. Sometimes you just need to step back, take a second to breathe, look at your results and realise, "hey, I did my best, and this is a good result." Your own health should always come above your studies.

Motivation

Motivation is a fickle, fickle thing. In my own case, motivation mainly came about from my own interest in Engineering. Since the subject itself and the problem-solving was so interesting to me, studying for it and learning about it became something that was quite fun. Even so, I sometimes found myself apathetic about study.

Here are some top tips for maintaining motivation:

- Take breaks: There's simply no way you can concentrate for hours on end...
- Reward yourself: You'd be surprised how much a treat at the end affects your mentality towards study!
- Think of the future: You don't want to regret the one chance you get at the HSC... Basically, I guilt tripped myself into avoiding procrastination.

If none of these strategies work, the unfortunate truth is you've just got to get it over and done with somehow. It may as well be sooner rather than later. Don't fall into the trap of putting something off for so long that you never do it. Like steel that's been slightly stressed, your strength will also increase with a bit of stress!

For the Love of Engineering

A small sub-note: I love engineering! Having a genuine passion for this subject will make studying so much more rewarding. Learn to enjoy the problem-solving and knowledge that comes with the subject, and good results will follow.

Goals

Having a goal, however vague it may be, is a good thing! My plans were basically to get above 96 ATAR so I could get into a co-op scholarship (of which there ended up being none), and maybe state rank in

Engineering. Knowing what you want to do gives yourself a goal to work towards, which acts as an excellent motivator for study. I always wanted to go into the field of engineering, so success in the subject was a major goal for me.

Generic but Useful Study Tips

1. Focus on understanding

Sure, memorisation is important and at times necessary, but understanding is the most important. Not only does actually understanding something solidify it in your head, but it also allows you a greater depth of knowledge to pull upon when you're in an exam.

2. Don't do the same thing 1000 times

If something isn't clicking, or if you just can't remember it - approach it some other way! Repeating something over and over again isn't going to force it into memory if that doesn't work for you. Different techniques will have to be applied at some point.

3. Prioritisation!

You need to prioritise your studying! Obviously, focus on fundamental concepts and methods over anything complex. There's simply no way you can expect yourself to understand something like work-energy on an accelerating body on a slope if you don't understand the relationship between power and force.

The Dos and Don'ts of Engineering Studies

Common Misconceptions

1. "Engineering is just memorisation"

    Whilst there is a vast amount of memorisation in the subject (as with most in the HSC), if you don't understand the concepts and are able to perform the mathematics and problem-solving then you're not going to do well.

2. **"You need to do Physics and Extension Maths to do well in Engineering"**

   While Physics and Extension Maths certainly do make your life much easier for Engineering, they aren't necessary. Yes, the concepts found in these subjects are applied in Engineering. However, they're also of such a calibre that someone doing just Engineering Studies, with the right study and understanding, can do just as well as someone who does these other subjects.

3. **"Concepts in Engineering are always universal"**

   This is an incredibly easy trap to fall into. With the nature of problem-solving in Engineering, it's easy to apply one idea that seems to fit another situation, when it really doesn't. It's important you differentiate and realise what concept applies to which section of the syllabus. For example, brass and steel can both be dual-phase materials, but the phases in brass are not ferrite and cementite.

4. **"Maths is the only way to solve a problem"**

   While maths will always lead you to the correct answer (providing you apply it correctly), the time-savings and elegance of a graphical solution to something like forces on a body can be a life-saver in an exam. Don't neglect your diagrams and solutions.

The Unfortunate Art of Rote Learning

Rote learning has got to be one of the most controversial topics in all of the HSC. Personally, I think relying upon it as the sole method of studying is idiotic. It's like cracking a nut with a sledgehammer. Sure, you'll get there in the end, but it's so unwieldy that you end up wasting time. Utilising it as a tool in your study arsenal rather than the only method is much more useful.

The reality is that there is an awfully large amount of content in Engineering, and most of that is going to involve some serious memorisation. The key to memorising all of this is understanding the concepts behind the content,. For example, you could choose to remember every application for hardening and tempering a piece of steel - or you could understand the changes it brings about to its structure and properties and how that could be useful for a given application. The latter method allows for easier application of your knowledge to more areas.

The downfall of rote learning is that it is utterly useless for any of the problem-solving questions in Engineering. There is simply no way to remember solutions to every problem you come across. The same way you do in Maths, the only way to succeed in these questions is to understand and apply the mathematics you have learnt to find the correct answer.

Ultimately though, as much as I dislike rote learning, it is indeed necessary for much of Engineering. You need to have rote learning in your study arsenal, or you won't be able to succeed. Even if you understand every single heat treatment of steel, the structure of stainless steels, composite layering, workings of a jet engine, there are going to be a million small details you just have to remember. Percentages of carbon in steel and how they affect phases, series of aluminium alloys and stainless steels, the processes of heat treatments, types of hardness testing; the list goes on and on. Memorisation is going to be inevitable, so you'll have to get used to it.

How to Not Fall Apart in and Before an Exam

1. **Keeping up momentum**

    Momentum is the most important thing you can have in an exam. We've all been 'in the zone', where you just go on and on with your answers and you feel like the test is going amazing… and then there's one question that stumps you. Give it some thought, and, if it doesn't go anywhere, skip the question and come back to it later. One derailed train of thought can lead to the whole exam becoming a foggy cloud of memory, so keep your momentum going.

2. **Multiple choice questions are your friends**

    Nowhere else in the exam are you going to find 20 free marks sitting there to be gobbled up in the span of minutes. Every now and again there'll be a curveball, but try to work through multiple choice as fast as you can. Usually they're quick memory checks, but the stray mathematical question can slow you down.

3. **Brush up on HSC keywords**

    Knowing what keywords such as 'identify', 'define' and 'analyse' can mean the difference between a band six response, a band four response, or a whole bunch of information useless to the question. Knowing the keywords allows you to perfectly tailor your response to the question, and in a subject as content heavy as Engineering, this is vital to success.

4. **Dot points are okay**

    Remember, you're doing Engineering Studies, not English. If a question asks you about the advantages and disadvantages of using Laminated Veneer Lumber in a structural beam, you can simply write dot points for each part. You don't need to write a mini-essay for every three-mark question.

5. **Materials are key**

    Most of the content-heavy questions in Engineering always circle back to materials. Be it ceramics, steels, aluminium alloys, wood, fibre composites, concrete, you name it, these will always be a major part of the test. You need to understand their structures, why they're useful, where they're used, how they're tested, and how they're manufactured, as well as the societal, ethical, and economic implications of their uses.

6. **Brief histories**

    Important historical developments usually come up in a six-mark question, or similar. As boring as this can be, you need to know important developments such as the internal combustion engine, fixed-wing flight, the advent of fibre-polymer composites, the automobile, and so on and so forth. This is one of those areas where you just need to remember - I don't really have any tips... sorry!

7. **Applying concepts to unexpected areas**

    Sometimes, an absolute curveball of a question hits you out of nowhere. You never learnt this. It's not in the syllabus. No one you know has seen it before. And yet, it's strangely familiar... That's because those cheeky Engineering test writers want to test your understanding of a concept, not just your memorisation of a use-case! For example, we all know aerofoils are used in planes, but they also find use in boats as hydrofoils and yachts as sails! Knowing the concept behind how something works and why it's useful can allow you to apply your knowledge to more than just the basic scenario. These are the questions that differentiate the top students, so practising applying your knowledge to unfamiliar scenarios is key!

8. **Always draw a diagram**

    This might sound obvious, but drawing a diagram in a problem-solving question can be the difference between a solution clicking and you staring at the paper for 20 minutes. This is an easy way to streamline the forces acting upon an object while removing frivolous information. This also allows the marker to see your thought process, giving them a chance to allocate you some precious marks.

9. Write down all of your working out

It's tempting to not write down some working out that you may see as simple, but this could be the difference between you ignoring a simple mistake that ruins all of your working. You should also write down any information you know from the question, such as pressure, force, mass, acceleration, useful formulas, etc. Always be extremely careful with your maths.

10. Have a solid grasp on SI units and their prefixes

You need to remember SI units, such as Newtons, Pascals, Kilograms, Volts, so on and so forth. All of the working in Engineering is based upon these, so you're basically setting yourself up to fail if you don't know them. If you know at least the 7 basic units then you can solve almost any question, but knowing derived units such as velocity and pressure are incredibly useful too.

Just as important are prefixes. Micro, milli, kilo, mega, giga may be confusing now, but what they represent in terms of mathematical powers is incredibly useful and should become second nature to you.

11. ALWAYS CONVERT TO BASE UNITS!

Base units are a wonderful thing, and you should always convert to them. Always write down the data you know in base units – this gives less chance for mathematical errors or oversights. For example, 10 Megapascals would become $10*10^6$ Pascals. This becomes extremely important, for forgetting a conversion could mean that you end up with a result about a million times off the right answer!

12. Don't spend too long on drawings

While drawings can be a major source of marks in an exam, they're also a major sink of time. You're not expected to have a perfect drawing in an exam. As long as the general shape, important details, and ideas are conveyed, you should be alright.

13. **Utilise Engineering language**

    You need to use the language of the Engineer when answering questions. You could pull any person off the street and they'd tell you, "carbon fibre is strong". Writing only that in an exam is asking to lose marks. 'Strong' is too vague in Engineering. You need to specify exactly what you mean, such as "carbon fiber reinforced polymer is strong in tension." Utilise this type of language to the greatest possible extent for maximum marks.

    In saying this, you must be wary of repeating yourself. Say a question asks for advantages of aluminium alloys, and you say it is "strong and light", "has a high specific strength", and "has an excellent strength to weight ratio". You might think you wrote three different answers to the question and had an excellent response... but those three things mean the exact same thing. Be careful of the traps that Engineering language can present in having multiple terms for the same thing.

14. **Flying high with syllabi**

    The syllabus is one of the most useful tools available to you as a student. Not only does it specify what you should have achieved by the end of the course, but it also specifies every single thing they can test you on. Every topic in Engineering is named in there, thus the syllabus becomes an excellent tool not only for revision before an exam but to guide your study as well as any notes you may choose to write.

15. **Take your study beyond school**

    Relevant modern developments and happenings in Engineering will always find their way into an exam. You need to be up to date on your knowledge and recent developments. For example, the increasing prevalence of electric cars, the Boeing 737 MAX and its MCAS issues, and renewable energies are all areas that are modern developments not found in the course but could be tested in an exam. Incorporating Engineering into your everyday life just by looking around can be an excellent tool to further your own understanding.

For example, take a mundane place like a train station. If you look around, you will see Engineering everywhere: galvanised electrical pylons with ceramic insulators, copper wiring providing power to trains, steel tracks, gravel, and geotextiles beneath the tracks... the list goes on. Noticing things like these means you're on the track to gaining an incredible understanding of the content in Engineering Studies.

16. Know and bring your equipment

If you walk into the exam and you're missing something as vital as say, a ruler - you're basically making your own job a hundred times harder. Remember equipment like compasses, circle templates, rulers, mechanical pencils... and your calculator.

Also, never have your calculator set to radians. Always check that your calculator is not set to radians. Don't be like me and have 20 minutes left in an exam and have to redo all your mathematical calculations because you realised your calculator is in radians. Let me tell you first-hand how frightening that experience is. You never want to be in that position.

17. And finally... practice, practice, practice!

Engineering is at its core, a memory and a problem-solving subject. By exposing yourself to as many questions as possible, you gain a greater grasp of both your own knowledge and its application. This is incredibly important for drawings and problem-solving questions, as the more you practice, the quicker you see a solution and the quicker you get it onto paper. Written questions also benefit from this, as the greater the pool of questions you've practiced, the more unlikely a question you've never seen before will come up.

Just remember - practice doesn't make perfect. Practice makes permanent. Always ensure that when you practice something, it's the right thing and you don't make incorrect solutions or knowledge permanent in your mind.

Sample Questions

The humble seesaw, and the importance of multiple solutions

"Find the force at C if the seesaw is balanced"

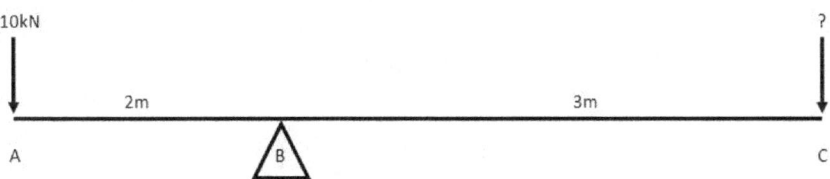

Diagram of a Seesaw

Here we go – the simplest looking question around. It's a seesaw! The reason I wanted to show this question is so that you could see that even for something this simple, there are multiple solutions.

Method A - Moments about B

$$\circlearrowleft_+ \Sigma M_B = 0$$

$$0 = (F_C * 3) - (10 * 2)$$

$$F_C = \frac{(10 * 2)}{3}$$

$$F_C = 6.67kN \downarrow$$

Above is arguably the solution that you should always take to a question like this. It's the least amount of working possible and is just a simple moments calculation. However, I'll show you a few other methods just to broaden your scope of solutions.

Method B
- Moments about C, and sum of vertical forces

As we know, wherever a force's moment arm passes through the point at which we sum moments, we can treat it as a zero number. This means that by summing moments about C rather than B, we can find the reaction at B, and, since the see-saw isn't moving, sum vertical forces. It's important to remember we can apply this in many cases — moments can be summed anywhere, as long as you know all the forces acting on it. This is also incredibly useful in truss analysis.

$$\circlearrowleft_+ \Sigma M_C = 0$$

$$0 = (R_B * 3) - (10 * 5)$$

$$R_B = \frac{(10 * 5)}{3}$$

$$R_B = 16.67 kN \uparrow$$

$$\uparrow_+ F_V = 0$$

$$0 = 16.67 - 10 - F_C$$

$$F_C = 6.67 kN \downarrow$$

There we go, another solution with different steps that have arrived at the same answer.

Method C
- Mechanical Advantage and Velocity Ratio

A completely different method now, where we use mechanical advantage to find the answer. As you know, the velocity ratio is equal to the distance the effort moves over the distance the load moves. When efficiency is 100%, it is equal to mechanical advantage. Mechanical advantage equals to load over effort. In this case, we can assume efficiency to be 100%.

Assume C to be effort and A to be load, where B is the pivot.

$$VR = \frac{2\pi * 3}{2\pi * 2}$$

$$VR = \frac{3}{2}$$

$$MA = VR * \eta$$

$$MA = \frac{3}{2}$$

$$\frac{L}{E} = \frac{3}{2}$$

$$E = \frac{2L}{3}$$

$$F_C = \frac{(10 * 2)}{3}$$

$$F_C = 6.67kN \downarrow$$

And, once again, the same answer! I know this is a really simple question, but it's the easiest way to showcase the validity of multiple methods of solving a question. These are just the tip of the iceberg, and if you can gain a solid grasp on these concepts and applying them, then you'll ace the problem-solving sections of the paper.

Tip 'N Slide – Visualising a Solution

"A uniformly loaded crate of mass 100kg is 2m tall and 1m wide. It is resting on a ramp and horizontal force 'P' is progressively applied as shown. If μ = 0.3, determine whether the crate first tips or slides and the force required."

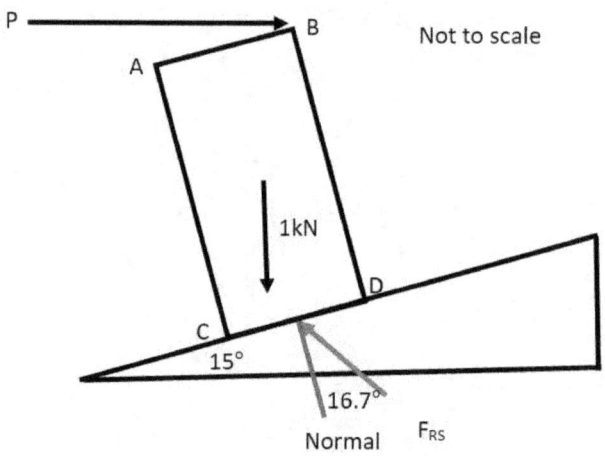

Diagram of crate on slope

This question is a very difficult one! Not only do you have two separate problems to solve, but they're also pretty hard.

$$\circlearrowleft_+ \Sigma M_D = 0$$

$$0 = (P\cos 15 * 2) - (1\sin 15 * 1) - (1\cos 15 * 0.5)$$

Let's go with the tipping first. We know that a moment will be induced about somewhere for it to tip, so you just have to figure out where. It's most likely going to be D, as P pushes the box up the slope. Therefore, by summing moments about D, we can find the force P required to tip the box over.

Hang on, where'd all these numbers come from? This isn't as simple as the see-saw, so let me explain. The quickest solution was to break the 1kN weight force and P into components parallel and perpendicular to the plane. Hence, the 15°. We know that the component of P multiplied by sin15 would be perpendicular and thus pass through D, so we can eliminate the term. The 1kN weight force is broken into parallel and perpendicular components, and 1 and 0.5 simply come from the weight force being halfway up the box and halfway down.

$$P = \frac{sin15 + 0.5cos15}{2cos15}$$

$$P = \frac{sin15 + 0.5cos15}{2cos15}$$

$$P = 0.383945962 \ldots kN$$

$$P = 383.97N \text{ to tip}$$

So, we have now found the answer for the crate to tip. The hard part with that is visualising where it will tip and the moment arms, but enough practice will make this intuitive.

Now, onto the sliding. Because P isn't parallel to the slope, it pushes the box down into it. This increases the reaction at the normal, thus increasing frictional force. Because P and friction now become related, solving this via pure mathematics becomes an extremely long, tedious process where simultaneous equations become required. I've done it before, and it literally takes pages of working. I never recommend it as it takes too long and there's too much room for error.

The easiest way to solve this is instead by using the angle of static friction, where $tan^{-1}(\mu) = \varphi_S$. I've visualised this on the diagram for you, where $\varphi_S = tan^{-1}(0.3)$, equalling 16.7°. Then we can simply create a force polygon where 'F_{RS}' (what I like to call 'the resultant' of static friction, the normal force and the friction force) is inclined at an angle of 16.7° + 15°, due to the normal being inclined as well.

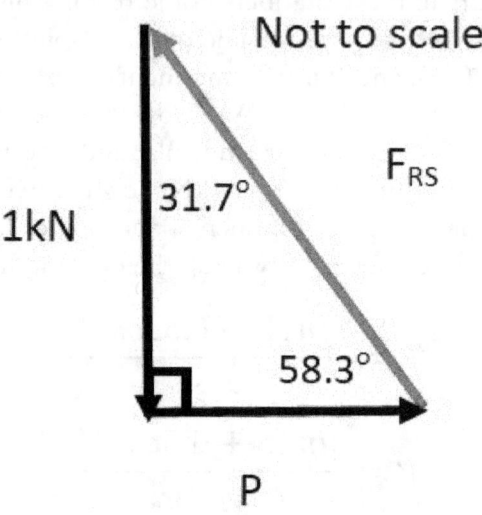

Force polygon of crate

The following calculations to find P for sliding are simple, being just the sine rule.

$$\frac{P}{\sin 31.7} = \frac{1}{\sin 58.3}$$

$$P = \frac{\sin 31.7}{\sin 58.3}$$

$$P = 0.6176125879 \ldots kN$$

$$P = 617.61N \text{ to slide}$$

Alright, so we finally got both our answers.

Since $P_{slide} > P_{tip}$, it will tip first, with a force of 383.97N.

If you can solve this question, you'll probably be able to solve any other mechanics in the HSC.

Knowing Your Maths

Things like work, energy, power, pressure, etc. are all maths based. While I could give you a sample question or two on these, there's nothing special that you really need to understand for them, as most of the time it's just manipulating a formula. Always check the reference sheet for these formulas, and simply practice these types of questions as much as you can. You're fairly unlikely to get a curveball with these questions. However, you should still watch out for things like double elongation and acceleration up or down a slope. Check your working religiously – one negative sign somewhere destroys your entire answer.

Remember your work-energy principle:

$PE_i + KE_i +/- W = PE_F + KE_F$

Applying this in a work-energy question with the right maths means you'll always get to the right answer. Basically, everything else is on the reference sheet.

Drawings

Unfortunately, I can't really guide you through drawings. All I can tell you is to know your AS1100 standards, especially sectioning and bolts. It's one of those things where you just have to practice many, many times. Make sure not to neglect things like isometric drawings either.

Electrical Questions

It is also important not to forget about electrical questions. Most of the time these questions do end up being maths based, but you have to still remember your circuit diagrams and symbols. All the formulas you need are on the reference sheet, except for Ohm's law. Just remember how it differs for parallel and series circuits and you'll be fine.

A Quick Guide to Written Questions

The key to written questions is identifying key information in the question, aligning it with your knowledge, and getting it onto paper as succinctly as possible.

"A 0.4% carbon steel is used for a go-kart axle. Describe the processes that could be used to produce a hardened and tempered structure. Explain the changes in structure and properties due to these processes and discuss why subsequent tempering is necessary."

This question would be worth approximately five marks. First, identify the HSC keywords. In this case, they are describe, explain, and discuss. Next, identify the key information we've been given. 0.4% carbon steel, go-kart axle, hardened and tempered structure and properties are what we have to tackle in this particular question.

Since we now know it's a medium-carbon steel used in a go-kart axle, we can immediately put this into the context of hardening processes.

From there, we can quickly plan a response in our heads. I'll use dot points here to highlight the important points.

Describe the processes:

- Steel is heated to above UCT and allowed to soak for the entire structure to become austenitic.
- This is then rapidly quenched in water to form hardened steel.
- This forms a martensitic structure, which is hard and brittle.
- To temper, the steel is heated to an elevated temperature (above 200°C) and held there, to break down some of the martensite.

Explain the changes in structure and properties:

- BCT martensite is formed due to FCC austenite trying to transform to BCC ferrite, where carbon atoms become stuck in interstices due to fast cooling, trapping the structure as BCT.

- This acicular martensitic structure is extremely hard but very brittle, breaking easily.
- Tempering results in a tempered martensite structure, which is slightly less hard but significantly less brittle, allowing higher toughness.

Discuss why subsequent tempering is necessary:

- Go-karts go over bumps and irregularities in tracks.
- Thus, the axle needs to be tough, otherwise it would instantly break.
- Therefore, to serve its purpose correctly without breakage, tempered martensite is required to maintain high hardness and toughness.

Essentially, you just string those together to get a response. Most questions will be along those lines, but perhaps with less keywords. The only ones you've got to lookout for are questions about roles of engineers or the like, where you really have to think about societal, economic, environmental and engineering impacts rather than just what you learnt in class.

A Small Thank You

Of course, I'd like to thank my teachers and my mum for getting me through the HSC year and everything… but there's one man I need to thank more than anyone.

My Engineering Teacher, Mr. Paul Copeland, was perhaps the only reason I managed to achieve a state rank. His teaching and passion for Engineering were simply sublime, and I know for a fact all of us in his class were incredibly lucky and grateful to be in it. Each lesson was incredibly enjoyable and packed with knowledge, which really made the subject so much easier. I strongly recommend his textbook

"Engineering Studies: The Definitive Guide" to anyone looking for a concise yet packed with information and easy to understand source of knowledge in Engineering.

The End:

In the end, it all boils down to you doing your best and seeing how it goes. If you apply some of the things I talked about, then I'm confident that you will have already improved your chances of doing well, not only in Engineering but the HSC as a whole.

The most important thing I want you to remember is that your HSC will be defined by how you manage pressure. Pressure can be what makes or breaks not only your marks but also you as a person during this HSC year. A wise man once said:

"Pressure can turn coal into diamonds, but it can also turn diamonds into dust."

I like to believe we all start out as coal. Let yourself be shaped into a diamond over this coming year and come out shining with an awesome result! Just try not to turn into dust in the process.

Good luck, and have fun!

Adam's Engineering Cheat Sheet

- Have a basic timetable for study
- Keep up momentum
- Don't overthink multiple choice
- Don't spend too long on drawings
- Know your HSC keywords
- Know when to use dot points
- Have a perfect grasp on Materials content
- Have a basic idea of Engineering history
- Apply concepts to unexpected areas
- Always draw a diagram
- Write down all of your working out
- Have a solid grasp on SI units and their prefixes
- Utilise Engineering language
- Take your study beyond school and textbooks
- Know and bring your equipment
- Practice everything as much as you can

Geography: How I achieved stress-free HSC success by eating SUBWAY® sandwiches (and studying)

By Lachlan Tran

> *"There is no way to happiness — happiness is the way."* — Thich Nhat Hanh

After reading the title, you're probably wondering what on earth this article is about. What does Subway, a transnational fast-food sandwich franchise, have anything to do with the HSC? How can a sandwich lead to success in anything? Don't worry, all your questions will be answered soon, but first, allow me to introduce myself.

My name is Lachlan Tran and I graduated from Sydney Grammar School in 2019. It has always been a dream of mine to study medicine and become a doctor, and I was very aware of the competitiveness and high marks required. However, I didn't have to lock myself in my room and study for ten hours every day. I didn't have to go cold turkey on social media. I didn't have to become a hermit and never go out with friends. I managed to thoroughly enjoy my last year of high school, despite constantly hearing that it's supposed to be the most stressful year of school.

Only you are in control of how stressful your HSC year is, depending on your perspective and attitude towards it. I've often heard top students talk about how much stress and suffering they had to endure during their final year, waking up early and sleeping late to fit in studying, but luckily it all ended up being worth it because they achieved the results they hoped for. Whilst this is certainly a viable method, my question to you is what happens if something goes wrong and you don't achieve the results you were hoping for? Would all the stress and worrying still be worth it? In this article, I want to share with you my approach to the HSC year that made it all worth it, regardless of the results at the end.

My Story

I ended up with an ATAR of 99.70, band 6's in all of my subjects and placing first in the state for Geography. At this point, it's easy to look at my photo at the top and my surname Tran and assume that I spent all my time chained to my desk studying. However, my HSC year was one of the years that I did the *least* amount of studying. In fact, I was studying far more in earlier years. During the holidays of Year 10 I was studying for 8 hours per day, and in Year 9 I once spent a ridiculous 13 hours in one day studying. Surprisingly, my marks had never been lower.

So, what was the difference? In Year 12 I used my time so much more productively and focused a lot on my mental health and wellbeing. I found that having good mental health and being happy was far more beneficial to my studies than actually studying, and this is something I want to try to emphasise throughout this article.

Sleeping well, staying fit and healthy and enjoying the year is so much more valuable than trying to squeeze in studying in every spare minute, or sacrificing your happiness for academics. I say this because I made that mistake and was miserable in earlier high school years. I also saw some of my friends make this mistake in Year 12, locking themselves in their rooms and choosing studying over going out with friends. They suffered during their final year because of this isolation mindset. Whilst some of them were able to achieve similar marks to me, what was the cost? Why not choose to be happy, as well as doing well at school? Please remember that your general health and happiness is so much more valuable than a number at the end of the year. You should always put your mental health first. This leads me onto my first study tip for Year 12.

Study Tips

1. Make sure you have a good time

Now, this can be some potentially dangerous advice. Please don't misconstrue my message and decide to throw your books out the window, put your feet up and turn the Playstation on. Don't get me wrong, I *still studied*. I stayed on top of my homework, updated my notes regularly and was flexible with my studying, knowing when I had to work more and when I was able to relax depending on my workload for the week. I'm not saying that you shouldn't study at all, I'm saying that you shouldn't veer to either extreme of excessive studying or relaxing. You must find the golden mean between the two, the equilibrium that delivers both happiness and academic success.

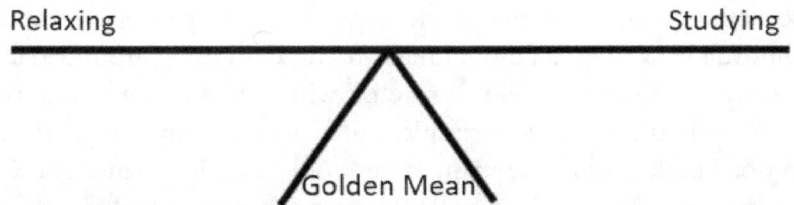

(In all aspects of life, school and studying included, there shouldn't exist any rigid dichotomies. Instead, find an equilibrium that delivers the most ideal results, as shown in the diagram. To quote the Marvel villain Thanos, you must find an equilibrium so that your final year is "perfectly balanced, as all things should be.")

The golden mean differs between individuals and it's up to you to find your own balance. This could mean that you need to put in more work if you're lagging behind, but also that you should consider studying *less* if things aren't working out. If you're not getting the results you're hoping for, studying more hours isn't necessarily going to get you better marks. If studying is interfering with your happiness and you're not enjoying your routine, then you won't be able to unlock your full potential. Returning to the quote at the beginning of this article, don't pursue a path of suffering with the hope of happiness at the destination. Happiness isn't an objective, it is a way of life. If you can understand this during your HSC, both your academics and your wellbeing will benefit.

What this meant for me was keeping up my fitness by going to the gym every morning, as well as going out with friends regularly. When I realised that I needed to work more, I found the solution at State Library, where I was able to combine studying with socialising by going there with friends every weekend. For you, this balance could be achieved by continuing a hobby or passion into Year 12. Ultimately, it's up to you to find the equilibrium by doing the things that make you happy. I promise you, if you're in a positive, happy mindset when you're studying, then you are guaranteed to do better at school.

Live in the moment

Something that really helped me during my final year was embracing mindfulness and meditation. I really focused on being grounded in the present moment and being aware of what I was doing at that point in time. This sounds very simple, but is actually surprisingly difficult to do. Think about how many times your mind has wandered whilst you've been reading this article. How many times have you checked your phone?

To make the most out of your studying, it is important to be mindful of what you're doing. That means that whatever it is that you're undertaking at any particular point in time is the most important task in the world, whether it be eating breakfast, or going out with friends, or playing sport. You only need to think about studying when you're actually studying. In this way you will minimise your stress because you won't allow it to bleed into the rest of your life. This also means that when you're studying you must be fully present and aware that you are studying, not allowing your mind to wander. This will make your studying so much more efficient, allowing you to cut down on hours and spend more time relaxing. Put your phone in the corner of the room, shut the door, and put your head down!

Another tip I have is to pay attention in class. Many people think doing well in exams is all about writing good notes and studying them, but I found that paying attention in class was by far my most powerful tool. I didn't have to study my notes nearly as much because I remembered learning the content the first time around. To make the most out of class, you have to be present and not just mindlessly copy down notes from the board word for word. I would summarise the notes given to us in class using my own abbreviations, acronyms and arrows, trying to make it as short as possible. Writing little notes on the side also helped me out.

> Hum: dev ~ thought of as unproductive, mosquito infested
> - Abattoir (1910), ↑ capacity (20k/day) in 1923, dumping of carcasses = eutrophication = algal blooms (invasion) ~ ↑ nutrients lead to mang dieback, disrupted energy flows in eco.
> - Union carbide plant (1955) = pesticides (DDT) + orange dumped = ↓ soil pH, dissolved carbs ~ $CaCO_3$ structure.
> - 4th most polluted waterway (1960)

(My Geography notes showing my use of abbreviations, symbols and arrows. Find your own unique style that works best for you.)

By doing this, it forces you to think about what you are writing. This helps solidify the content in your mind.

3. Eat Subway sandwiches

It's finally time for me to acknowledge the meaning behind my clickbait title. Let me share a little anecdote with you. In the Year 11 annual exams I had an hour and a half break before my Geography exam which most students used to cram in some last minute knowledge at the library. For whatever reason, I instead decided to head into the city with my friends and sit down at Subway for an Italian herbs and cheese pizza sub. Despite minimal study, I managed to pull off my most miraculous result in Geography ever. The only plausible explanation was the Subway. Before each Geography exam following that, I would go to Subway and order the exact same sandwich. I came first in every single exam. Whilst the Subway sandwiches had no correlation whatsoever to my exams and this little routine of mine made no logical sense, it allowed me to go into the exams feeling confident and having luck on my side.

Many professional athletes also have unique rituals and idiosyncrasies that work for them. For example, tennis player Rafael Nadal always arranges his bottles diagonally with the labels facing the court and never steps on lines when he walks, always crossing them with his right foot first. He's won 19 grand slams and has made over US$120,000,000 in prize money. Are these rituals responsible for his immense success? No, of course they're not. His talent and hard work to back it are the main factor causing his success, but these rituals are *scientifically proven* to improve performance. When going into something unknown that causes uncertainty or anxiety, performing familiar tasks helps ease one's mind, improving attention and increasing confidence and emotional stability.

To maximise your chances of success, you should consider finding your Subway sandwich. Whether it be waking up at a particular time or wearing a particular shirt, these rituals will help you feel more comfortable, which is when you perform your best. One of the greatest pitfalls of top students in exams is being too stressed beforehand. Despite studying so much, they lose their marks from silly mistakes and mental blanks. I found that putting the notes aside and meditating for 15 minutes before every exam helped me enter the exam hall calmly. Through this, I was able to drastically minimise marks lost due to silly mistakes.

Geography

Before I offer my advice on the subject, I'd like to take the time to thank my teacher Ms Chloe Robson, who was by far one of the greatest teachers I've ever had. Her enthusiasm and effort was always appreciated, going above and beyond to mark our notes and essays. She would always bring in chocolates and Tim Tams to give us the sugar rush we needed to survive the last period on a Friday. She made the subject thoroughly enjoyable, inspiring all of her students to work hard to make her proud. I was so lucky to have such an amazing teacher, which can make all the difference. Thank you for everything, Ms Robson.

Now, onto the subject Geography.

Unfortunately, Geography doesn't receive the respect it deserves as a subject. I often hear students calling Geography 'not a real' subject and only choosing it as a 'bludge' subject because it's easy. The truth is, if you bludge Geography, it isn't going to be easy. The exams for Geography are actually quite demanding, 3 hours long, consisting of 20 marks of multiple choice, 40 marks of short answers (with some longer responses up to a page long) and 2 essays. The students who choose Geography thinking it's easy will struggle with the demanding paper. Thus, preparing well for the subject will give you a huge advantage over these students and can propel Geography into your top 10 units.

Geography is a content heavy subject (similar to Economics and History). If you want to do well, you need to find a good way of memorising lots of statistics and case studies. Your best friend in the subject is statistics, because backing up your answers with evidence immediately strengthens it (even if you have absolutely no idea what you're talking about). My method for learning my stats occurred in 3 steps.

1. Type out a stat sheet

I would gather all my stats together for a particular topic and have a short explanation beside the number to show what it meant.

Example: A section of my stats sheet for viticulture and wine making

7.6m ha of vineyards
250m HL prod (historical low, ↓ 8.6% ~ climate) 243 hL consumed (wine glut 7m hL)
Italy = biggest cons (42.5m hL)
7.4 acres avg vineyard size in France
EU leading prod – 175m hL/yr, 45% wine growing area, 60% prod
167 ha ave size in Aus

I would read over the stats a few times and then move onto the next step.

2. Type out another stat sheet, but with only the numbers

The next step was to remove the explanations from the stat sheet. I would look at the numbers and say out loud what the stats were for. I would repeat this until I got them all right. It would look something like this:

Example: stats sheet with just numbers

```
7.6
250
42.5
7.4
175, 45, 60
167
```

3. Start with a blank sheet and type out the stats and explanations from memory

The final step to completely cementing stats in your memory is to type everything up to the best of your memory over and over again until you start seeing the numbers in your sleep.

Making Notes

Making your Geography notes is a very time consuming task, so I would recommend constantly updating them every day or at least every week, so that the work doesn't pile up. But, before you think about maintaining your notes, you must first begin writing the notes, which can be a very daunting task. Where do you begin? How do you structure your notes? Have a look at a sample from mine.

Example: A Large City in the Developed World (Sydney)

Sydney's Characteristics and Nature as a WC

Spatial Location

- 34°S, 151°E
- 12,367.7km²
- Situated in basin (Cumberland Plain), surrounded by Woronora Plateau (S), Blue Mtns (W), Hawkesbury Plateau (N)
- Greater Syd radiates from Port Jackson, includes Blue Mtns + Central Coast

Characteristics

- Pop – 5.48mil, growing at rate of 1.76%/yr
- Pop density of Greater Sydney – 407/km², density of built up urban area – 1,237/km²
- Topography shapes Syd's morphology (fn + character)
    - N Shore slower to develop ~ hilly topography, mostly quiet backwater until Harbour Bridge, most of N Shore part of Hawkesbury Plateau, overlaid by hilly ridges + gullies
    - E Suburbs on coast, containing iconic beaches (Bondi, Coogee), lie on steep slopes + prominent seaside cliffs
    - W Suburbs on Cumberland Plain, relatively flat, situated on rain shadow = drier

World City

- 1 of 3 most multicultural cities, attracting ppl from all over globe, bringing huge range of languages, cultures, cuisines, ideas
- Contains 7/10 most popular visitor attractions, hosted nearly half of all intn'l visitors during 2011-17, who spent on avg $2,400 each = $8.6bil (1/3 of Aus' intn'l tourism earnings)
- Alpha WC, ranked in top 10 most connected cities
- Global Financial Centres Index (measures competitiveness) ranked Syd 4th in Asia-Pacific region
- >3/4 of all foreign + domestic banks in Aus have HQs in Syd
- 2015/16, GDP of Greater Syd = $400bil, ¼ of Aus' GDP

The best way to structure your notes is by the syllabus dot points which I have underlined at the top. I then have subheadings that acknowledge each part of the syllabus dot point, with relevant information (also in dot points) below. Note that I have statistics in almost *every* line. I studied my notes by stats because, if you know your stats, then you will know the content that goes along with it.

Case studies are also very important in Geography to use as examples to strengthen your answers. You do not need to know them in excessive detail. Be logical and only learn relevant information that you think could be useful in an answer, otherwise you're just increasing your workload and making it harder for yourself.

Example: Case Study on a Large City in the Developed World (Greensquare)

Case Study: Greensquare (urban renewal)
- Inner-east of Syd, 4km S of CBD
- Alexandria, Zetland, Waterloo, Roseberry, Beaconsfield
- Oldest industrial heartland transformed through urban renewal
- 278ha urban renewal
    - $13bil construction
    - 30,500 new residential dwellings, expected to house 61,000 ppl by 2030
    - Modern library, streets for walking/cycling
- Waranara Early Education Centre
    - Old outpatient building transformed into colourful, state-of-the-art childcare centre
- Banga Community Shed
    - Prev pathology building, now place to learn new skills repairing + reusing household items
- Gunyama Park Aquatic and Recreation Centre
    - Heated + powered by on-site energy w/ green space for sports + relaxation

I have the name of the case study (Greensquare) and what it can be used for (any question asking about urban renewal) in the brackets. Underneath is some pretty basic information: location, size and an overview of what it is. I also pulled out 3 specific examples of the project. However, for the exam I only memorised 2 of them. Your case studies don't need to be extensive, you just need to find the key information that's useful for you. Don't mindlessly copy down everything that you see. I read through pages of information and watched videos on Greensquare, and then condensed it into that small box above. Ultimately, that's all that I needed. You're going to need lots of case studies, examples and stats to cover all the syllabus dot points, so be smart about your study and minimise your workload by picking out only the most important parts.

Exam Techniques

1. Multiple Choice

There's really not much to say here. Your exam has 20 multiple choice questions, mostly on mapping skills and a few on definitions. The only way to prepare is to find the skills you're shaky at and do lots of practice. The most common mistakes are dropped from silly mistakes. So, pay attention to what the question is asking, whether it's *Area Reference* vs *Grid Reference*, or *from* a location vs *to* a location. Work on the skills you aren't as good at, ask your teacher, use the internet and learn your definitions. You should be constantly doing skills papers throughout the year so that you don't get rusty. The multiple choice is the easiest part of the paper, so don't worry about it too much.

2. Short Answer

The short answer section is worth a whopping 40 marks (as much as the essays) and is the easiest place to get marks. If Geography is one of your weaker subjects and you're looking to give it a boost, working on short answers first is the best place to start because you can pick up marks so much easier than in the essays.

The first step to answering this section is to break down the question to make sure you acknowledge each part of the question to get the full marks. There are two parts to this step:

1. Directive/Key Term

    - What is the question asking you **to do**?

    - Almost every question begins with a directive term (e.g. outline, explain, describe).

    - You must know what the question expects of you as soon as you see the directive term (if you're unsure what they mean, you can find the glossary of key terms for Geography on the NESA website and familiarise yourself with their meaning).

    - Stick to what the question is asking. If it asks to *describe*, there is no need to *explain* and doing so won't get you extra marks.

2. Syllabus Terms
   - What is the question asking **about**?
   - Have a look for any syllabus terms in the question – these will help you structure your answer.
   - Eg "functioning", means you're writing about energy flows, nutrient cycling and biodiversity, "vulnerability and resilience" means you're writing about biodiversity, extent etc., "importance of management" means you're writing about heritage value, utility value etc.
   - If you're not quite sure what you're expected to write about when these syllabus terms come up, then you need to *read the syllabus* (it's that simple!).

My last tip for short answers is going to get its own line, in bold, italicised and underlined, because it is so important:

<u>For every point you make, use a stat or an example to back it up!</u>

Stats and examples are your most powerful weapons in Geography. You wouldn't go into a gunfight with just your fists, so don't go into your Geography exam without stats and examples. Sure, the stakes aren't as high and you won't end up dead if you ignore my advice, but you'll most likely end up with a mediocre mark in Geography.

Now, here's a sample question from my trial exam and how to break it down.

> *Q: Outline the nature and rate of change in the functioning of an ecosystem at risk you have studied as a result of natural stress. (4 marks)*
>
> 1. Directive/Key Term
>   - *Outline* is the directive term and according to NESA it means to "sketch in general terms; indi-

cate the main features of". This basically means to describe with specific examples.

2. Syllabus Terms

- *Nature and rate of change* refers to what type (natural/human) and how fast (gradual, rapid, catastrophic) the change is.

- *Functioning of an ecosystem* refers to the biodiversity, energy flows and nutrient cycles.

- *Ecosystem at risk* means that you need to talk about a specific case study that you've learnt.

- *Natural stress* means you're talking about stress caused by natural or biotic factors.

I've broken the question down and now know how to answer it. So, let's look at my answer.

> A: Tidal inundation is a regularly occurring change in the Homebush Bay Intertidal Wetlands (HBITW) that occurs twice a day. It is a natural change, and thus the ecosystem is well adapted to it. The tides allow decaying mangrove leaves to decompose and form biofilm, which is deposited further up the bank when the tides recede. This biofilm provides nutritious sustenance to Red and White Claw Crabs and enables energy flows, as it provides fixed energy to a heterotrophic being, allowing the flow of energy through the food chain. The inundation has also become responsible for nutrient cycling as it causes soils to be waterlogged and anoxic. Thus, bacteria in the soil have adapted by using denitrification, which removes nitrogen from nitrates and uses the produced oxygen for respiration, an example of nitrogen fixing and the functioning of the nitrogen cycle.

I've identified the natural stress of tidal inundation, commenting on its nature and rate of change, even throwing in a stat ("occurs twice a day") to support it. I've then linked this natural stress to ecosystem functioning, using specific examples of biofilm, Red and White Claw

Crabs and denitrification by bacteria to support my answer and talk about energy flows and nutrient cycling. Note that I didn't need to talk about biodiversity as the question was only worth 4 marks, and so choosing nutrient cycling and energy flows was adequate.

Now, all you need to do is follow my structure and practice it until you feel comfortable.

3. Essays

This section is worth 40 marks and you have to pick 2 essays to write out of a choice of 3. Essays are not difficult. They are essentially the same as short answer questions in that you follow the same steps when breaking them down with directive terms and syllabus terms. The only difference is that they are worth more marks, so you need to discuss more things in more detail with paragraph structure. If you are prepared for your short answer section, then you are prepared for your essays. This is because almost all the questions in your short answer section can be turned into essays. For example, the sample short answer question I gave you above can be slightly tweaked to become an essay question.

> *Q: Outline the nature and rate of change in the functioning of TWO ecosystems at risk you have studied as a result of natural and human stress. (20 marks)*

This question works in the same way as the previous short answer question, except, you'll have to talk about one additional case study and also talk about human stress. In essays, you don't have a specific number of lines limiting you. Since you have more room, you would also define all the important syllabus terms in your introduction.

Essays are your chance to 'flex' to the marker by showing them how much relevant information you know. The information is only relevant if you are able to link it back to the question. So, in this case, every point you make has to draw back to how it affects the functioning of ecosystems. When writing your essay, if you have the question in mind for every sentence that you write, you will do well. Once you've got this downpat, all you need to do to get the top marks is to throw in your stats and evidence to strengthen your points. Finally, don't hold back! It doesn't matter if your essay begins to look like a mathematical proof. Stats are good and they will distinguish you from the other students.

Ending Note

If you've made it this far in the article, then you are clearly a motivated individual and conscientious student who deserves to do well. Even if you don't get the marks that you're hoping for, the most important thing is your attitude and approach towards Year 12. Life is erratic and unpredictable and sometimes won't go your way, even if you do everything right. Regardless of the number at the end of the year, if you put in your best effort with the right techniques, then you should be proud of yourself because you have the foundations to achieve success. Life will reward you eventually, I promise. Look after yourself, be happy with what you do, and, if all else fails:

There's always an Italian herbs and cheese pizza sub waiting for you at your nearest Subway.

Lachlan's Geography Cheat Sheet

- Lots of memorising is required, so discovering the technique that works best for you will be hugely beneficial. If you can't find one, then try my technique: minimising your notes little by little until you're left with a blank page and it's up to you to type it out from memory.

- Structure your notes using the syllabus and summarise large chunks of information into as little words as possible. Consciously doing this ensures you understand what you are writing and makes you think more when you read the information.

- Don't have excessive information about your case studies (unless it's for Ecosystems at Risk, because then your case studies are the entire topic) and only note down relevant information that will help you answer questions.

- Don't worry too much about multiple choice, just find the ones you're weak at and practise them.

- For short answers, identify directive and syllabus terms to ensure you're answering the question.

- For essays, treat them the same as short answers, but with more structure, detail and evidence.

- **USE STATISTICS.**

The Rules of Law - Getting through HSC Legal Studies

By Zair Ahmed

"When you don't like how the tables are set, turn over the tables."

Part A: Character Testimony

On the outside, this quote may seem funny or even obnoxious, but it touches a fundamental yet hidden truth about the HSC experience. Year 12, just like this quote, is about **control,** because the HSC is a beast that will consume every aspect of your life if you lose control of it. This year is about taking control of your life and the HSC itself - that is the key to success.

Now, I know it's very easy to make such wild proclamations having already undergone this trial . However, having come out the other side in one piece, it's the most important lesson I learned from the times I failed to maintain **control.**

That isn't to say that my Year 12 was full of regrets; the contrary, actually. I made several mistakes in Year 12, such as starting the year off poorly in terms of academics, personal health, balancing extracurricular and study time, and social life. These mistakes were just that, mistakes from which I learnt more about my strengths, weaknesses, as well as guidelines on how I should conduct myself in the future. All of these were important lessons, not regrets. Realising that this is the end of your high school experience and that you only get one go at it, I made a special effort to join all extracurriculars and involve myself in the wider high school community.

Finishing the HSC was a relief, and the future holds exciting possibilities as I transition to studying Law and PPE (Politics, Philosophy, and Economics) at ANU. Year 12 is what you make it. To make it easier, I hope that some of the following advice helps you on your journey!

Part B: The Trial that is Year 12

Motivation

Maintaining motivation is one of the hardest challenges throughout Year 12. The subjects you choose are an important first step in this process, since you should be loving what you do and have an interest in what you study. However, motivation has a tendency to deteriorate over the year, so I decided to gamify my study.

This involved 'delayed gratification,' where I would only allow myself to do something I wanted (whether that be watching a show, movie, playing something, etc.) if I had completed certain tasks. Not only did this incentivise studying, it also provided me a greater sense of contentment when I had received my 'reward.' The source of motivation doesn't necessarily matter, as long as it's always there. I was often motivated by other people's work ethic, whereby I felt guilty for not working. This in turn spurred me on to work, so it's important to have friends that work hard and help you stay motivated.

These were all temporary strategies I used to motivate myself, but there was always one overarching strategy. At the beginning of the year, I visualised what my perfect job and day looked like. From that point on, every decision and piece of work I did contributed to achieving that perfect day. I decided what I wanted in the long-term and knowing that was a significant motivator throughout the year.

Stress and Organisation

There are three inevitabilities in life: death, taxes and stress during Year 12.

Managing workloads, keeping up with deadlines, and balancing every aspect of life were all very stressful for me. Thus, organising my day transformed not only my wellbeing, but also my productivity. Initially I began with to-do lists, and even this small task was something I had to learn to adapt to my own strengths and weaknesses. I found that I wasn't intimidated by long to-do lists but just needed things to be constantly checked off. Therefore, I eventually composed lists that were broken into smaller tasks which provided me with a desired sense of progress, but also were also worthwhile and rewarding.

Establishing breaks is also vital to maintaining productivity, and I aimed to vary up my breaks as much as possible. This was especially with regards to location. Taking long walks and listening to music is a fantastic way to clear your head and relax yourself - plus, you get exercise (an oftentimes foreign concept in Year 12). Yet, despite the activity, I changed the location to enjoying my breaks at any place other than my study table. I would read and write in the backyard, watch Mad Men on my bed, play a game on another table. Whatever it was, it wasn't to happen on my study table. This meant that whenever I did sit at my study table, my body was tuned to only studying.

Creating a timetable is extremely helpful in clearing your mind and organising yourself. While there are several apps and programs you can use to craft one for you, I preferred making my own for all potential customisation. This is my timetable from a random week in Year 12:

Time / period	Monday	Tuesday	Wednesday	Thursday	Friday
Recess	Green Group Meeting	Tutorial Service	Mod B Critical Reading	Mod B Critical Reading	
4:30-5:00 pm	Lunch		Finish Mod C Notes	Prefects Meeting	Prefects
5:00-5:30 pm	Walk	Walk	Walk	Walk	Walk
5:30-6:00 pm	Walk	Walk	Walk	Walk	Walk
6:00-6:30 pm	Walk	Walk	Walk	Walk	Walk
6:30-7:00 pm	English Extension 1 - Practice Paper		English Extension 1 - Finalise Essay	Biology - Consolidate Mod 6 notes	English Advanced - Finalise Mod A and B Essays
7:00-7:30 pm		Legal Studies - Sentencing Essay			
7:30-8:00 pm	Dinner	Break	Break	Dinner	Dinner
8:00-8:30 pm		Dinner	English Advanced - Mod C Discursive Piece	Legal Studies - Complete Crime and Human Rights Questions	English Advanced - Mod A and B Practice Questions and Theses
8:30-9:00 pm	Society and Culture - Finish PIP Bibliography				
9:00-9:30 pm		Extracurricular - Finish Schedule	Dinner		Break
9:30-10:00 pm	Break		Break	Break	English Extension 2 - Refine and Finalise Assignment
10:00-10:30 pm	English Extension 2 - Finish Assignment Draft	Biology - HSC Sample Paper	Binge Mad Men	Society and Culture - Proofread PIP	
10:30-11:00 pm					English Extension 2 - Peer Marking
11:00-11:30 pm	Break				
11:30-12:00 am	Legal Studies - Finish Homework Questions	Break		Break	Break
12:00-12:30 am			Break		Extracurricular Event Planning

I always attempted to have at least hour-long blocks of study, often allocating more time than what was needed (especially during non-exam periods). This was so that I could realistically stick to the timetable, as missing the deadline for one study block can spiral into procrastination caused by the 'Oh, I've messed up my timetable so why bother sticking to it for the rest of the day?' mentality. As you can also see, there are ample breaks and the subjects I study are varied, which helped productivity tremendously. This was supplemented by subject-specific to-do lists I made with due dates, so that, at all times, I knew what I needed to do and what to insert into my timetable. This would look something like this:

Subject	Description	Due Date
Legal Studies	Complete World Order Notes	Monday Week 5
	Finish World Order Essay Scaffold	Friday Week 5
	Exam Revision – Crime Multiple Choice Questions	Wednesday Week 4
	Exam Revision – Finish 1.5 Case Studies	Friday Week 4
Society and Culture	Finish Popular Culture Notes	Wednesday Week 4
	Social and Cultural Continuity- Complete Worksheets	Monday Week 4
	PIP – Refine Introduction and Submit	Friday Week 4
	PIP – Complete Progress Repost	Friday Week 4

Part C: Obiter Dicta (On Legal Studies)

Legal Studies can seem like a daunting mountain of information that you can never surmount, but there are always shortcuts you can pave to the summit. The content you need to memorise is quite extensive, so it really helps to have an interest in the subject.

The Court Clerk - Making Notes

The easiest trap to fall into when making notes for Legal Studies is to fail to write concisely, especially considering the abundance of information provided from all resources. My most helpful resource in this regard was textbooks; Legal Studies textbooks are structured by the syllabus and are quite comprehensive. I chose two textbooks - a comprehensive one as well as another one that was more succinct with more summaries. By cross-referencing the two, I was able to pinpoint what information was important, along with being able to access a wide range of cases and statistics. I structured my notes similarly to textbooks, but far more concisely (thus being more helpful during exam study periods).

The defendant acted in defence of self, another, or property; only accepted in limited circumstances and only for reasonable force.
Crimes Act 1900 – s419 – Self-defence – onus of proof
In any criminal proceedings in which the application of this division is raised, the prosecution has the onus of proving, beyond a reasonable doubt, that the person did not carry out the conduct in self-defence.
Risky because consideration of reasonable force by defendant and jury might be different. The force used must be proportional to the perceived threat and cannot be vengeful.
Zecevic v DPP (1987) 162 CLR 645
Zecevic had an argument with his neighbour, returned to his flat, got a gun and shot his neighbour. He claimed self-defence, explaining that the neighbour was moving towards his car, where the accused believed his kept a gun, when Zecevic shot him. The trial judge said the jury could not consider the defence of self-defence because unreasonable force.

An excerpt from my notes - separated through colour coding and tables.

My tendencies to colour-code my notes were initially fuelled by a desire to make my notes look pretty (some call it procrastination, I call it art). Ultimately, however, distinguishing cases, stats, legislation, definitions and so on in this manner was tremendously helpful in allowing me to find and understand everything comprehensively.

While the questions relating to your optional topics (other than Crime and Human Rights) are always 25-mark essays, creating theory notes as you would for the mandatory topics is vital for developing a holistic understanding of concepts. Formatting your notes for these topics also ensures that they are more convenient for you to browse through, extract, and ultimately formulate essay arguments based off of the concise notes you have collected. After this, browse through the internet to gather all updated information and then do a final do-over of your notes with any new evidence of law reform.

My notes ended up being my go-to resource, since they were an amalgam of all the important information I had found from every resource compiled into one summarised package. Note-taking styles vary depending on your strengths and weaknesses, but I found that with the content style of Legal Studies, extra information never hurt.

Formulating a Case Strategy – How to Study

There is no universal way of studying. So, going in with this knowledge, I tried out several methods. Eventually, I found myself wired to certain tasks through memory association. Whenever I had to memorise certain information, I would always stand and walk around. Whenever I put on certain music (e.g. 'The Social Network' soundtrack), my mind would automatically be in study mode. Thus, through these tasks and changes in my immediate environment, I conditioned myself to study and be more productive.

With a subject like Legal, it's easy to succumb to paranoia and memorise more than is necessary, which can result in a failure to uphold your standard or even neglect other subjects. Thus, it was imperative that I knew what I could easily recall and make links to, as well as identify weak points. Certain things, such as definitions or obscure historical context behind legal concepts, don't need to be memorised but simply understood. Cases, evidence, legislation, statistics and evaluations are things you do need to be able to recall on the spot during the exam. You don't need to memorise entire essays; essay plans and frameworks will suffice. Whether it be through jingles, acronyms, or everything in between, I had a method for everything just to store everything I needed in my brain.

Year 12 is also disruptive in terms of classes, with carnivals and extra-curriculars meaning that we had less time in class than what was required. Since Legal is a heavily theory-based subject, I created my notes for each topic in the holiday before each term, concomitantly gaining somewhat of an understanding of what I would be learning. When school continued, I used classes to consolidate my information and clarify anything that was needed. However, the bulk of the work was already done beforehand. This repetition further helped me ingrain information into my memory and thus allowed for easier studying.

Essentially, I would aim to understand all the concepts and general evaluations for the entire topic within the holidays, followed by learning all major legislation/cases and the finer details during the term. Before exams, I would have my notes and essay plans all completed. Then, I would revise the content before completing practice questions. Multiple choice questions made for easy, quick practice that allowed for a clear identification of any gaps in knowledge. Furthermore, Human Rights short answer questions are predictable and answering them during crunch time before exams can be time-consuming, so I wrote dot points to plan out my answer in filling the required criteria for full marks. As for the Crime and Options Essay, I memorised all possible essay plans for the former and a list of paragraphs that I would mould for the latter, regardless of the question (Options questions tend to be more encompassing).

Right before an exam, I would sleep and eat a healthy amount (unlike the rest of the time), and hope for the best. Invest in a good pen and, if an exam is in winter, use hand warmers.

Differentiate Yourself

It is vital to use whatever is at your disposal to succeed in Legal Studies. Everyone will use similar textbooks and provide similar evidence. To achieve high-range marks, it's important to distinguish yourself from everyone. Stand out and go far and beyond. An easy way to do this is to keep up with current events and new legislation - incorporate these into your essay and link them to the concepts you learned in Legal Studies. This demonstrates to the marker that not only are you going beyond the textbook and actively engaging with the subject in day-to-day life, but also that you can apply it to what you have learned.

The HSC is also designed to benefit you individually if your peers do well, so working collaboratively was significant in allowing me to succeed. Working in study groups, sharing cases/evidence, and peer-marking essays got me through so much of Legal Studies.

Use whatever is at your disposal and take control over your knowledge and studies. That was the most important lesson I took away.

Writing Essays

Essays make up 65 out of a total of 100 marks within the HSC exam, and it is crucial to get into a habit of writing them throughout the year. Crime essays are diverse and more specific in the questions they can ask, but can still be predicted using the syllabus. I jotted down the 6 topic-based questions, questions based on the Themes and Challenges, and past essay questions. After this, I crafted essay plans for each possible question, which was minimalist and only consisted of vital information I would otherwise not remember. To save up on workload, I attempted to make my paragraphs as flexible as possible so as to be usable for multiple essay questions. For example, my paragraph on Mandatory Sentencing was usable for an essay question on the criminal trial process, discretion, law reform, non-legal methods, as well as balancing the rights of offenders, victim, and society. This lightened my workload as there are many possible Crime essay questions.

As for the Options essays, which make up 25 marks each, my method of preparation was simpler. I would prepare seven paragraphs that could encompass any possible question and choose the four or five that applied the most for the question that was asked in the exam. I didn't originally intend to memorise my essays. However, after studying them thoroughly, phrases, wording, and sentences began to imprint themselves into my memory.

The structure for Legal essays is relatively simple, consisting of an introduction that answers the question, followed by a small overview of the points you will discuss. Following this are your paragraphs (I wrote three for Crime and four to five for the Options questions), which are then wrapped up by a short conclusion that summarises your main stance and answer to the question.

A dilemma often arose for me in attempting to discuss the positives and negatives within a paragraph (markers want you to be able to acknowledge the moral 'greyness' of the legal system), but also put forward an argument effectively. I modelled my paragraph structures depending on the argument I put forward. For example, if I was to argue that Jury reform was ineffective, I would, in a sense, 'sandwich' my opposing points within the paragraph. That is to say that I would present evidence for its ineffectiveness after the topic sentence, followed by counterpoints that highlighted its effectiveness. I would then counter these again by more evidence for its ineffectiveness, thus ensuring that I acknowledged both sides of the argument but still provided an argument with a final impression to the marker that coincided with my view. I also avoided using judgements along the lines of 'moderate effectiveness' or 'somewhat effective,' since the marker wants you to argue a position strongly.

Unlike English, I avoided grandiloquence within my Legal essays. All links to larger legal concepts (e.g. justice, equality, fairness, the rule of law) and judgements were clear and explicit - leave no room for interpretation. Furthermore, while having two-three pieces of evidence per paragraph is more than sufficient to score well, I always incorporated at least five or six pieces. The most obvious reason for this is to demonstrate a greater understanding to the marker, whilst also providing backup if you forget anything.

Another advantage of having more evidence is in the off-chance that you get an extremely specific essay question. For example, my essay plan for the criminal trial process included a paragraph on the effectiveness of criminal defences. The paragraph itself outlined 4 different defences, alongside 2 pieces of legislation with each. These weren't extensively elaborated upon as this paragraph still had to be succinct enough to be able to be written under exam conditions and finish the essay. However, when a 15-mark essay question asked the student to evaluate the effectiveness of criminal defences, I could simply separate that one paragraph into 3 or 4 different ones, each with their own evidence. I would pad each paragraph out with more conceptual information and elaborations, but I wouldn't be completely helpless for specific questions. The same occurred during my HSC exam, when I had to stretch my post-sentencing considerations paragraph (which was originally under an overarching Criminal Sentencing Process essay plan) into an entire essay.

Interweave evidence seamlessly and use it to supplement your arguments and judgements, not the other way around. Write quickly (this was an issue for me) and legibly. Stick with a clear structure and answer the question.

Part D: Cross-Examination - The Legal Exam

The Legal exam is 3 hours long, with various sections and question types. I always set a routine for my 5 minutes of reading time, as well as custom time allocations for each section tailored to my writing speed. This practice only comes from doing past papers and questions, as doing these allowed me to realise which questions I needed to spend less time on. For the first minute of reading time, I would browse through the short answer and essay questions, allowing me to ease my mind and subconsciously stow away the information I wouldn't need. For the next four minutes, I answered the multiple-choice questions, remembering the answer in my head. As writing time began, I would spend 3 minutes on multiple choice questions, 20 on Human Rights, 40 on the Crime Essay, and 55 minutes each on the Options essays.

Multiple choice questions arise from general information gathered from the fundamentals of the subject and topics that essay questions aren't asked on (e.g. The Nature of Crime). No matter what, I would attempt every question. This section was by far my weakest, as there are instances when there are two correct answers. Remember that you must choose the 'more correct' answer in line with the syllabus.

The next section, which consists of short answer Human Rights questions, is often where a large majority of people lose marks, either directly or indirectly. Overwriting is an issue, as I would sometimes write too much and for too long in questions that were only worth 5 marks. Planning the response in your head and dove-tailing the question with the mark requirement to identify what you need to cover are both very useful strategies. Don't neglect cases, treaties, and legislation in this section as it will elevate your marks. Avoid answering in dot points - use full sentences and only write the amount that you need to.

As for Crime essay questions, I would always write three body paragraphs unless I had extra time left over at the end (in which case I would add another). I decided to keep introductions and conclusions to two sentences each so as to ensure that my arguments were fleshed out. It's important to pay attention to the wording of the question, as extra caveats (e.g. merging a Theme and Challenge with a topic point, or adding 'for offenders, victims, and society' at the end of a general justice question) need to be acknowledged and integrated into your response.

There are always two questions to choose from for Options essays. Generally, one of these is more open and the other more specific - what you choose depends on your prepared material. I always chose the general question since I could apply my prepared paragraphs more effectively, but keep in mind that since the question is easier, so will the threshold for top range marks. The easier the question, the harder it is to distinguish yourself. It is always helpful to craft an essay plan (even the simplest possible plan can suffice) for organisational purposes, but also because it indicates to the marker that you have the required knowledge to complete an essay should you not due to time restrictions. Markers do look at essay plans, so making one is always beneficial.

If you still have time left over, I would always go through the exam again. I would recheck all of my multiple-choice questions and short answer responses. Since essays are often too long to make meaningful changes to, I would scan them for grammar and legibility issues.

Part E: The Verdict

That's that.

Year 12 is not fun. Yet, despite all of this, it's the year I will remember the most from high school. Keep your friends close and maintain the relationships you have. They will help you get through the year and beyond, and there will always be that shared experience you all went through. You're all in this together.

Whether it be with regards to balancing your life, extracurriculars, studies or anything else, remember that if you don't like how things are set, take control of your life. All the best for the HSC and beyond!

Zair's Legal Studies Cheat Sheet

Preparation

- Don't memorise more than what you need to. Have a clear understanding of what needs to be remembered and what doesn't.
- Use notes as a succinct consolidation of textbooks and class resources.
- Colour-code your notes and make all aspects of them instantly discernible by the eye.
- Practice multiple-choice questions: they're an easy way to pinpoint weaknesses.
- Plan out the structure to Human Rights questions.
- Always stay up to date with the news and add recent reform into your notes. Try to integrate current affairs into your essays through an intertwining with fundamental legal concepts.
- Vary your study environments – wire yourself to perform tasks in certain locations or while performing certain actions (e.g. memorising essays when standing, doing sample papers when in the living room).

Essays and Exams

- Create essay plans for possible questions. These you should craft using the syllabus (don't forget the Themes and Challenges).
- Write a small essay plan for all essay questions. When practicing before exams, don't write the entire essay but simply a skeleton of it.
- Prepare flexible essay paragraphs that can be applied to multiple essay questions.

- Use more pieces of evidence (cases, legislation, stats) than you need.
- When attempting to present an argument, keep in mind the marker's expectations. 'Sandwich' your argument like below to formulate a good final impression supporting your argument but also one that is cognisant of the multifaceted nature of the legal system:

  Judgement: System X is Effective in achieving justice

  Point/Evidence 1: Supports effectiveness

  Point/Evidence 2: Counters this point and presents ineffectiveness.
- Point/Evidence 3: Supports effectiveness.
- During the exam, attempt all questions and plan out your responses. Use reading time to answer multiple choice questions in your head and browse through the essay questions.
- Write legibly but also as fast as you can.

Good luck!

Hacking Modern History

By Seohyeong Lim

"Never, never, never give up."-- Winston Churchill

We all dread the HSC; an experience full of stress and anxiety, yet it can bring so much joy and be rewarding. My name is Seohyeong Lim and I attended Ashfield Boys High School. Though I pursued academic excellence, I genuinely never thought that I would receive the results I did. I will be forever grateful for those who were a part of my journey.

I was dux of my school with an ATAR of 97.85, as well as placing 3rd in the state in Modern History. My mindset fluctuated consistently throughout the year, but I always had one goal: to achieve success and do myself proud.

Ashfield Boys High School provided a basis for success which I was very fortunate to have. Amazing teachers and supportive peers greatly enhanced my abilities to gain such an amazing achievement. Despite this, I, like many others, faced many ups and downs during the HSC journey. From the lowest of lows to the highest of highs, you should always surround yourself with positive, supportive peers to face these challenges. Do not leave any regrets in high school, pursue everything you want, and you will achieve it.

General advice for Year 12

Here I will outline some general advice which you can use to improve your overall HSC experience. Maintaining a high level of motivation, creating habits, looking after your mental health, organising and loving what you do are the most important factors which will affect your HSC journey.

1. Motivation

Maintaining a high level of motivation is easier said than done. Harsh, tough periods are inevitable in our lives. Having supportive and positive surroundings will greatly maintain your motivation as you can combat these times together, as one.

Having an end goal can also have immeasurable benefits for your drive to success. Write down what you want to become and what you want to achieve as motivation. Put your favourite quote on your desktop or change your wallpaper to someone you aspire to become. This will ignite a flame within you which will motivate and inspire you to be better. Complete your HSC without regrets. You only get one shot, don't waste it!

2. Habits

Building a habit can do wonders to keep you in focus and achieve your goals. This is really enhanced by a personalised timetable, though your desires and willingness to actually act will decide how successful you become. Habits of study should be figured out from Year 11, where you begin to understand the tactics that work best for yourself. Build a habit, and eventually your habits will create a lifestyle change which will do wonders for your studies. You cannot study one day and then just not do anything for another two. Building a habit and sticking to it will make the HSC much more manageable.

3. Timetable

While most students create a timetable to use, most do not stick to it. Plenty of personalised timetable templates are available, but tips on how to use them are not. So, here are some of my tips as to how to use a timetable:

1. **CAN YOU REALLY DO IT?** – are you planning to study 12 hours per day? 5 hours straight? NEVER do this. You will lose focus and study inefficiently. Though this may begin positively, this cannot and will not be sustained throughout the year. Input break times, space subjects out, and be realistic when creating your personalised timetable.

2. **BE FLEXIBLE** – following on from the previous tip, you should create flexibility within your timetable. It should not be constrained to time limits where you must rush to complete a task. Instead, create flexible working hours which will not pressure you and will instead provide a platform where you are in a comfortable headspace to work.

3. **EQUALITY for all** – give all your subjects equal amounts of attention. While this can vary during exam periods, you should pay equal attention to all subjects instead of over-studying a few subjects. Remember, 8 units plus English are all calculated for the ATAR, so give each subject the equal treatment whether you like it or not. However, do note that if there are some subjects where there is a specific weakness then you should focus on that. The HSC is, after all, an aggregate of every subject. Therefore, if you can lift the marks in one particular subject more significantly than another, allocate time accordingly. You are only as strong as your weakest link.

4. Organisation of Documents

Organisation of documents, such as notes and handouts from teachers, can also greatly improve your study habits. $2 binders from Kmart are extremely useful, where you can use dividers to differentiate subjects. A physical document organisation space is very rewarding and useful. However, if you do not want to use such tools, just properly organise your files on your desktop. Create logs by theme, date, lesson, etc., so in the future when you look for documents, they are easy to gather.

5. Procrastination

I am not going to tell you to stop watching YouTube, stop playing games, or get off Instagram. However, what I will tell you is to track the time you spend on such activities. We all need a rest and can have a small duration of time watching and enjoying such activities, but make sure you do not get dragged into a pit of procrastination. Moderation, as with everything, is key.

Modern History

Modern History is a peculiar subject which receives polar-opposite reactions from individuals. Those who like it, love it, while those who do not, find it completely useless. You really should enjoy learning about history if you have picked it. It becomes more and more interesting as you delve further and see the connections between different events. Indeed, learning Modern History enabled me to have a greater appreciation of life as a whole, and where we as humans have come from.

To begin, there are some misconceptions about Modern History which I would like to address:

- **"Modern History is boring"**

    Entering the course with a close-minded outlook will create a sense of boredom and disinterest. Enter it open-minded, for if you try to really understand and appreciate history you will enjoy it far more. Contrary to its name, this course also provides some brief outlooks into the future, such as the Nuclear Age module, which creates an interesting (if terrifying) vision of the future.

- **"Modern history does not scale well"**

    At the end of the day, your ATAR results will only be a reflection of the amount of work, dedication and passion you have shown for the subject. If you are really passionate and willing to learn about history, you should definitely select it. It is without a doubt possible to achieve a great ATAR choosing Modern History.

- **"If I failed Year 11 Modern history, I have no chance in Year 12"**

    Year 11 is the chance for you to make as many mistakes as you want without having any effect on your final results. Unless you dislike or feel opposed to studying Modern History, you should not drop it. You receive a clean slate at the start of Year 12 from which to improve, so do not stress about preliminary marks.

General Modern Advice

There are no shortcuts to learning Modern History. You need to put in the work. While these tips will provide advice on how to attack Modern History, ultimately there is no better way to achieve success than to work hard.

1. Memorisation

Memorising 20 different essays are a no-go, but this does not mean you should neglect it altogether. For me, memorisation came pretty easily as I constantly edited and redrafted my essays through feedback from teachers. This provided a great opportunity to memorise the content before it was even time for exams.

Always try to remember important dates such as battles and the signature of treaties, as well as terminology from foreign countries. This specific knowledge enhances your essay's sophistication immensely. Furthermore, errors on dates are mistakes that a marker will easily pick up on and will relish in correcting you over!

2. Writing Faster

This is probably the most important tip for all subjects. You should always try to improve how fast you write. This enables you to write every bit of knowledge you have acquired onto paper in a restricted time period. Imagine the frustration of knowing every detail yet not being able to put it all down on the page. Detail and information are extremely important, and the greater the amount of RELEVANT information you write, the greater chance you will have of getting that Band 6.

Preparing for this can take many forms. Practice writing essays in restricted time periods, decreasing the amount of time you have every time with the same amount of words. Test new pens and new positions to write. You have to become strategic and find the best possible way for you to succeed. However, do keep in mind that your writing must be legible, otherwise you will receive no marks at all!

3. Practice

Cliché, right? But seriously this is so IMPORTANT. Following on from memorisation and writing faster, always practice, whether it be your short answer, source analysis or essays. Hand in essay drafts to your teachers every week. Make this a habit, not a grim task. Your teachers will provide important feedback which will be vital for your growth and understanding of areas in which you need to improve.

For source analysis responses, you should practice even more. Answering random, unseen questions will enhance your understanding of gaps in your knowledge which you could then fill to get that Band 6.

4. Terminology/Statistics

You have to use ACCURATE, RELEVANT terminology and data to enhance your responses. Words such as Volksgemeinschaft, Treaty of Versailles and Gestapo must be entrenched within your mind with their meanings. Having an extended knowledge of such terminology will greatly benefit and enhance your position within the cohort.

5. Connect 4

You must find connections between an event, its significance, its time period, and links to the syllabus. By finding these connections, it shows the marker that you have an in-depth understanding and knowledge of different events which will create a cohesive and structured response.

6. Avoid Generalisations

A Band 6 response is said to be 'sophisticated' and specific. Statements such as 'democracy was always good' (during the early 1900s, democracy was not the common system such as seen today), and 'dictators are all the same' (no, all dictators faced and grew from different circumstances) should not be used. Act like the marker does not know a single piece of information, adn create a detailed account of your own judgement to provide a powerful argument for the marker. Never ever make generalisations.

Exam preparation and techniques

Being quick, understanding the syllabus, utilising your time efficiently and preparing tactics for the exam will greatly increase your chances for success in the Modern History exam. Here are some tips to ace that exam:

1. Taking Advantage of the Syllabus

Preparing your notes by taking full advantage of the syllabus will be vital for your success within Modern History. I would advise that you take your notes in one of two ways: chronological order (where you take notes based on the time of events) or thematically (where your notes are based and grouped by different themes relevant to each other). While you should write notes on the 'CONTENT' section of the syllabus, you should also consider revising and taking notes based on the 'OUTCOMES' section at the top of the syllabus.

Timelines, Venn diagrams, mind maps and tables are extremely useful tools to visualise as well as make connections between different themes or events. These tools I used repetitively throughout my notes to see connections and similarities between different aspects within the syllabus.

2. Answering the Question

Always reference the question in your answer. This is such an obvious thing, yet many students neglect to do this. Always take time to figure out what the question is asking for and write according to those guidelines.

3. Your Way

Prior to going into the Modern History exam, you should have a plan of how to attack the exam. Your way: how you will start, where you will start and what you will read first. For example, are you going to begin with the essay and put down all your knowledge first, or begin with the source and go from sections 1 to 4? Deciding this will greatly reduce the amount of time wasted on trying to figure out what to do, as you are already prepared for it.

'Common Module' (Power and Authority)

This module is the only section which all Year 12 students will do commonly, and hence is a great opportunity to differentiate yourself from the other students sitting the exam.

1. Don't rely on the source

Do not, EVER, rely on the source. The source is only there to support and justify your answer. Hence, when you begin a source analysis question, you should first attempt to answer it without even looking at the sources. If you do not provide adequate enough knowledge beyond the sources, the markers can easily see that you really did not put the effort in. However, this does not mean you do not talk about the source at all. You should refer to all sources throughout your responses to show how it supports your judgement.

2. 5 W's

There will almost always be an "account for the perspective" question within the Power and Authority section of the Modern History exam. For this you should just remember the 5 W's.

- Who – primary or secondary source? Which side of the conflict is the person a part of?
- What – what type of a source is it? Newsletter, letter, journal, recount?
- When – when was the source written? Could it have been affected/manipulated by time
- Where – where was the source produced?
- Why – what is the content of the source? What motive does it present?

Essay

You will write two essays in the Modern History exam. For each, you should aim to write a minimum of 1000 words. Writing a lot enables you to substantiate an argument and really show the marker your knowledge and understanding of different topics. Here are some general essay tips:

1. Structure

Plan the structure of your essay before beginning to write. Whether it be chronologically or thematically (e.g. social, political, economic), a proper structure should be created. This will set the foundation for the introduction, body paragraphs and conclusion, and you will have an easier time communicating your argument. Below is a brief summary of how you should structure your essay.

Introduction – short and concise (between 100-150 words)

- Get to the point of what you are going to write about.
- Reiterate your judgement throughout the introduction. Using terms such as "meanwhile", "yet this shows", and "this supports" allows you to form links to your thesis.
- End with a strong summary of your thesis.

Body Paragraphs - 3 to 4 paragraphs (200-300 words approximately)

- Begin with an introductory sentence about your stance on the theme/event and what you will cover in the paragraph.
- Your thesis/argument should be maintained throughout the paragraph. You should aim to mention it once every three sentences.
- Each paragraph should conclude with a variation of a thesis relevant to each point made in the paragraph.

Conclusion – 50-150 words

- This is basically a copy of your introduction.
- Restate your thesis and make your judgement clear.
- End with a resolution, a sentence which brings in all of your points made within the essay and ending with your judgement.

2. Importance of a Thesis

The creation of a thesis is one of the most crucial factors when writing essays, as it sets the foundation on which you can express your point of view/judgement on a topic. In my opinion, you should have at least one thesis for each topic covered in a module. This enables you to see the broad nature of the Modern History course, as well as enabling you to view the connections between different themes and events. It should be complex and incorporate different factors, setting a foundation for the body paragraphs and conclusion. The thesis is by far the most important aspect of the essay which addresses your argument towards the question.

The thesis should be one to two sentences long and must be sustained throughout the essay. When writing the essay, constantly refer back to your thesis. Also, the body paragraph should consistently refer back to the thesis, as it 'supports' and 'solidifies' your argument. The thesis sets the foundation for your argument, so make it strong and clear.

3. Don't recount

Do not recount, I repeat, DO NOT RECOUNT. The marker does not want to hear a story of what happened, but rather they want a story of why and how something happened and its implications. Spend a sentence or two providing a brief, concise explanation of events, and then delve into its implications and how it affected the eventual outcome. Again, you will have to link this back to the thesis and provide your own perspective. You can say a certain event happened, but you must always link different events and its eventual outcome on such events.

4. Your Judgement

A point which my Modern History teacher emphasised was the need to establish my own judgement. You have to provide your own point of view, whether it be correct or not, against or for the status quo, as long as you are able to back it up with substantiated, relevant evidence. Whilst some may suggest to go against the status quo, as long as your essay is backed by evidence and maintained, it will not really matter.

5. Historiography

Historiography, if you do not know, is opinions/references to historians. You should get used to seeing the names Richard Evans and Ian Kershaw, as their opinions will constantly come up in your textbooks. While historiography is a good way to support your argument and show that historians have the same view/argument as you, historiography is not needed if your argument is sustained and supported by evidence. Do not stress over historiography, but if you can have some references, it can greatly elevate your essays.

6. Taking your learning above and beyond

I tried to take my learning above and beyond the syllabus, something which was made easier by the resources provided by my teachers at school. Extra reading material, study plans, advice, etc. should all be taken with two hands. They will provide an opportunity to further enhance your knowledge as well as your understanding. Borrow books from the library, watch documentaries relevant to your course, do every bit of research possible to widen the gap between you and your cohort. Our school even used two Modern History books (KEY FEATURES OF MODERN HISTORY 2 4th and 5th Edition) which provided an abundance of knowledge and understanding. At the end of it all, all the extra hours and research you have put into your study will pay off. To gain that edge, it is paramount to go above and beyond.

Sample questions and my approach

Here are some examples of how I would approach exam-type questions. Planning is vital for this.

Example: Power and Authority Short Response with Sources

I am only providing a guideline on how to target this question, so I will not include any actual sources.

> Study Sources B, D and G. To what extent do these sources provide evidence of the methods of control used by the Nazi regime? **10 marks**

My approach: Remember that this is a 10 mark question, so it should really feel like a mini essay. However, you should spend at most 20 minutes on this question. The first step is to read through the question thoroughly and underline key points.

(a) Study Sources B, D and G. (b) To what extent do these sources provide evidence of the (c) methods of control used by the Nazi regime?

   a. You will have to make references to sources. However, as mentioned previously, let the sources support your argument, not the other way around. In this way, you can showcase your knowledge and in-depth understanding of the syllabus.

   b. 'To what extent' – this means to evaluate, provide your opinions on the positives and negatives. Maintain your evaluation or judgement throughout your response and constantly refer back to it.

   c. 'Methods of control' – While you will gain a sense of these through the sources, this is the section where you will need to utilise your own knowledge. In your plan, you should create concise points which could be used as follows:

- Methods of Control
  - Terror and repression – concentration camps, Gestapo, SS
  - Legislation – 'aryan' race, Reich Citizenship Law 1935, KDF
  - Propaganda – Nuremberg Rally 1934, Berlin Olympics, censorship

These steps will take less than a minute when you constantly practice. Whilst they are important, make sure that you do not spend too much time creating your plan. Now that you have all my resources, you can begin your response. I will provide a hypothetical introduction which could be used.

- The <u>Nazi regime implemented various methods of control, which was used to manipulate and control the German population</u> (**references to the methods of control and how it benefitted the Nazi regime**). *Terror and repression, through the use of concentration camps and the Gestapo, new legislation such as the Reich Citizenship Law 1935 and the creation of the KDF, as well as propaganda as <u>evidenced by the sources</u>* (**reference to sources, though it is not needed in the introduction**) *instilled discipline and control over the German population which <u>enabled the Nazi regime to thrive</u>* (**evaluating the role of methods of control**).

Essay Plan – Peace and Conflict (Conflict in Europe)

How significant was the conflict in North Africa to victory of the Allies in Europe?

As in the 10 mark question, read through thoroughly and underline every key point in the question.

(a) <u>How significant</u> was the (b) <u>conflict in North Africa</u> to the (c) <u>victory of the Allies in Europe</u>?

- a. **'How significant'** – Again, you have to make a judgement, evaluating the important of a certain situation

b. Since the question asks for a specific event/battle, you MUST address it. Since it is specified, it should constitute at least 30-40% of your essay.

c. **'Victory of the Allies in Europe'** – now you must explore all the other possibilities and events which could have also led to such an event.

This would be my very concise, dot point plan for this essay:

- **North Africa** - Control of Mediterranean Sea, control of Suez Canal (link to wider world), British control sea and air, straining German supply lines, three-front war, Boost British morale.

- **Air War** – Morale, two-front war, destruction of industries/Luftwaffe.

- **Russia Campaign**
    - **Barbarossa** – Severe losses to Wehrmacht/Luftwaffe, ended Hitler's uninterrupted victories.
    - **Stalingrad** – Communications hub, industrial centre, morale boost.
    - **Kursk** – Final offensive, 'beginning of the end', Red Army involvement.

- **D-Day/Liberation of France** – end of the conflict – technical battle which led to end of war.

For your introduction, follow the example as shown for the short response. Make connections between the main points (E.g. the Russian campaign drained Germany's resources which was then taken advantage of in the North African campaign) and sustain your judgement throughout the essay. Each of your body paragraphs should address the points in bold above. You should then conclude using the structure guide from my first tip.

A message for those who were a part of my HSC journey

To all my teachers, peers, and my family, thank you for sticking by me through the highs and the lows. It really would not have been possible without you. Always follow your teachers' guidance, as they will have your greatest interests at heart and will want the best for you. Family, whether it be parents or siblings, are vital support within your home life. Always communicate with them, and don't be afraid to ask them for either space or support if you need it. Your peers are your family outside of your home. You will no doubt have arguments or bad blood, but remember your highs, all the laughter and joyful moments, as those relations will be the most memorable after school.

Conclusion

Again, I will repeat, "Never, never, never give up." I, as well as everyone else from Top Achievers and all those who you know, are rooting for you. You can do it. You will succeed. I believe in you. So, let's make it happen. As one famous magician said "We are in the endgame now."

Seo's Modern History Cheat Sheet

General Tips

- MAINTAIN a high level of motivation throughout the Year by having an 'END' goal.
- DEVELOP HABITS to maintain your study pattern throughout the year.
- TAKE CARE of your mental health and stress, it is OKAY to rest if you need to.
- Organise EVERYTHING, from your timetable to your documents to the amount of free time you have.

- Finally, ENJOY what you do. The more you enjoy it, the better you will perform.

General Modern Advice

- MEMORISE the key dates, battles and terminology from foreign countries.
- Try to WRITE AS FAST AS POSSIBLE while still being legible.
- PRACTICE, PRACTICE, PRACTICE – this will bring everything you have done together
- Use terminology and statistics to ENHANCE your responses.
- Connect EVENTS, its SIGNIFICANCE, TIME period, and links to SYLLABUS.
- BE SPECIFIC, NOT GENERALISED.
- Find out what TYPE of a learner you are (audio, verbal, visual).

Exam Preparation and Techniques

- TAKE ADVANTAGE of the syllabus – utilise mind maps, tables, etc., to make connections.
- Remember to always ANSWER THE QUESTION.
- Find YOUR WAY of attacking the exam.

Common Module

- Use the source to ENHANCE your response, not the other way around.
- Remember WHO, WHAT, WHEN, WHERE, WHY.

Essays

- PLAN your structure first, then begin writing.
- CREATE a persuasive thesis and MAINTAIN it.
- ALWAYS evaluate and show your judgement, NEVER recount.
- Make YOUR judgement clear.
- DO NOT STRESS too much over historiography, but it can definitely enhance your essay.

PDHPE: How to make studying your new favourite sport

By Emma Scroope

> *"When life gets you down, do you know what you've gotta do? Just keep swimming. Just keep swimming. Just keep swimming, swimming, swimming ..."* Dory, Finding Nemo

The HSC period often feels like an endless cycle. No matter how much work and effort you are putting in, the final exams still feel like an eternity away. It's often hard to see the end in such an overwhelming and daunting experience. However, if you simply tell yourself to *"Just keep swimming, swimming, swimming,"* you will be able to slowly progress towards the finish line. My name is Emma Scroope and I graduated from Loreto Kirribilli in 2019. I achieved an ATAR of 99.55 and placed 1st in the state for PDHPE.

I've lost count of the amount of people who have told me that high school was the best time of their lives. Consequently, I often felt pressure to ensure that I was enjoying my experience and that it lived up to its name. I struggled to understand how such a stressful time could possibly be one of the best years of my life. However, by applying the right mindset, it eventually became this for me!

MY TOP 2 GENERAL STUDY TIPS

1. **Have a distinct 'study space'**

    Personally, I hardly ever did work at home as I found it incredibly difficult to concentrate. Instead, I regularly went to the local library as I found it motivating to be amongst people who were also going through the same process as me and were engaged in their studies. Having an established 'study space' helps your mind to recognise that it is time to study. When you are out of this 'study space' you will be able to relax more easily and enjoy your break. Trying to do work in front of the TV or while in bed is not an encouraging work environment and only enhances the distractions.

2. **STAYING ORGANISED**

    I never liked to plan too far in advance. It's hard to know what your workload will be like in three weeks' time or how long a task is going to take you. I preferred to physically write out my weekly planner on paper at the start of each week (I used the Kikki.K weekly planner). This provided a rough guide of when my extra-curricular activities were and when I would be able to fit in study blocks. At the end of each day, I would list all the work I had been given that day and add this to the existing list I had of ongoing tasks. I would then plan my afternoon based on the following principle which helped me prioritise my tasks:

    1. Urgent and Important things (e.g. assessment due the next day that I need to edit and submit)
    2. Urgent but not important (e.g. homework task that is due tomorrow, such as daily maths homework)
    3. Important but not urgent (e.g. an assessment task that is due in two weeks that I received that day)
    4. Any other additional homework I may have received that day (if I have any time leftover)

MONDAY	TUESDAY	WEDNESDAY	THURSDAY	FRIDAY	SATURDAY	SUNDAY
30/9	1/10 English Maths XI	2/10 PE Religion II	3/10 Legal Maths 2U	4/10 WILD-CARD	5/10 English Maths XI	6/10 PE Religion II

In the lead up to the Trials and HSC I placed my 6 subjects on a rotation system. I studied for two subjects each day and then on the fourth day I allocated it as a 'wildcard' day. This was recommended to me by a study skills speaker, which suited me as I often did not manage to complete everything I wanted to on those previous days. This allowed me to dedicate my 'wildcard' day towards catching up on anything I felt behind in or wanted to do more practise on. At the end of the three-day cycle, I then planned my next three days.

PDHPE ADVICE

PDHPE was undoubtedly my favourite subject due to its practical nature. I particularly loved the way that I could apply what I was learning to my own everyday life.

PDHPE is what inspired me to choose to study a Bachelor of Nursing at the University of Sydney this year and I am excited to deepen my knowledge about our healthcare system. My two options were Sports Medicine and The Health of Young People, however my advice can translate to the other options as well.

Misconception: If you know the syllabus and the content then you'll be fine.

Having a comprehensive understanding of the syllabus and the content are of paramount importance. However, this is simply the foundation. Without applying this knowledge through practise, you are making it harder for yourself to achieve results in the top bands. At the beginning of each topic, I made a table to ensure I had a practice question for each area of the syllabus (I usually found them from past HSC papers). As we were taught a particular area of the syllabus, I would try to complete a past HSC question and hand it into my teacher for feedback. It's one thing to know the content but being able to use your knowledge to respond to questions in a convincing and effective way requires a different level of thinking.

It's important to not leave all your practise until just before the HSC, but rather to ensure you are building on your writing skills as you go. PDHPE questions are very repetitive throughout the years and often are taken directly from the 'learn to' area of the syllabus or are slightly reworded. By employing this study technique, hopefully it can help you to consolidate what you have learnt on that particular day and potentially highlight if you need further clarification on a particular area. I have attached a sample for the Sports Medicine option below (I have had to reword the questions due to copyright reasons). This helps act as a checklist to make sure you have covered all the necessary areas in the lead up to an exam.

FQ2 - How does sports medicine address the demands of specific athletes?

AREA OF SYLLABUS	PRACTISE QUESTIONS
LEARN ABOUT Children and young athletes - medical conditions (asthma, diabetes, epilepsy) - overuse injuries (stress fractures) - thermoregulation - appropriateness of resistance training	How does sports medicine address the demands of children and young athletes? (12 marks)
LEARN ABOUT Adult and aged athletes - heart conditions - fractures/bone density - flexibility/joint mobility	Explain the sports participation options available for aged people with various medical conditions. (8 marks)

LEARN ABOUT	To what extent do iron deficiency and bone density affect safe sports participation? (8 marks)
Female athletes • eating disorders • iron deficiency • bone density • pregnancy	

HOW TO MAKE NOTES THAT HELP WITH MEMORISATION:

1. Gather relevant and credible sources. I used a combination of our teacher's class notes/lesson plan, our textbook and the website PDHPE.net.

2. Read all the information across the different sources that correlates to one point on the syllabus.

3. Pull up your notes and write down everything you can remember. Try to be concise, using dot points and only including relevant information. You are not required to know statistics in depth. However, you must have an overall understanding of the trends.

4. Go back to your sources and read the information again to ensure you have not forgotten anything that is also necessary to include.

5. Add in supportive examples that help explain the content. This may include any links to newspaper articles that apply the content to current situations (e.g. an article about the psychological strategies Michael Phelps uses to enhance performance).

6. Go to the 'Learn to' side of the syllabus and make sure you have enough information to answer any potential questions that may be drawn from that side of the syllabus. If you are struggling to answer these questions, then it is a good indication you need to add more depth.

7. After you finish making your notes, print them out and read your notes one syllabus dot point at a time. After you finish a

dot point, go back and highlight the important parts (try not to highlight as you are reading as you will tend to highlight more. Instead, highlight once you have read the whole dot point).

8. The highlighted part has now become your 'second draft' of notes and should somewhat mimic a 'fact sheet'. You should then be ready to start memorising!

Rather than having pages and pages of notes, try to break down them down using pictures, tables, mind maps etc. This will make your notes less intimidating so you are not overwhelmed with the amount of content you must memorise. Using visual aids is also better for memorisation as it is easier to form a 'mental picture' in your head of what your notes look like when trying to recall something in an exam. I used a table format to lay out my notes:

How are sports injuries classified and managed?

WAYS TO CLASSIFY SPORTS INJURIES

Direct and indirect

- Direct injuries = caused by direct forces generated from outside the body e.g. fractures, dislocations, sprains and bruises
- Examples include a shoulder dislocation due to tackle in rugby
- Indirect injuries = caused by an intrinsic force (within the body) as a result of excessive strain being placed on muscles, tendons and ligaments causing irritation and possible damage to body structures
- Usually a result of inadequate warm up, ballistic movements, excessive movement or fault in execution of skill e.g. tear of hamstring during a race

Soft and hard tissue

- Soft tissue = damage to muscles, tendons, ligaments, cartilage, skin, blood vessels, organs and nerves
- They may be acute (occurring suddenly) e.g. sprains, strains, dislocation, subluxation, torn cartilage, contusions and abrasions or chronic (prolonged) e.g. same type as acute but severity necessitates a long rehabilitation
- Hard tissue = causes damage to bones and teeth e.g. fracturing a bone

Overuse

- Overuse injuries result from intense or unreasonable use of joints
- They are provoked by repetitive, low-impact exercise such as jogging or stepping as they cause pain and inflammation around the site of injury
- Examples include anterior shin splints and tendonitis
- Overuse contributes to stress fractures which are indicated by local swelling and tenderness

APPLY

- Identify specific examples of injuries that reflect each of the classifications (included in notes)

SOFT TISSUE INJURIES

Tears, sprains, contusions

- Tear = when tissue is excessively stretched
- Two types:

- Sprains e.g. rolled ankle or ACL rupture in knee
  - stretching or tearing a ligament resulting in pain, swelling and inability to perform normal joint movement
  - Ligaments are strong and inelastic tissue, which connects bone to bone
  - Ligaments have a relatively poor blood supply meaning it is a slow healing process
- Strains e.g. torn hamstring
  - Muscle or tendon is stretched or torn may cause bleeding or discolouration around the injury
  - There are three types: First degree, second degree, third degree
  - Stretching or pressure around the injury will result in sharp pain
- Contusion = Caused by the rupture/bursting of capillaries. Which leads to internal bleeding (i.e. the crushing of soft tissue which interrupts the blood flow to surrounding tissue) Normally referred to as a deep bruise

Include acronyms and mnemonics in your notes. This is an effective way to memorise syllabus terminology and it often was the first thing I scribbled on the page in an exam to make sure I didn't forget it. They can be as silly as you want! Some examples include:

The Ottawa Charter (D.R.S.B.C)

Developing personal skills	Did
Reorienting health services	Rachael
Strengthening community action	Save
Building healthy public policy	Bobby's
Creating supportive environments	Cat

The Principles of Social Justice (P.E.A.R.D.S)

Participation	Please
Equity	Everyone
Access	Avoid
Rights	Ruining
Diversity	Dan's
Supportive Environments	Special sauce

Tips for memorising:

- Read one page of notes at a time, then turn the page upside down and write out and much as you can remember on a blank page.

- If trying to learn a particular trend, definition etc., say it out loud 7 times (this supposedly is the equivalent of writing it out once). My reasoning is that if you can say it out loud and explain it to someone else then you can write it down in an exam.

- Use flashcards and write questions on the front to test yourself (e.g. what's the leading cause of death for males?).

- Use A3 mind maps to summarise your notes (e.g. put a focus question in the middle and draw arrows coming off it).

EXAM PREPARATION AND TECHNIQUES

<u>Timing</u>

- The PDHPE exam is 3 hours long and there are 100 marks all together. If you break that down, you should be roughly spending about 1.8 minutes per mark.

- Although the exam allocates 40 minutes to spend on multiple choice, it generally will take around 20 minutes.

- Our teacher would often go around the classroom and ask us how long we should spend on a 3 mark question, 5 mark question, 8 mark question and so on, and we would have to tell her using the 1.8min/mark principle. By the time the HSC came around I could recite how long each question should take me to avoid wasting time figuring it out in the exam.

- This definitely helped me ensure I was being concise in my answers and ensured I made it to the end of the paper without missing out on any questions. If ever a question took me longer than the 1.8min/mark principle I simply left it and came back to it at the end.

- When completing practise responses, I would time myself and write how long it took me at the top of my page. It's important to mimic the exam conditions rather than giving yourself an unrealistic scenario of unlimited time.

Understanding the key terms

- Understanding and appropriately responding to a key term of a question (e.g. explain, investigate, analyse etc.) is essential in achieving a mark in the top band.

- For example, the key term of a question is 'explain' then the criteria for a top band response will say 'makes clearly evident the relationship between.' If you do not recognise what the question is asking you, then you cannot construct a higher order response.

- A complete list of the meaning of the key terms can be found on NESA. In class we would have to match the definition of each word to its corresponding key term. I recommend printing these out and hanging them up around the house.

- E.g. If a question asks 'to what extent…?' you must explicitly implement the wording of the question in your answer by using phrases such as to a paramount extent, the extent is tarnished by…, to a limited extent, or to an immense extent.

- In an exam, the first thing I did after reading a question was highlight the key term and physically write out on the page what it meant. This helped to ensure I constantly asked myself while writing my answer if I was directly answering the key term.

Multiple Choice Questions

Multiple choice was definitely my worse section! I always seemed to over analyse the answers. A simple way to think about multiple choice is that the answer is given to you. The answer is on the page, all you must do is pick it out. It was hard to train myself to not overthink my answer and learn to trust my instincts. The best way to practise is to expose yourself to a range of differently styled multiple-choice questions. PDHPE multiple choice often consists of interpreting and applying graphs, data, tables, etc., so it is important to include relevant graphs in your notes (e.g. upside-down U hypothesis for optimum arousal), so you are familiar with them.

Short Answer Questions

A great strategy that one of my school teachers constantly instilled in us was 'facts, not fluff, make five.' This basically infers that in order to write a 5/5 response (or any full mark response) you must prioritise facts over fluff and be concise.

Here's a sample question that I pulled straight from the right-hand side of the syllabus:

> *Explain the relationship between the principles of training and the physiological adaptations in response to training. Use examples to support your answer (8 marks)*

How to attempt this question:

1. Identify the key term and understand what the question is asking you to do.

Explain = *"Relate cause and effect; make the relationships between things evident; provide why and/or how."* (Glossary of Key Words, NESA).

- Before starting, it is a good idea to brainstorm possible 'connecting words' to emphasise the relationship between two things.
- I often resorted to using the thesaurus to prevent myself from being repetitive and to find new words to express myself. Some examples include consequently, as a result, therefore and thus.
- Ensure you consistently use these throughout your response, not just at the beginning or the end.

2. Identify the area of the syllabus it wants you to talk about.
    - It's important to note that this has been taken directly from the 'learn to' section of the syllabus. This states that you must be able to: Examine the relationship between the principles of training, physiological adaptations and improved performance.
    - I often wrote the syllabus dot points down on the page in the top right-hand corner as the marker must read everything on the page, and it may be useful if you don't have time to cover all the dot points.
    - TIP: Highlight or underline the syllabus dot points in your response to draw attention to them. The HSC marker will be reading your response on a screen, which scans in colour, and it instantly shows you have included the relevant information and are aware of what is expected in the answer.
    - After identifying the syllabus dot point you then will need to recall your information on that topic. You may also pull up your notes if you are in the early stages of practising.

- For this response you are required to talk about (you do not need to go into comprehensive detail on all of them):
- Principles of training:
  - Progressive overload
  - Specificity
  - Reversibility
  - Variety
  - Training thresholds
  - Warm up and cool down
- Physiological adaptations in response to training:
  - Resting heart rate
  - Stroke volume and cardiac output
  - Oxygen uptake and lung capacity
  - Haemoglobin level
  - Muscle hypertrophy
  - Effect on fast/slow twitch muscle fibres

3. Come up with relevant examples. This question specifies to use examples to support your claims. However, even if the question doesn't specify to do so, this is essential. You cannot get in the top bands if you are not using examples, no matter how many marks the question is worth. An example helps demonstrate to the marker that you are not simply dumping your content on the page but can apply what you know to practical scenarios. Examples strengthen your argument and help respond to the key term (e.g. justify or demonstrate). Generally, every 2-3 sentences you need to be including an example.

In this response I have applied the basic three-step approach of:

- Including explicit judgement to ensure I was consistently fulfilling the requirements of the key term 'analysing.'

- Including the relevant syllabus terminology.
- Including supportive examples.

Sample answer:

There is an inextricable connection between the principles of training and the subsequent physiological adaptations that an individual develops. The principle of training thresholds implies that the magnitude of improvement is approximately proportional to the threshold level an athlete works at. Working above the aerobic training threshold in the training zone (65% - 80% of Maximum heart rate), for example going for a thirty-minute jog, stimulates the body to produce up to 20% more haemoglobin. As a result, this increases the oxygen carrying capacity of the blood and thus increases the level of the workload at which the athlete reaches their anaerobic threshold (90% of Maximum heart rate). This allows the athlete to maintain higher intensities for longer periods of time, because they remain within their aerobic training zone. This extended period in the aerobic training zone e.g. lengthening a thirty-minute jog to an hour directly utilises the slow twitch muscle fibres, as they contract slowly and for long periods of time. Aerobic training causes an increase of capillary supply and myoglobin content within the slow twitch muscle fibres and therefore enhances its efficiency in transporting and storing oxygen. The principle of progressive overload allows an athlete to gradually increase resistance, repetitions and/or sets. For example, if an athlete training for rugby league was previously doing 3 sets of lifting 110 kg with a 2-minute rest between sets, the progressive overload principle can be applied by increasing the load to 5 sets of 120 kg with a 1 minute rest. This undoubtedly leads to increased muscle hypertrophy as muscles are forced to work at higher intensities after adapting to the previous standard. The increased resistance and regularity of training stimulates growth of muscle fibres by increasing the mass of the connective tissue surrounding the muscle and the actin and myosin filament that produces muscle action. The principle of reversibility implies that in the absence of training (e.g. due to injury of the ACL), all the physiological adaptations will be lost just as quickly as they were attained. Muscle atrophy, specifically the leg muscles such as the quadriceps, will occur due to the inability to continue strength training (e.g. no longer being able to do a barbell front squat). No training will inevitably lead to decreased stroke volume and cardiac output, as the heart will not be able to have as forceful contractions it did while training considering the left ventricle walls are no longer being strengthened. This will naturally contribute towards a higher resting heart rate as more contractions are required to pump out the same amount of blood as before. Evidently, there is a distinct relationship between the principles of training and the physiological adaptations.

Here's another sample question:

Analyse the impact of a growing and ageing population on Australia's health care system. (5 marks)

The growing and ageing population has a detrimental impact on Australia's health care system. An increase in elderly people undoubtedly negatively impacts the amount of health care available such as general practitioners, palliative care etc., as there will be less people within the workforce to pay taxes to allow the government to cover these health care costs through Medicare. Consequently, the government will be forced to spend excessive amounts, which they don't have, on building new health care facilities such as nursing homes. This will undoubtedly increase tax and the overall cost of health care for the general Australian population. An increase in elderly people further unfavourably impacts the health care system as there will be an increase in the number of people suffering from chronic conditions such as Alzheimer's which increases the need for specialised health care (e.g. having an assigned nurse help the elderly bath and eat). This will produce work force shortages and drastically hinder the availability of health care as there won't be enough trained medical professionals, for example occupational therapists, to account for this rise. This increase of elderly people suffering from illness also negatively impacts the health care system as there is limited growth projections for volunteers who manage volunteer organisations (e.g. meals on wheels). This further reduces the amount of services available to elderly people to account for their needs such as if they are homebound and cannot cook for themselves, as these organisations don't have the resources to compensate for this exponential rise in demand. Overall, a growing and ageing population triggers a vicious cycle which adversely impacts the health care system.

Options: Longer response questions

- Longer response questions still follow the same principle as the short answer section. You need to be concise and to the point.
- In longer response questions (i.e. the 12 markers) use paragraphs to separate between the different syllabus dot points that you are talking about.
- Have one introductory sentence that outlines all the syllabus dot points that you are going to be discussing. This also helps ensure that if you run out of time the marker will be aware that you understand what parts of the syllabus are relevant.
- Longer response questions often use more demanding key terms such as investigate, critically analyse and examine. It is important that you are aware of the transition from the short answer section to the options part of the exam.
- You must ensure you are going in depth while still including only necessary information.

FINAL POINTERS

The take home message of this article is to just keep going! Try to remember that this is just one year of your life. Slowly chip away at what is before you and you will eventually get there in the end. No feeling compares to when the HSC exam supervisor says 'pens down' for the final time. In order to experience that satisfaction, ensure you are putting 100% of yourself into your final year of school. Ultimately, you only get out of it what you put in. I'm sure you'll surprise yourself in the end when you see what you are capable of achieving. Try to enjoy the experience by making sure the HSC doesn't completely take over your life.

Best of luck for the year ahead, and remember *"Just keep swimming, swimming, swimming!"*

Emma's PDHPE Cheat Sheet

- Don't ignore the key terms of a question. They have been carefully chosen for a reason and they don't all mean the same thing. You can't answer a question successfully if you are unsure of what it is asking of you.

- Examples, examples, examples! You need to be constantly reminding yourself to put examples into your response. You cannot do well if you don't include examples to support what you are saying.

- The syllabus and memorisation are only part of the PDHPE equation. You need to be practising your content from right now! It takes time to develop your writing skills.

- Don't ignore the right-hand section of the syllabus. It is just as important as the 'learn about' section. If your notes do not cover this area, then this must be rectified immediately.

- Make your notes concise to avoid having to memorise excessive amounts of information. Use dot points and include pictures, tables, mind maps etc to make your notes more appealing and less overwhelming.

Physics: The High School Uncertainty Principle

By Daniel Monteiro and Wenquan Lu

Introduction - Wenquan Lu

> *As our circle of knowledge expands, so does the circumference of darkness surrounding it. – Albert Einstein*

Modern physics has told us that there is nothing faster than light. However, I believe that there may be exceptions, such as the growing of knowledge itself and simultaneously the expanding of the unknown. Most of us are now still very near the centre of the circle, and studying is an effective way to shift you towards the circumference. I am Wenquan (David) Lu from Barker College and I topped 2019 HSC Physics, state ranked in Chemistry, Maths Extension 1 and Chinese Literature, and graduated with an ATAR of 99.95.

My high school experience at Barker was exceptionally good because all my hard work paid off. In this world of uncertainty (proved by Heisenberg's uncertainty principle), hard work doesn't necessarily equal a good result. I topped all of my 20 internal school assessments in Year 12, so I felt really blessed to be rewarded for my consistent performance. Of course, when I say hard work, I mean really, really hard work.

Introduction - Daniel Monteiro

"The definition of insanity is doing the same thing over and over and expecting different results" – Albert Einstein

My name is Daniel Monteiro and I was the School Captain and Dux of Cherrybrook Technology High School in 2019. In the HSC I got a band 6 in all my subjects, received an ATAR of 99.85 and placed 8th in the state for Physics and 5th for Science Extension.

Throughout my early years in high school I did relatively well across the board in multiple subjects. I was never the best at any one aspect of schooling life, but my consistent high achievements earnt me a reputation as a 'smart kid.' As such, I felt the pressure to do well and maintain the standards that I set for myself. This, of course, culminated at the start of Year 12 in late 2018 where everything suddenly felt very real.

At this point in time, everything I did would be set in stone. If I failed, then all I would be is some kid that used to do well in a couple of tests. These anxieties and thoughts slowly poisoned my outlook on the future and my work ethic. I spent a lot of time punching the walls of my room, procrastinating on studying and worrying more about the results than the work before me. After my first round of assessments my results were by no means terrible, but they were definitely not at the level of the top-achiever that I wanted it to be.

After the first term of Year 12, I was both mentally and emotionally exhausted… but that was about to change. Over the summer holidays, I went with a friend of mine to volunteer in Cambodia, teaching English to grade 1 students. Travelling overseas gave me a sense of independence and perspective that I had lacked for the past few months. Whilst it sounds like a cliché, sometimes you can't see the big picture when you're stuck doing high school work. For me, it literally took travelling across the world to realise what I truly wanted. So, when I returned to school the next year, I resolved myself to maintain the following mindset:

- I would learn for the sake of education and knowledge;

And

- My marks would serve only as a reflection of how hard I worked, not as a symbol of my own identity or value

Once I did that, I found that not only was I genuinely happier throughout the HSC, but my results were significantly better as well. With that in mind, let's get started!

General Tips

1. *Work as hard as you possibly can, so that when the opportunity to do something fun comes up, you don't feel guilty taking it.*

    Every day after school, I'd go to the library and put in three or four hours consistently. However, after that I'd go grab dinner with my friends at the shops (a strategy that ended up eating – pun intended - through my savings). Don't work ridiculous hours, otherwise you'll burn out. Make sure that when the opportunity to have fun comes up, you are prepared enough that you can take it.

2. *Stay on top of things.*

    As a school captain, I had an extremely busy schedule. I found that if I fell behind on my school-work, I'd quickly be drowning in it. To mitigate this, I began working on every task as soon as I received it. Unlike many other high achieving students, I am not organised at all. However, for me it didn't matter, because I finished all my work before anyone else. If you're a bit of a mess like me, put in the hours and stay on top of things. Many people spend more time planning on how they're going to study than actually doing the work. Don't make that mistake. Prioritise what works and get rid of what doesn't. This leads me on to my next tip…

3. *"The definition of insanity is doing the same thing over and over and expecting different results"* – Albert Einstein

   If you get your results back from an assignment or test that you aren't happy with, look for where you went wrong. This may be a conceptual lack of understanding, but quite often the error arises in other areas. Change your study methods and don't let yourself get stuck in a routine that doesn't work. These can also come from lifestyle choices. Perhaps you aren't getting enough sleep, are skipping breakfast or going on social media while studying. Your results aren't necessarily a reflection of how many hours you're putting in, so if something isn't working don't keep punishing yourself. In my case, I completely separated my home and school life. I'd study at the library, but whenever I'd get home I wouldn't think about assessments or subjects. This meant that I was stressing less, sleeping more and enjoying my free time.

4. Love what you do!

   Ultimately, I credit my success with the genuine love that I have for science. A lot of people warned me not to do 7 units of science through high-school, but I loved every second of it and found that each subject helped (in some way or another) with the other ones. If you can find an interest in the content that you're learning, you'll end up understanding the content and enjoying the experience a lot more. I found myself reading up on things that were beyond the scope of the course but nevertheless enhanced my grasp on the material. This ultimately reflected itself in my responses and set me apart from the cohort.

Physics

General Landscape of Physics

HSC Physics is a pre-calculus, elementary but comprehensive course that covers topics from quarks to the universe. The HSC Physics exam for 2019 heavily emphasised, analytical and memorization skills, meaning that a well-rounded student must be good both quantitatively and qualitatively. A common misconception among students is that with the introduction of the new syllabus, HSC Physics is becoming more quantitative. However, if you take a look at the 5, 7 and 9 mark questions, there are still many long-responses. In my opinion, the new syllabus merged two types of questions into one, consisting now of long-response questions embedded with calculations. As a result of this, analytical skills, (the ability to apply theoretical knowledge and formulae you have memorized), are of a higher value than blind recounting of content.

Working Scientifically

Working Scientifically is another highlight of the new syllabus. It is an individual module included in many textbooks like Pearson, Nelson, and it is usually placed at the very start, indicating its significance. To succeed in this section, you need to carefully read through this module in your textbook, and "Working Scientifically" in NESA's syllabus. The definitions and usefulness of buzz-words such as 'validity', 'reliability' 'accuracy' ('precision' is not included in the new syllabus) should be memorized. Depth study and daily experiments conducted in school are opportunities for you to practice your 'Working Scientifically' skills. Try to associate systematic and random error with these buzzwords while conducting the experiments: systematic error, validity and accuracy are often interrelated; random error, reliability (and 'precision') are usually correlated. Furthermore, processing data and information is also an important skill in Working Scientifically, which demands the ability to draw graphs, tables and use a variety of visual representations.

In graphs, conventionally, the independent variable is put on the horizontal axis, while the dependent variable is put on the vertical axis. However, if it is specified as A vs B, variable A is always on the y-axis and variable B is always on the x-axis. Don't forget to include all of the elements in your graph, including a detailed heading, axes, axis labels, units, crosses and a line/curve of best fit. BE VERY CAREFUL OF (x 10^k) NOTATIONS BESIDE THE UNITS, UNDERLINE THEM, AND TAKE THEM INTO ACCOUNT IN CALCULATION!

Incorporating Mathematics

Mathematical derivation is another core skill in studying HSC Physics. Understanding Physics is much faster through mathematical derivation and calculation than qualitative description. When I encounter a new formula in Physics, I always think of its relationship with other more basic formulae or experiments I have learnt before. I then try and derive this new formula from its very root. For example, Kepler's 3rd law can be derived solely from Newton's law of universal gravitation, and force acting on an electric wire can be derived purely from the Lorentz force formula. Moreover, there are clear parallels between Newton's law of universal gravitation and Coulomb's law, as well as similarities between gravitational fields and electric fields and their associated equations. Different modules and fields of Physics can be drawn together by inspecting, deriving and interconnecting formulae.

Physics is probably regarded as one of the most difficult subjects that you can study in high school. Rumours like this cause people to avoid it because they're afraid of coping with the difficulty. Alternatively, they choose it because they intend to rely on the scaling to bring up their ATAR.

There are a few specific rules that you should bear in mind when studying physics.

> *Rule 1:* **Open your eyes.** Physics is everywhere. No one can artificially manufacture enthusiasm, but if you start seeing what

you learn applied in the world around you, it becomes a lot more interesting and will motivate you to keep working. Whether you're on the bus or going for a walk, think about the forces acting on you. When you feel your computer charger start to heat up, curse the eddy currents that are forming within the transformer.

Rule 2: **Assume that nothing is real. Question everything.**
Over the year you'll learn so much that will change your understanding of space, time, matter and energy. It's a lot to process and if you don't have a rock-solid grasp of what's going on, you'll quickly fall behind. In physics, the questions that you receive in the HSC look for you to apply concepts to random scenarios. Memorisation does not work. You have to completely understand the concept in order to apply it to the random scenario conjured up by NESA. So, even if you think you understand what's happening, try to come up with a new question for your teacher that will expand your understanding even further.

Rule 3: **Don't rely on maths to carry you through physics.**
Many who study physics will also do extension 2 maths or something equivalent, expecting their talents in mathematics to translate to success in Physics. This is anything but true. I've always considered Physics to be more of a writing subject than a mathematical one. The maths that you do encounter is very simple, often requiring you to simply substitute in variables to equations. Rather than expecting mathematical understanding, the difficult questions will ask you to explain a concept or scenario. Here, you've got to be able to express your ideas and communicate complexity concisely, using an equation or calculation only as evidence for the point that you're trying to make. Spend most of your study time doing practise questions that ask you to outline, explain and analyse, because these are the questions that will differentiate you from the rest of the cohort.

Rule 4: **Throw the syllabus out the window.** Controversial. I know. In my HSC, I think I read the syllabus maybe twice or three times. Now this might not work for other subjects (please read the other articles in this book for that information!), but in Physics, you are very rarely asked to regurgitate information. Instead, they ask you questions which require application of your knowledge. If you aren't prepared to go beyond what they expect from you, it's very difficult to get a band 6. Learn for the sake of knowledge, not because it's a syllabus dot point. I've seen many other students obsess over the syllabus and it has trained them to think linearly and not be creative. This ultimately limits their ability to successfully answer the difficult questions.

By now, you're probably starting to realise that I'm not like most high achieving students. I'm messy, I don't make timetables, I don't look at the syllabus and most importantly, I never use highlighters. The most important thing is that you find something that works for you. If you're like me and can't obey a strict structure of study, then don't force yourself into one particular method just because it's worked for other people.

Preparing for Exams

1. **Questions, Questions, Questions.** I was part of the first cohort to deal with the new HSC syllabus for Physics. This made it extremely difficult to find past papers that were applicable. I'd meet people in the library from other schools and constantly ask if they wanted to exchange trial papers or samples that would give me more exposure to a range of different responses. I didn't write a concise set of notes in Year 12 for Physics. Whenever I encountered something that I didn't know, I'd go and research it in depth and then write out my answer. Once you've done enough papers, all of the questions start to follow a similar pattern and you don't need to explicitly force yourself to memorise the content – it'll just be muscle memory at that point. That being said, I did put together a list of extended responses that I could refer back to…

2. **Build a bank of extended responses.** While I don't think you should keep a set of generic notes, a range of extended responses (7-9 markers) can be invaluable when you're doing past papers. You can refer back to these and see the best and most concise way of expressing a certain physics concept. Share this with your friends and get them to collaborate, adding more depth and complexity to the responses so that you eventually perfect them. You shouldn't memorise these as you would an English essay, but rather just refer back to them while doing trial papers.

3. **Teach a friend.** If you've gotten tired of writing out all of these lengthy responses, pull a friend aside and start asking each other questions about physics. If you can articulate and teach a concept to a friend of yours, then you'll be able to do the same for the HSC markers. Albert Einstein once said that *"It should be possible to explain the laws of physics to a barmaid"*. If you can teach physics to someone else, you can ace the HSC.

Answering Questions in the Exam

The thing that differentiates Physics from other subjects (even other sciences) is that you'll find yourself having to analyse a completely random scenario that you've never seen before. This won't be in the syllabus and you won't even know what you have to write about, but if you keep calm and step through what's happening, it's easy to see the solution.

If you absolutely have no idea what's going on, start writing about whatever relevant physics principle that could possibly apply. Just quoting some of Newton's laws can help you scrape a couple of marks, especially if you find a way to link it to the question. At every chance that you get, you should try to slip in some physics terminology that can impress the marker and show sophistication.

Experiments

Before practicing questions, I always summarised and memorised all the experiments first. The aim, hypothesis, diagram, method, tables, graphs, analysis, sources of error, ways to improve it, reliability, accuracy, validity, historical implications and connection to other experiments were all considered and memorized whenever I revised an experiment. Thorough understanding of every experiment is necessary for answering experiment questions and long-response questions in the HSC exam. I know memorizing experiments is a very tedious process, but it is a must for HSC Physics.

Long-response Questions

The way my school helped me to prepare was by collecting a range of long-response questions from the trial papers from different schools and projecting them on the board, letting the whole class share their ideas, thoughts and structures to answer the questions. Along with the teacher's contribution, the responses became close to perfect with everyone's help. However, individual essay time is also necessary. For my study, I included as many things as possible in order to touch on all of the relevant experiments, theories, applications and diagrams. Every practice question would cover a certain area of knowledge. Practising a variety of questions enabled me to cover the entire syllabus comprehensively, and ensured that there was nothing that could surprise me on the day.

When it comes to the exam, planning is extremely important. As soon as the exam started, I would look at the long-response questions and plan them during the reading time.

- The first step is brainstorming to develop any relevant ideas. If you have memorised and practiced enough, the ideas will naturally come to you.
- The second step is trying to establish the connections between concepts, experiments and theories.

- The third step is scaffolding a coherent structure based around those connections. This is so that, as soon as the writing time starts, you can jot down the specific events, experiments, calculations and theories that will be included in your response before starting on the multiple-choice section.

Once this is all done, I will start writing. Let me show you an example question from module 5.

Sample Answer

The ISS space station orbits Earth at a constant speed. Although both the astronaut and the space station have a force acting on them, the astronaut feels weightless and the space station moves perpendicularly to the force.

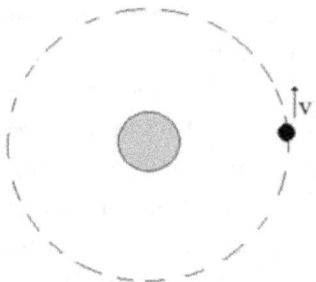

Explain why the weightlessness of the astronaut and the motion of the ISS do not contradict the laws of physics.

4

> *Ironically, we don't feel 'weight' due to the presence of a weight force, instead we feel weight from the normal force. For the astronaut to feel weightlessness, there must be no normal force acting upon them. This occurs because the ISS is accelerating at the same rate ($a = \frac{GM}{r^2}$) as the astronaut. Both the astronaut and the ISS are in free-fall which provides a sense of weightlessness, however due to some tangential velocity, instead of moving towards the Earth, both the astronaut and ISS instead move in a circular motion as the effects of gravity act perpendicular to the velocity thus making it a*

centripetal force ($F = \frac{mv^2}{r}$). As such the laws of physics hold true, despite the astronaut possessing some weight force due to the gravitational force of attraction provided by the Earth, the astronaut will feel weightless as there is no normal force because the ISS accelerates towards the Earth at the same rate.

In this answer I've addressed the cause and effect, talked about weightlessness and the motion of the ISS and finally, included an equation in my response to consolidate my knowledge of the subject.

Outside of the Syllabus

My extracurricular activities also contributed greatly to my success in Physics. In Year 10, I successfully passed aeronautics and astronautics engineering courses offered by TU Delft and MIT respectively with edX. In those courses, I learned university-level aerodynamics, mechanics and explored the usefulness of calculus in Physics and Engineering. Moreover, I participated in the Imperial College London Global Summer School 2018 Physics stream, studying coding, damped simple harmonic motions and coupled oscillators, which afforded me an appreciation of computational power when solving Physics problems. From my personal experience, succeeding in Physics doesn't necessarily come from several months of intensive study. Instead, it emerges from years of accumulating knowledge in this subject and incorporating Physics into your daily life, so that you are familiar enough to tackle all types of questions that the exam throws at you.

Some Final Thoughts on Year 12

Despite my change in attitude at the start of Year 12, I still faced a lot of doubt and uncertainty through my HSC journey. When you succeed, it becomes addictive and you start to wonder how your success will be measured out of high school. This led me to believe that money was the ultimate measure of success. So, for a large chunk of year 12, I considered studying finance and becoming an investment banker; an area that definitely interested me. However, there was something wrong about abandoning my love for science and the world around me that I couldn't overcome. I owe it to my parents who ultimately convinced me not to follow money but to do what I love. They said that if you work hard (and still work smart) in any profession, you can be financially successful. And so, I am excited to start at the University of Sydney in 2020, studying a double degree of Engineering and Science, where I can continue studying physics and the ways in which it can be applied.

Werner Heisenberg truly was right in his uncertainty principle. There are always limits to what we can know. The doubts and uncertainties that follow are inevitable and I won't try to give you advice on how to get through them because, at the end of the day, it is your very own personal journey that I couldn't hope to understand. The key to success in the HSC is a strong willpower that will let you keep working even when you think you're about to burn out. This is what kept me motivated through the HSC. It's who I am. I don't like to quit. Even when I want to throw in the towel, I dig deeper and keep going. If I can do it, then you can too!

Daniel Monteiro's Physics Cheat Sheet

- Always be the one asking the most questions in class
- Physics is a difficult subject, that means you might have to write more to fully explain yourself. Don't be scared of a long response.
- Start from the ground up and build your skills up from there. If you're stuck on a question, check your fundamentals and see where they lead you.
- Focus on the physics, not the syllabus
- Use your maths as evidence in your responses, just as you'd use a quote in an English essay. Explanation is far more important.
- Don't study the night before the exam. If you don't know it by 8pm the previous night, you won't be able to apply the concept in the exam

Wenquan's Physics Cheat Sheet

- The new syllabus tests both analytical (problem-solving) and memorization skills. A top-achiever needs to be confident both quantitatively and qualitatively.
- Long-response questions embedded with calculations will become increasingly common. PLAN before writing a long-response question!
- Carefully read through the "Working Scientifically" module in the textbook.
    - Daily experiments and depth studies are very valuable opportunities for practicing and consolidating Working Scientifically skills.
    - Participating in experiments and writing great reports on a daily basis are necessary for achieving top marks in HSC.

- Mathematical derivation is a crucial method for understanding Physics. A certain degree of proficiency in maths, whilst not necessary, will most definitely help you to succeed in high-school Physics.
- Memorising details of every experiment is very useful when revising.

Science Extension: How to Get Ahead of the Pack

By Nicholas Fakira

Introduction

Hi. I'm Nicholas Fakira, I graduated from Barker College in 2019, and I came 4th in the state for Science Extension during its debut year. I've always had a passion for all kinds of science from a young age, a passion which only grew as I was introduced to new branches with each passing year approaching the HSC. I remember my ears perking up as I heard about the new course that I couldn't wait to start as soon as I left the subject overview prior to starting Year 12. It is hardly a surprise that Science Extension ended up being one of my favourite courses, an enjoyment which I believe was the primary factor in making it my strongest subject.

I completed the 2019 HSC and received an ATAR of 94.45. This may be lower than many of the other ATARs featured in this book, but keep in mind that it just means you don't have to be a 99.95 student to succeed in Science Extension! I have enrolled in an Advanced Science (Honours) Degree at the Australian National University in Canberra to further my passion for Science.

One of my favourite quotes that I would like to share with all of you is the following:

> "*Much to learn, you still have.*" —Master Yoda

This is a great piece of advice to keep in mind for the HSC in general, but specifically for an Extension subject such as Science Extension. It reminds us that there is always more we could learn to further improve our knowledge on the subject at hand and make us stand out from others to a marker. It represents our ability to learn both inside and outside of class. My teachers loved to emphasize that an Extension subject revolves around the ability of the student to perform independent research and take their learning into their own hands as required. This is especially true for a newer subject, as the teachers don't have the history and past experience to answer every question thrown their way. In addition, the research project that makes up a core element of the course is going to be specific and individually tailored. Thus, self-led research is the most effective way to learn new ideas about the new concepts you will be discovering. My research paper on capillary action and plant-based implications of fertilizer usage wasn't common knowledge to any teachers I had available, so I primarily learned through reading research papers — as many as I could get my hands on.

How to Keep Up in the HSC
Study tips:

1. Start studying as early as you possibly can

Consolidating notes that were taken in class and rewriting them into your study notes either at the end of week or a few days after they were taken in class will make your life so much easier. Create a big study notes file, one for each subject, and make sure you edit it at least on a weekly basis, by adding more information to it or making the current information more concise. This means that when you get to your Trials and HSC exams, you are already set up perfectly and can revise efficiently rather than waste time organising and collating your study notes.

2. Do whatever you can to <u>start</u> studying

The hardest part of studying is doing it in the first place. If you struggle with procrastination, then set rewards for starting, or pretend you are only going to do 5 minutes. Whatever you do or however you do it — make sure you start. Once you do start, it usually won't be as hard as you were expecting or dreading, and you won't feel the need to stop.

3. Don't be afraid to reach out for help

This is probably one of the tips that I could have paid more attention to throughout my HSC year. All of your teachers and support networks are there to help you and give you whatever tools/advice you need to keep on going, and many of your teachers will bend over backwards to make sure that you do as well as you can. Your teachers will usually be happy to find you extra past papers from other schools, give you out of class marking feedback or run exam technique sessions.

4. Share concepts that you understand with others

You've probably heard it a million times by now but teaching others about concepts for any subject is the easiest way to solidify it in your brain and ensure you don't forget it. You will have to command a greater level of understanding than the regular student in order to teach it in a relatable way that other students can understand, which means that A) you know the content better and B) you are less likely to forget it. Win-win!

Dealing with stress:

Throughout my HSC year I always had the mentality that walking into an exam stressed would decimate your exam technique and make you forget everything you had carefully studied for. Due to this, I always made it a priority to ensure that, if I felt stress creeping in before exams, I would take a break and remind myself that I would get through it. One specific question I used to ask myself a lot is: *"What can I do in the next 60 minutes that will help me the most for my upcoming exam?"*. The answer might be to study a certain weak topic, or look through an assessment to find common mistakes, or to eat a good meal (the night before) or go to bed and get 9+ hours of sleep. This process breaks down your upcoming time into manageable chunks, and allows you to make a simple decision on what is a good short-term plan and stick to it. It also stops you from thinking exclusively about the exam, as you will have a specific goal for the next 60 minutes.

Goal Setting:

I recommend setting both long-term and short-term goals over the course of your HSC year. The long-term goals could relate to university course entry requirements, HSC Top Achiever status, or first-in-course/NSW ranked in course. For these goals I recommend setting some 'reach' goals, that are above your current skill level, but you could feasibly achieve if you improved your attitude, work ethic, and academic skills. For myself, this was the Bachelor of Philosophy course, a high-achievers course at ANU that required a straight ATAR of 99 or higher and was essentially the highest level of science research course available to undergraduates. Another reach goal of mine was to top the state in Science Extension.

You should also set some 'primary' goals that you are working towards if you stay on track and don't have any issues that cause you to fall short. This is where I had my Advanced Science (Honours) course, which required a 95+ ATAR (which could be boosted by +5 bonus points for achievement in relevant courses). Finally, have some 'panic' or 'fallback' goals. These ones are your backup plan if everything goes wrong and falls to pieces. While you never want to rely on these, they give you a safety net and stop you from thinking all is lost if you have the occasional bad assessment. Some people tend to lose their cool after having one or two bad assessments and because of this fall into a downwards spiral that causes them to do worse in their assessments for the rest of the year. Instead, with this system, you just have to understand that you will need to make up for the bad assessments to keep on track for your primary goals.

When setting short-term goals, I would suggest a combination of both results-based goals (like achieving 95% in that upcoming assessment, or being in the top 10 students for one subject by Term 2) and action-oriented goals, such as studying 15 hours for that in-class assessment, or practising your speech perfectly 5 times before you perform it in class. A combination of these will allow you to understand both how much work you are putting in and what results you are getting out. This will leave you in a better position to adjust your learning/studying style based on where you need to improve. If 5 hours of English quote memorisation + 15 hours of essay practise can get you a 90%, then it gives you a strong baseline to work off of for future English assessments. This method can also give you a better idea of how much more time you might need to dedicate to English to improve that 90% to a 95% for example.

How to get ahead in Science Extension
What is Science Extension about?

Science Extension as a subject is concerned about a few 'questions' that are answered throughout the entirety of the syllabus.

- What is Science?
- Why do we need Science?
- How do we carry out Scientific Research?
- How can we use Scientific Research?

How is Science Extension different?

The most important part of performing exceptionally in Science Extension is understanding that it is not like most other subjects. Many subjects like Mathematics, Physics, Chemistry, Economics and English can all be easily improved by working as many waking hours as possible on nailing every variation of every question that could be asked.

Science Extension is different because the exact opposite is a far more reliable method of improving. Instead of rote learning and mass practice questions, it is instead far more helpful to use logical and critical thinking to analyse a few types of question in great detail. This will aid you in understanding exactly what is required, as well as being the best way to learn how to analyse *any* question thrown at you in an exam scenario.

Regardless of the module that the question is drawn from (or the primary verb in the question), almost all questions should have a direct correlation to the scientific method. Even if not explicitly asked, I recommend that your responses always circle back to the impact on the quality of the scientific research being performed. If a question asks you to find errors, explain why these errors harm the scientific method and risk the validity of the research, and give brief examples of what would make the research more reliable/valid, as well as how. If the question asks you to analyse the effectiveness of a source, decide how it ties in with the scientific method and give baseline examples of both great and terrible examples as a point of reference to compare the source against.

These additional above-and-beyond responses will set you apart from the majority of students that simply answer the question in basic terms without understanding the interconnectedness of all of the modules.

Exam Techniques:

1. *Understanding your cohort:*

One exam technique that I believe to be beneficial is answering each question by first estimating the criteria and predicting what the majority of the Science Extension cohort will write. You then have to figure out what specific and hidden parts of the question you can refer to in order to set yourself apart from the cohort and place yourself into the top band range for that particular question. You will need to have some idea of what a basic answer may look like and how you could extend and improve on that — what information most people will miss that you could add. For most questions, a basic answer will answer the question with limited depth and little specific reference to the source supplied. A good answer will have better depth and mostly relate to the specific source in question. A top band answer will have a great level of depth that is specifically tailored to the source supplied, as well as precise additional details about the source that could improve clarity.

An example of this relates to the essay in the 2019 HSC exam. The question pertained to the sources presented and the methodology of my research project. However, I knew that a more impressive answer would draw from the entirety of the syllabus. So, in addition to writing on these topics, I brought in an additional paragraph on the history of science which mirrored my arguments in the other paragraphs to strengthen the essay (which received full marks).

2. Typing Skills:

Another important way to improve where your peers most likely won't is in your keyboard skills. It may sound quite silly, but practising your typing is almost as important as knowing what to type. I can type on a computer keyboard at 90 words per minute, granted that I know what I'm going to type. When writing by hand, this slows to a measly 35 words per minute. This allows me to spend a lot more time planning responses before I write them, touching up other answers, or making sure I can read through the source material an additional few times. Compared to an English exam where I can't stop writing if I want to finish with full length essays, I have a considerable amount of time to think and plan responses and go over sources additional times to ensure that I write much better answers. At the end, I also had extra time, allowing me to go through and add a lot more detail to answers and ensure that my worst questions received sufficient touch-ups before I submitted my responses. Many of those touch-ups could have improved a question by a mark or two, a significant amount in a 50-mark exam.

Learn how to touch type if you don't already and improve your speed (even just a one-minute typing test every week will improve it significantly!) whenever you can. I was able to write approximately 25% more words than the expected amount in the exam, meaning that there was a lot more 'meaningful answer' for the markers to mark, setting me aside from the average answer.

3. What question order should you follow?

I think that after reading all of the questions and sources (in the reading time), you should complete questions in order from easiest (i.e. the questions that make the most sense and you already have a clear plan for the answer) to hardest (i.e. any questions that you are confused about or unsure how to start). This means that you can let your subconscious mind work on the harder questions while you don't have to focus as much on the easier questions. In contrast, if you start on the hard questions, you will sit there thinking before you start writing. You also want to keep the extended response/essay question in the back of your mind and have a thesis by the time you get around to answering it.

Once you start on the essay, ensure that your first paragraph has a connection to the general concept of the scientific method. My essay opened with a paragraph relating the question to the foundations of science and how they affected the scientific method, before adapting to introduce my other paragraphs in brief.

Appreciation

I'd like to thank my wonderful teachers, Dr. Katie Terrett and Dr. Michael Hill, as well as a supporting Agricultural teacher Dr. Alison Gates. Without their help throughout the year I would not have performed anywhere near as well as I did. They helped nurture and inspire my continued passion for Science through their teaching styles and enthusiasm.

I'd like to thank my loving parents, who understood that I had my own ways of getting through the HSC and didn't stay on my back about studying or working throughout the entirety of the year. They gave me the room to perform the way I wanted to and in the end it all worked out as well as I could have asked for.

Conclusion

Hope after reading this article you have a better idea of how to tackle the HSC, and specifically how to stay ahead of the pack in Science Extension. Not everything in this guide will work for everyone. I am very aware that all people have different learning styles. However, these strategies have worked well for me and, even if you don't think they will work, give it a shot and see how it goes. I wish you all the best of luck in the coming HSC, and I hope that you achieve those 'reach' goals that you've set in place for yourself.

Nick's Science Extension Cheat Sheet

- Your learning never stops. Outside of class make sure to use as many resources available to you as possible.
- Try and enjoy as much of the HSC as you can. It will reflect in your marks.
- Stay organised with a large expanding file pocket for all handouts, spare notes and assessments – never lose anything again!
- Reach out to people such as students, teachers, parents, siblings, mentors or tutors for help – even if you think you don't need it.
- Help others by teaching them in order to strengthen your own understanding.
- Don't let the stress get on top of you! Life will go on and you will get through it.
- Keep long-term goals and look at them every day. Don't forget what you are working hard towards. I kept mine written on a year planner that I ticked off every day.
- Don't put life on hold just to get through the HSC year. Continue to go out and see friends, go to parties and keep on exercising.
- Understand that the HSC is about sorting the entirety of NSW Year 12 into a long line from highest academic skill to lowest. You have to improve and become better than people above you in order to overtake them.
- Learn how to touch type and/or type faster. It is a blessing to have the first computer-based test in the HSC, and use it to the fullest potential.

Society and Culture: It's So-WHY-ity and Culture

By Lara Hather

> *"Hard work beats talent when talent doesn't work hard."*- Kevin Durant

To me, the HSC always seemed like some sort of mythic creature. It was around every corner and behind every door. It was always there, looming, even after I graduated from my six years of schooling at Manly Selective Campus. Nonetheless, Year 12 was a year that both pushed and rewarded me, and allowed me to realise how much I was truly capable of. Similar to many of those before me, and no doubt many after, I finished the HSC with little-to-no knowledge of what I wanted to do in life. I ended up with a 99.50 ATAR, a 5th in the state ranking for Society and Culture and no idea of how that would translate to the real world.

GENERAL Tips

1. Balance

I always called the HSC exams the 'home-stretch' because, as I'm sure you've all heard before, "it's a marathon, not a sprint!" My marathon was more than just schooling. Struggling with anxiety and perfectionism throughout my high-school life, Year 12 helped me clarify what matters most. Balance. To those entering Year 12, think about what matters most to you and always look after yourself. For me, routine played a key role. Indeed, I would have an evening swim the night before exams (yes, no matter what the weather) and stop off at the beach the morning of to take a minute to relax and de-stress. Balance is absolutely everything.

2. Reflect

For this, I learnt an awesome tactic called KSS: Keep, Stop, Start. Simply put, after every block of assessments, I sat down with a list of all my subjects and figured out what studying/revising/learning tools I wanted to 'Keep', which ones didn't work so well ('Stop') and what tools I thought could work better or have heard friends/high achievers used ('Start'). See below an example of a real table I did for Society and Culture in Year 12.

Keep	Stop	Start
• Doing practice responses for every dot point • Staying up to date with news • Practice essays • Flashcards for stats and examples memorisation	• Typing everything (start handwriting to pace) • Writing so many essay *plans* • Ignoring research methods and *Continuity and Change*	• Written practices INCLUDING essays • Timing responses • Writing essays not just plans • Learning C&C more thoroughly • Simplifying notes

3. Take off the pressure

Pressure can come from everywhere in Year 12; friends, family, school and YOURSELF. Take pressure off by scheduling in activities between studying. If necessary, force yourself to take time off and plan for fun! Not only does this help studying seem less never-ending, but I found if I had dinner out with friends one night I would be more motivated to finish studying or assignments that morning to reduce my stress in the afternoon. Following on from that, I believe studying should be task-oriented, not time-oriented. That way, if you're super into something, you can continue. Contrarily, if you're struggling with something, you can take a 15-minute break to refresh your brain without feeling the guilt of having to re-write your timed study plan. Because of this, my study plans were more like checklists than schedules. It also meant that I had the great satisfaction of being able to cross out tasks as they were completed.

SOCIETY AND CULTURE

Society (or Soc as we fondly named it) was my favourite subject by far at school. I loved the style of sociological learning and found it aptly relevant to my life. My school's entire focus was on India - our case study for *Continuity and Change* was India, we studied Hinduism (India's dominant belief system) for *Belief Systems and Ideologies* and Bollywood for *Popular Culture*. This partly fuelled my desire to go on a month-long journey to India two weeks after the end of HSC (finding out my HSC results at 4am on an overnight train through the desert is a memory I'll never forget). However, Soc is challenging, a major work is stressful and the need to stay up to date with current affairs can be challenging.

Tips

1. The syllabus is a resource

Unlike other subjects, the syllabus actually has answers that you can **directly quote,** such as the characteristics of social and cultural literacy, definitions for key terms, information about research methods and research types - all of which can be asked in multiple choice or short answer questions. I made flashcards of all this key information and knew it back to front by the time that exam day came.

2. Stay up to date

Society is a tricky subject because culture, and the world generally, is ever-changing and adapting. As soon as you find out which country your depth study is on, **download a news app**. Read the news for that country and find out what's happening in their day to day lives. This is because a relevant and up-to-date example will get you much stronger marks than an outdated one. Even on the morning of my HSC exam, I was reading Indian political news as fluctuating tensions between Pakistan and India often changed on a dime, so I wanted my example to be absolutely up to date. Examples are absolutely key - have a list of them (ones that work for multiple syllabus dot points are great) that you can whack into any paragraph to support an argument.

3. Stay neutral

It's often really hard to not be ethnocentric when looking at aspects of other cultures. For example, I found *sati* (an ancient Indian funeral tradition whereby a widowed woman would throw herself onto the burning body of her dead husband, effectively committing suicide) misogynistic, which made it challenging to justify this tradition in a cultural sense. Keep in mind that diverse cultures have diverse backgrounds, so focus on the social or cultural reasons why these people behave in such a way without applying the norms of your own culture. This will ensure you remain socially and culturally literate throughout all your responses, indicating a deeper understanding of the subject.

First, the Personal Interest Project (aka the PIP) ...

The one piece of advice I cannot stress enough is **do it early.** Post your questionnaire on as many Facebook pages as you can, email it to as many people you know and send it out on Reddit. Whatever you decide to do, do it EARLY. You know about the PIP very early on, far before assignments are ramping up. During that lull, get as much done as you possibly can. My PIP's leading question was *"How do socialisation agents develop adolescent perceptions of menstruation, forming a gendered sense* *of identity?"* I released my questionnaire a week after deciding on my topic and did my content analysis that same weekend. Anticipate how long each research method will take you. For example, I did a content analysis of menstrual product advertisements and that was easily the most time-consuming in comparison to my expert interviews, which were as simple as an email to a renowned professor. Plan out what you want to do as early as you can and then DO IT.

This leads me on to my next point: just start writing. I had friends who really struggled to start writing because they were so obsessed with over planning their chapters to the point of insanity. A great way to plan so you have a loose idea of your structure prior to writing the real thing is to make a scaffold. This ensures that you are balancing your inclusion of primary and secondary data as well as unique ideas or conclusions. Below is a real example of my scaffold for Chapter 2 of my PIP.

CHAPTER 2

Idea/ Finding	Over time, social values have become less conservative with regard to menstruation, as periods become more normalised.
CONTENT	NOTE: SELF-SELECTION BIAS OF DATA AS PARTICIPANTS ARE VOLUNTARY (may reflect liberal views and willingness to talk) • Economic autonomy of women as the division of labour is adjusted as the workforce widens due to technological advancements from modernisation spread from globalisation • The media and broadening access to technology has allowed for more rapid change to occur concerning the growing acceptance of menstruation • FUNCTIONALISM THEORY (school serves an implicit function to socialise gender norms, roles and status)
Primary A	**Focus Group** *"Older generations, in general, are just more conservative… but that's for most things… younger generations are more liberal"* *"I think it might be like… people will think it's still weird but it'll become less extreme"*

Primary A	*"I think we as a generation will be able to bring institutional policy type things... combatting lack of awareness etc."* "Women are much more a part of public life... in terms of being a significant amount of the workforce so it wasn't as much of a home issue... it came into the forefront of something that had to be discussed" **Questionnaire** *Periods are a natural biological process but should be kept private to each individual* - Gen X → 65% (most clicked) Over time society has become more comfortable discussing menstruation - Gen Z → 76% (most clicked) Concerns regarding menstruation are of interest to women only - Gen Z 12% - Gen X 23%
Primary B	Content Analysis "You feel cleaner, and feeling cleaner is more comfortable" (1985 Tampax ad) to "Periods happen. We might as well be real about it." (Carefree 2014)
Secondary A	Dunnavant, Nicki, and Tomi-ann Roberts. "Restriction and Renewal, Pollution and Power, Constraint and Community: The Paradoxes of Religious Women's Experiences of Menstruation." *Sex Roles* 68.1-2 (2013): 121-31. Web. - Prescriptive religious women feel greater levels of embarrassment - Western secular women are more liberated Discuss SECULARISATION Bobel, Chris. ""Our Revolution Has Style": Contemporary Menstrual Product Activists "Doing Feminism" in the Third Wave." *Sex Roles* 54.5-6 (2006): 331-45. Web. - Reappropriation, humour and culture jamming (menstrual activism to reconstruct menstrual ads) - Resists androcentricity Peranovic, T. & Bentley, B. 2017, "Men and Menstruation: A Qualitative Exploration of Beliefs, Attitudes and Experiences", *Sex Roles*, vol. 77, no. 1-2, pp. 113-124. - This finding may reflect improved equality in modern relationships and increasing involvement of men in reproductive decision-making. Men's role in menstruation may arise from

		the notion that the "modern man" is becoming more sensitive and thoughtful and emphasizes reciprocity in intimate relationships
SYNTHESIS		To write as a part of response

So, as you can see (apologies for my shorthand in some places), I start off with a very broad hypothesis or idea and then separate that into sub-sections. My idea is that periods have become more normalised (an example of social change). This then branches into social values such as secularisation, which I then have a secondary resource for, and some data from my questionnaire which backs up my assumption (such as that 76% of Generation X respondents said that 'Over time society has become more comfortable discussing menstruation'). My table is pretty loose and messy and, as you can see, my synthesis section (where I would write an overall conclusion or summation statement) is left blank. That is because I found I prefer to write that statement after my chapter was drafted so I could ensure that it directly related to what I ended up discussing. However, some dot points or basic scribbles in that section could be really useful if you need it. See below my conclusive statement for this Chapter:

> *"Accordingly, the researcher hypothesises that the stigmatised nature of menstruation arises from the enculturation occurring from society in a holistic sense, not as a result of the actions of one cultural group but rather as a combination of interpersonal and media interactions that create a social symbol, formulating a binary gender division that affects every day conduct of life."*

Note how I use the language of the syllabus (enculturation, interactions, symbol, gender etc.) and explain that I believe that menstrual stigma arises from a plethora of enculturation agents, rather than a singular phenomenon. The most important thing about the PIP is to back it up with evidence. In other words, FOOTNOTE, FOOTNOTE, FOOTNOTE! It flags to the marker that you are continually referencing secondary data and makes your arguments appear grounded in fact, rather than speculation. In my whole PIP, I ended up having 123 footnotes (obviously I footnoted articles or primary research more than once) which demonstrates the consistent reliability and validity of your work. Do this process of footnoting as you go, as it will save you the headache at the end!

At the end of the day, the PIP should sustain your interest by being something you are passionate about, so be smart with what topic you pick and make sure that it means something to you.

Now onto exams...

1. Multiple Choice

- Society multiple choice is tricky and often ambiguous. Eliminate ridiculous or incorrect answers, and, if you are still unsure, go with your gut. Because so many concepts are linked, questions can seem like they have more than one answer. Pick the **best** answer and stick with it.

- Don't spend too long on multiple choice. In a society exam you have 2 minutes per mark, which leaves 16 minutes for 8 multiple choice questions. If you can go through the multiple choice relatively quickly, you're giving yourself more time for short answer and extended response, where extra time can really make a difference.

2. Short Answer

1. **Use the language of the question.** It clearly shows the marker that you are directly answering the question and continually referring back to its key ideas.

For example, in this question for the *Popular Culture* module: "Explain how the consumption of ONE popular culture is influenced by mythology (5 marks)," the key words might be consumption, influence and mythology.

"Furthermore, internal mythologies often actuate the triumph of 'good' over 'evil' such as in Chennai Express (a 2013 masala film with mass Bollywood star SRK) whereby the tag line "Don't underestimate the power of a common man" relates to the densely populated middle class in India, as heroes such as SRK obtain a deified status due to their relatability to consumers, accelerating consumption.

This statement within my response both integrates an example and directly relates to the question as I discuss internal mythologies, their relation to India (which relates to key word 'influence') and how this propels consumption. Even if you don't do Popular Culture as your elective module, you can always integrate and elaborate on the framework provided by each individual question.

2. **Follow the PEEL structure.** This was really helpful for longer responses in the Continuity and Change section where I struggled to not waffle and spout irrelevant information that wouldn't get me marks. The structure goes as follows: Point (make a succinct argument in one sentence that directly responds to the question with more specificity), Elaborate (in the next few sentences, flesh out the argument using language of the question and of the syllabus explaining how and why), Example (include a relevant and recent example that demonstrates your argument), Link (summate and link your response back to your 'Point' and the question).

A pretty basic example:

Describe ONE example of how technologies have affected micro interactions within society. (4 marks)

POINT → Communication technologies, namely social media, have catalysed evolutionary change as localised face-to-face interactions are replaced by digital communication, enabling the acculturation of diverse worldviews.

ELABORATION → Social media platforms, like Instagram, Facebook and Twitter, have affected micro-level interactions by increasingly shifting them to online, reducing the importance of non-verbal aspects of communication (such as haptics and proxemics) in expressing one's cultural norms and values.

EXAMPLE → For example, social media giant Facebook has over 1.49 billion daily active users across the globe [Brandwatch.com 2018], demonstrating the move to digital platforms that allow the integration of different cultures.

LINK → Thus, social media has altered the nature of micro-level interactions to become less culturally homogenous and more digitised.

3. **Write the right amount.** In other words, don't write too much or too little. Based on the amount of marks given, I would usually write double and a bit the number of lines that I would fill (so for a 5 marker that's roughly 12 lines depending on the demands of the question). The best thing you can do to prepare for SA is to write practice responses *as you learn the syllabus* rather than just at the end, so you are constantly writing responses for each niche area of the topic to pace and with a clear idea of how much you need to write.

3. Extended Response

The structure I learnt for extended response was to have a short introduction and conclusion and then, effectively, three 5 markers in the middle (following PEEL), each with a different 'Point' in relation to the question. Just after the reading time, I found it helpful to scrawl down what my three paragraphs were going to be for both extended responses. This allowed me to focus on short answers without stressing.

Intro

- Answer the question straight off the bat and directly explain what your depth study/example is, justifying the relevance of your particular area of study.

- Your first sentence should clearly outline an overarching argument and use the language of the syllabus to highlight your knowledge of the subject.

E.g. Manly 2019 Trial Q: *Discuss the impacts of a popular culture on society and how these impacts contribute to social change (15 marks)*

> First Sentence of my Introduction: 'Bollywood, a film popular culture originating from India, impacts society by acting as a representation of consumers' views, contributing to social change through the socialisation and enculturation of norms and values within society.'

Body

- Follow the same structure as short answer responses BUT make sure your 'Link' ties to your 'Point' AND the question to ensure that your response is cohesive.

- Examples, examples, examples… the more evidence (statistics, legislation, data, anecdotes, quotes etc etc.) you have for your argument, the more believable and valid it will appear to the marker.

- Don't waffle. It's easy to try and fill space in an essay, but if that information is unjustified and not clearly laid out, it won't get you marks. Indeed, it may detract from other points made - keep it all clear. A succinct, strong response will do much better than a longer one which confuses the marker.

- I usually write 3 PEEL paragraphs in an extended response. However, there is no strict guide. Always remember that if you have a new argument, make a new paragraph. Four or five shorter paragraphs can still totally get you top marks if you are following a more condensed form of the PEEL structure.

Conclusion

- If you're running out of time on an extended response, WRITE A CONCLUSION. You need to have a full-bodied 'essay' structure even if you haven't finished the paragraph. Scribble out a few lines of conclusion wherever possible.

- Your conclusion should summarise concisely your points to relate to the demands of the question, without introducing new information.

- This should kind of be a 'drop the mic' moment, so have a final line that's punchy and clear to leave the marker the impression that you have a well-rounded and complete essay.

E.g. Manly 2019 Trial Q: *Discuss the impacts of a popular culture on society and how these impacts contribute to social change (15 marks)*

Last Sentence of my Conclusion: 'Hence, Bollywood's omnipresence in society inevitably initiates social change, altering depictions of gender to become less heteronormative and more egalitarian, socialising new philosophies regarding the roles and status of women versus men within India. Thus, Bollywood popular culture has a profound role in engineering social change.'

Overall

Year 12 is always going to be a demanding year, but you will get through it! There will be highs and lows, but, in a year's time, you'll be standing on the other side of what has been a massive hurdle, and that's a feat within itself. Just do what you can and enjoy your last year of high school! Good luck guys… :)

Lara's Society and Culture Cheat Sheet

Overall → Don't let study consume your life; a balanced mind is a brilliant one. Learn from your previous mistakes rather than dwelling on them. You can only go up, so focus on what you can do rather than what you can't.

General

- USE THE SYLLABUS (it is almost as good as a Society and Culture textbook and is a resource in itself).
- Know current affairs (watch the news, read articles, know what's going on in the world and how it relates to your studies).
- Be empathetic to other cultures and set aside personal biases.

The PIP

- Just get it done! Send out your questionnaire, write the chapter even if you're a perfectionist or have no idea where you might go with it. Write it and then tweak it, because then at least you've started.
- PLAN - plan a timeline for your research and writing your chapters. Plan your research and how you're going to use it and create scaffolds to make it all run smoothly.
- Footnote as you go, doing it at the end is an ordeal and a half. It'll save you time and a tonne of frustration.
- Pick something you are genuinely passionate about, because you're going to be drowned in research about it. Caring about your topic is evident in how you write it.

Multiple Choice

- Eliminate obviously wrong answers
- Your gut knows best. Trust it and don't second guess it (dwelling

on a single mark loses you time and usually you end up overthinking it).

Short Answer

- PEEL!!!! (Point, Elaboration, Example, Link).
- Use the language of the question.
- Think 'So-WHY-ity', tell the marker HOW and WHY.

Extended Response

- Jot down ideas for your points right after thinking about it during the reading time (it made me feel more organised and less stressed when I hit the big writing chunks).
- Examples. Always.
- New argument, new paragraph.
- Highlight the keywords of the question and have it next to you as you write. You should know the question off by-heart when you walk out of the exam from referencing it so much.

Taking Standard Maths Seriously

By *Finn Vercoe and Tallulah Adams*

Introduction - Finn Vercoe

Despite what cynics will try and tell you, the HSC is **not** a game, and there is no definitive formula for success. The sooner you realise this and begin to play by your own rules, the more successful you will be.

Sitting here on a calm summer's day, over two months since I bounced out of my last exam, with my dream university course secured for 2021 and a gap year of interminable possibilities before me, it would be easy to say the HSC wasn't all that difficult. However, if I said so, I would be lying. The HSC was an onerous grind, a continual struggle. You are speeding towards an inconceivable destination with the unshakeable belief that only oblivion could lie beyond that last exam. After all, for the duration of your sentient life, you haven't known anything other than 6am alarms, sombre commutes, incessant bells, the scratching of pens, and the doing-it-all-over-again.

So, from a guy who achieved a 99.20 ATAR, 1st in NSW for Standard Maths, 18th in NSW for Legal Studies and a Band 6 in 10 units of study, here is some pragmatic, no-nonsense advice on how to succeed in the HSC, without trying too hard.

Introduction - Tallulah Adams

> *Successful and unsuccessful people do not vary greatly in their abilities. They vary in their desires to reach their potential. — John Maxwell*

My name is Tallulah Adams and I graduated from Wenona school in 2019. I was always one of those people who really enjoyed school, but like everyone, I dreaded doing my HSC. I didn't need a super high ATAR for my course – I have no desire to be a doctor, lawyer or engineer, but I still worked as though I was aiming for that 99.95.

The biggest thing that kept me motivated was the idea that I had spent 12 years in school and would be at school 35 hours a week for the next year; I could choose to completely waste these hours mindlessly playing games on my laptop, or I could make the most of them and see just how far I could go. I can now look back on my high school experience and know that I gave it everything I had.

General Advice

1. Scaling Doesn't Matter

Scaling. I hate that word. Throughout the HSC, it was assigned immeasurable levels of influence. It was some omniscient, all-powerful being that presided over your academic fate. It was a deity for whom you would sacrifice your sanity by choosing subjects rumoured to please its sadistic desires – Physics, Chemistry, etc. For those who dared to risk its wrath by following their passion - be that Drama, Art or Geography – well, their destiny was predetermined, and it wasn't appealing. In my experience, the superfluous amount of power assigned to the word allowed it to wrongly be used as an infallible answer to questions such as, *"But you really enjoy PDHPE, why didn't you study it for the HSC?"*, or, *"Why can't I get into a Law degree with my subject selections?"*

It was all nonsense. Supposedly none of my subjects *'scaled well,'* but the impact of scaling is ridiculously overstated and should not even be a consideration in your HSC subject selection, let alone the defining factor.

🔍 what hsc s
🔍 what hsc **subjects scale well**
🔍 what hsc **subjects scale the best**

A quick Google search returns damning indictment of just how much emphasis we place on 'scaling.'

Ultimately, I cannot stress this point strongly enough – if you choose courses you are passionate about, you will be intrinsically motivated to study harder and predisposed to achieving a deeper understanding. Due to possessing this intrinsic motivation and deep understanding, you will achieve marks that make the (already negligible) impact of scaling **redundant**.

2. Find Friendly Competition

The HSC is essentially a competition, in that you are competing with roughly 70,000 students across NSW for the highest possible ATAR. However, this thought can often be overwhelming and unmotivating. So, in order to best evoke and capitalise upon your competitive side (everyone has one), try to create a friendly competition with one or two people per subject.

Personally, the competition I had with my friend, Jesse, is ultimately what pushed me to coming equal 1st in NSW for Standard Maths. She beat me comprehensively throughout Year 11, and, by the first assessment task of Year 12, and I was sick of losing.

The desire to win gave me the extra motivation to concentrate more in class, always complete the homework and prioritise Maths when studying. By creating this competition, I had turned the typically arduous task of revising into something of a game. By taking advantage of my aggressive competitive streak, I had essentially tricked myself into working harder.

It is important that the competition remains friendly and doesn't get so competitive that it compromises the relationship, or prevents you from helping each other out with certain topics that you find challenging. If the person is a good friend, this shouldn't be a problem.

Overall, creating a friendly competition with a close friend can be an effective method of motivating yourself to put in the extra hours of study, especially if you are a naturally competitive person.

3. Fix Your Attention Span

According to recent studies, our attention spans have decreased by roughly 33% since 2000. This has manifested in the rise of seven-second Vines and TikToks as the primary source of entertainment for teenagers. Gone are the days when free time would be spent settling into a novel. Now, we constantly cycle through Twitter, Facebook, Instagram and Snapchat to make sure we don't *'miss anything.'* The impact of such habits upon your attention span is severe. In turn, this will affect your academic performance.

How can you concentrate through a 3-hour exam or a one-hour class when you regularly split your day into 10-second chunks?

This is by no means scientific advice, but in order to retain your attention span I recommend trying some of the following activities:

- Go for a 30-minute walk without your phone or music.
- Read for an hour uninterrupted.
- Cook and eat a meal without looking at a screen.
- Go camping overnight with no electronics.
- Do a Sudoku.

4. Don't Burn Yourself Out

The HSC is a marathon. As such, it is important to conserve your mental energy for the final stretch by ensuring that you don't burn out too soon. The HSC Trials in August and the HSC itself in October are the key months of the year where you need to be in peak condition in order to achieve the best results.

Obviously, everyone has different ambitions when embarking upon their HSC journey. My study schedule was very reasonable, and shows that you do not need to give up all your hobbies and free time to get an ATAR in excess of 99. You will also see below how the intensity escalated throughout the year in order to peak at the appropriate moments.

For me, this is what my rough weekly schedule consisted of throughout term time:How much study to do during the 6 to 8-week summer break is a topic of much debate. In reality, you have only been studying HSC content for one short term, so as long as you kept up to date with all the key concepts and your study notes, there is absolutely no need to go over the top. Personally, I did no schoolwork from the 1st of December to the 10th of January, and all the work I did from that point to the re-commencement of school was only necessary because I slacked off towards the end of term. I recommend that you use those holidays to rest up for the big year ahead, enjoy the luxury of reading books that aren't textbooks, and spend all your time outdoors before you move into the library for the next year of your life.

Disclaimer: The time table on the right was my aim and, in reality, I probably actually studied a little less than this due to my chronic procrastination and incorporating mealtimes and family time into the schedule.

	8am-4pm	4pm-6pm	6pm-8pm	8pm-10pm
Mon	School	Study		Study
Tues	School	Football		Study
Wed	School	Study		Football
Thurs	School	Football		Study
Fri	School	Study		Free Time

	8am-1pm	1pm-5pm	5pm-11pm
Sat	Football	Study	Social
Sun		Study	Free Time

In the weeks leading up to, and during, the Trials and the HSC, you have time off school to prepare for the exams. This is the point where I really upped the volume of hours that I was putting into studying on a daily basis, and my schedule became similar to the one below.

In order to keep morale up during these long days of study, try the following tricks:

5. There's always hope

It sounds cliché, but my number one tip would be to never give up, even when you think there is no hope. I say this because I've come to realise first-hand just how much you can turn yourself around. Up until Year 12 I was always that person who everyone would ask "how'd you go?" after getting results back to make themselves feel better. My Year 10 ROSA grades were predominantly C's and I got 50% in my English Year 11 prelims...

At the beginning of Year 12, I realized that with my current study habits there was no way I'd even be scraping band 5s. I could have given up and accepted defeat at this point, but instead I used this to motivate me. I worked for around 5 hours on weeknights but gave myself a break for social time on the weekend. I ended up getting an ATAR of 97.7, 4th in the state for Standard Maths and band 6s in five of my subjects. It's fair to say my teachers, family and friends were rather surprised...

6. Find the study environment that works best for you

To begin with, there are two main venues which can facilitate your study habits: the library and your own home. Personally, I did both – at the beginning of the year I used the library so that I could collaborate with my peers, but, as Trials approached, I decided home was the best place for me as it was quiet and free of distraction. I found there were a number of pros and cons to each:

	Home	Library
Pros	• Comfort food readily available • Less people around to distract you • No need to carry around books and resources • No need to pack up study material – can leave notes in an organized mess	• People around to collaborate with and ask questions • Friends to keep you motivated • Better/larger study space • Possibly less distraction – no bed, no pool etc. • Better balance between working and relaxing – can leave the library knowing study is done for the day
Cons	• The constant need to lie down in bed • No peers around to collaborate • May not have an appropriate study space	• Often very noisy • Travel time • May get distracted by friends • Have to carry books around and may accidentally forget essential resources

If you decide to work at home, make sure you have a good study space set up. I found that setting up a desk in a room separate to my own bedroom was very beneficial as I could retreat to my bedroom at the end of the night without being surrounded by constant reminders of the HSC. Furthermore, it took away the temptation to get back into bed when I was sick of studying.

7. Figure out what type of learner you are

The way in which you learn will most definitely impact the way in which you should study. Think about whether you learn visually, auditorily, through reading and writing or kinesthetically (physically).

I found it very much depended on the subject. For Biology, I watched YouTube videos and learnt through hands-on experiments. For something like English, however, the only way I learnt was through reading articles, books and essays, and then writing my own essays. I have made a table below with some ideas:

Learning style	Ideas
Visual	- Watch educational videos - Get an A3 piece of paper and make supersize mind maps in nice colours
Auditory	- Podcasts - Ask your teacher if you can record them explaining a particularly hard concept and listen to it again later - Record yourself in a voice memo summarizing your notes and listen to it as you fall asleep - On Microsoft Word, if you click "review" then "read aloud", you can have your notes read back to you
Reading/writing	- Look on JStor and Google Scholar for articles regarding the topic you are studying, print them and highlight key information - Make flash cards (even online ones are great) - Hand write your notes (make sure to only include key information otherwise you'll be there for years) - Buy study guides with writing activities

Kinesthetic	- Make physical models of concepts – e.g.
	  - Ancient history: Build Pompeii out of lego and label each of the public buildings
	  - Biology: Use paper cut-outs, lollies, spaghetti etc. to model concepts such as protein synthesis and the immune system
	  - Standard Maths: Make a network out of spaghetti – use this to find the shortest path, minimum spanning tree etc.

8. Make use of your resources

Teachers, tutors, past papers and online resources are all there to help you. Don't be afraid to schedule some time with your teacher to go over a topic you don't understand – their job is literally to help you learn. Tutors can be expensive, although they're great for going over topics in details or assisting you with assessments.

Often, I would have a session with my tutor when I received an assessment notification, and this helped me overcome the mental block of not being able to begin. They can help break down an assessment into small tasks and help you understand exactly what you need to do.

Getting Subject-Specific: An Examination of Standard Maths 2

Subject Selection

Now, let's get more specific and discuss Standard Maths 2. This is a subject you will often hear endearingly referred to as 'Genny Maths' or, simply, 'Genny,' as the course was officially named 'General Maths' until 2018.

A key question surrounding this course for many students is whether to choose this or Advanced Mathematics (which introduces the concept of Calculus). Personally, I started Year 11 doing Advanced Maths and changed to Standard after two terms, so I have experience and knowledge of the pros and cons of both courses. By nature, Advanced is far more challenging, and thus will require more work both in and out of class in order to keep up. While there are less concepts to learn in Advanced, those that you do study are far more complex. I found Advanced Maths to be extremely theoretical, whereas Standard Maths was very practical and had substantially clearer links to real life applications. This helped make the content less alienating. In addition, when I changed from Advanced to Standard Maths, I had far more study time to allocate to other subjects and found that my grades in these also improved significantly.

Of course, competence in Advanced Maths is a prerequisite for a range of university courses such as aeronautical engineering, whilst at the University of Sydney it is even a prerequisite for commerce. If your dream university course requires Advanced Maths, then you should definitely give it a shot. However, keep in mind that a range of bridging courses exist, meaning that your dream is not over if you choose Standard Maths and still want to pursue such a degree.

Another key issue that I experienced regarding Standard Maths is a prejudice towards the course from other students. This may not be the case at other schools, but I certainly felt an elitist attitude from those that did Advanced and Extension Maths, in a way that was not mirrored by those who did Advanced and Extension English towards the Standard English cohort. Obviously, the concepts in Standard Maths are easier to grasp. However, it was the commonly held belief that if you did 'Genny' you were automatically 'dumb', and this misconception made me feel uneasy about changing courses back in Year 11. Ultimately, it is important that you ignore what other people say about your subject selection and just focus on doing your best in whatever course you take. Trust me, those with an elitist attitude stop looking down on you when your Standard Maths mark converts into a higher ATAR score than any of their own courses.

The most important thing to take away from this discussion is that there is absolutely no shame in taking Standard Maths – it was the most popular HSC elective course in 2019 with over 34,000 students choosing it! If you aren't pursuing a career in Mathematical fields, then choosing Standard will allow you to stay motivated through the practicality of the content whilst creating more study time to evenly distribute amongst your other courses. And, as I mentioned earlier, **scaling doesn't matter!**

How to Succeed in Standard Maths

Now that I have shared my general HSC advice and examined some of the misconceptions surrounding Standard Maths, it is time to share some of the strategies that I used to get 100/100 in the 2019 HSC exam.

1. **Eliminate Silly Mistakes**

    They happen to the best of us. In my HSC Trial exam, I lost four marks to silly mistakes and almost forfeited my #1 rank in my cohort. Following this, I embarked on a mission to not let such complacency tarnish my HSC score. Silly mistakes in Maths derive from rushing, over-confidence and lack of concentration.

    The first of these issues can be addressed by having a thorough understanding of the timing of the examination. The

HSC exam lasts 2 ½ hours, which averages out at 90 seconds working time per mark. Whilst this may sound intense, in the HSC I had enough time to complete the exam without rushing, as well as being able to double-check around 75% of the questions. This is because I did over 10 HSC practice papers under timed conditions and noted how many seconds it took me to complete each type of question. Recording this data will give you confidence that an abundance of time is provided to complete the exam, thus preventing you from feeling rushed and therefore eliminating silly mistakes that could have arisen.

Overconfidence is linked to rushing in that when a question appears straightforward, you can be thrilled at the prospect of 'easy' marks and dive in without reading it thoroughly. The best approach is to not take any marks for granted and treat every question with respect.

Furthermore, it is really easy to lose concentration over the course of a 2 ½ hour exam. The best way to counter this is to make sure you are well-rested and hydrated. On the night before the exam I tried to get around 10 hours sleep (9pm to 7am), as this is infinitely more beneficial than cramming. On the morning of the exam I completed two or three moderate difficulty questions to get my mind into gear, but not enough to burn out and confuse myself before the exam began. Also, the three-minute malpractice warning that the NESA invigilators read out before every exam has the potential to put anyone to sleep, so I often found myself slapping my face afterwards to make sure I was fully awake and that the adrenaline was pumping for the big event. Even though I definitely looked like an idiot, it worked.

In my experience, the most common silly mistake made in Maths is forgetting to round your final answer to the requirements of the question, e.g. *'to the nearest two significant figures'* or *'to the nearest metre squared.'* I addressed this by taking a highlighter into the exam and underlining this aspect of the question upon first reading to make sure I didn't forget it by the time I obtained my final answer.

2. **Don't Neglect the Year 11 Content**

   In the vast majority of HSC subjects, the content from the Preliminary course (i.e. Year 11) is just foundational and isn't actually tested in the final exam. However, in Standard Maths NESA reserve the right to insert up to 30 marks worth of Preliminary content into the HSC exam. Therefore, it is critically important that you stay engaged throughout the entirety of Year 11, make thorough notes, and remember to revise this content before your Trial and HSC exams.

3. **Write Notes on Palm Cards.** Standard Maths is not a subject that requires pages and pages of thorough notes. As opposed to there being a few topics that you must know in-depth, there are a large volume of concepts that you must have an adequate understanding of. Therefore, I wrote my revision notes on 7.5cm x 12.5cm white palm cards, available at your local Officeworks or Big W for a reasonable price. Using these ensured that I was concise and that my notes were well organised. Also, breaking down the content into palm-card sized chunks made it far more manageable to learn.

Example: Data Classification

> Data Classification
> - Categorical = category
>   → Nominal: NO intrinsic order, e.g. blue, yellow
>   → Ordinal: intrinsic order, e.g. average, good, e
>
> - Numerical = numbers
>   → Discrete: EXACT values, e.g. 1, 2, 3 etc.
>   ◦ Q: How many siblings do you have
>   → Continuous: ANY value, e.g. 172.8 or 23.4
>   ◦ Q: How many centimetres tall are

4. **Know Your Calculator.** In Maths, your calculator is your best friend. It is worthwhile investing a few hours in getting to know exactly how it works. In topics such as 'Bivariate Data Analysis,' you need to memorise quite complex combinations to insert into your calculator to use certain functions. I recommend asking your teacher for a sheet that summarises all the key calculator functions you must remember. If they won't provide one, go through the textbook and create one for yourself.

> How to Find $\bar{x}$ from Data Set
> 1) MODE
> 2) STAT
> 3) 1-VAR
> 4) Insert data
> 5) AC
> 6) SHIFT
> 7) STAT
> 8) Var
> 9) $\bar{x}$

5. **Consider a Tutor.** I believe Maths is one of the courses whereby having a private tutor is most beneficial. In class, by virtue of there being over 25 students and only 1 teacher, the communication flow is predominantly one-way and the individualised tuition you receive is limited. Having an hour of private tuition each week is a brilliant way to address all the questions you had from the week's classes. It also allows you to take advantage of alternate resources, opinions and methods, thus strengthening your knowledge and understanding. Furthermore, due to the Standard Maths syllabus being widely revised prior to 2019, a student who just graduated Year 12 has as much experience with the new content as your class teacher, so their credentials should not be underestimated.

6. **Show Neat and Comprehensive Working.** In order to make it easier for both markers and yourself, it is worthwhile to show **every** step of working when solving a question, even those you have done in your head or on your calculator. This will ensure you maximise the marks you receive and allow you to double-check your answers if you have spare time remaining in an exam. I have included an example below of how I organise my working when solving a simple simultaneous equation to ensure that full marks are achieved.

Solve: $2x + 8 = y$ and $x + y = 0$

(i) $2x = y - 8$ and $x = -y$

(ii) $x = \dfrac{y-8}{2}$

(iii) $\dfrac{y-8}{2} = -y$

(iv) $y - 8 = -2y$

(v) $y = -2y + 8$

(vi) $3y = 8$

(vii) $\therefore y = 2.666$

(viii) $\therefore x = -2.666$

This question would be worth 3 marks but requires 8 steps of working. In steps (i) and (ii) you isolate x by rearranging the equations. Step (iii) is possible because both equations are now equal to x. In steps (iv) through (vii) you isolate y to determine its value by rearranging the new equations. Finally, step (viii) is possible because in step (i) we determined that $x = -y$. This demonstrates the importance of writing down every step of working in a clear manner!

Exam preparation

Past papers are great for familiarizing yourself with all the types of questions you can receive. However, there does come a point where you're beginning to waste your time. Think about it - if you're doing thousands of papers, and getting similar marks in all of them, this may suggest there's certain topics you need to work on, and certain topics which you know inside out and are now wasting your time on.

To get around this, I began doing past papers to establish my areas of weakness. I would then screenshot/cut out the questions I got wrong and put them in a folder. I'd use these to make my own past papers which were only made of questions I'd gotten wrong and would keep redoing the questions until I got them right.

Topic tests are also great for overcoming difficult topics. You may have them in your textbook, or your teacher may be able to give you some. Our school used Smarter Maths and Project Maths, which was great as it organized previous HSC questions into individual topics and gave worked solutions.

In the Exam

You will begin with an allocated reading time in which you can look through your paper however cannot write or use a calculator. Use this time to take note of any difficult or long questions so that you can ensure you leave enough time to complete them.

Multiple choice

The first section of your HSC exam will include 15 multiple choice questions. That is 15 marks in which the answer is either right or wrong – there's no marks for working. From my experience with multiple choice, I've found there's always one right answer, a trick answer and two completely wrong answers. The trick answer is the one that will catch you out, so make sure you read the question and the four options carefully.

The greatest advice I ever got for multiple choice is to do all the questions twice. I always did my multiple choice at the beginning of the exam. Then, once I had finished, I would redo it. Turn over your multiple choice answer sheet so you cannot see your previous answers and do every question from scratch, writing down your answer on the back of the sheet. You can then compare your answers and if there are any disparities, and finally do a question a third time if you have to just to be sure This can save you from so many silly mistakes!

Short answer

When it comes to the writing section, SHOW YOUR WORKING! In my trial exam, I did the correct working for a 4-mark question but put it in the calculator wrong – I still got the full 4 marks because my working was right. Without working, the marker would have had no idea where that answer came from. If you are given a question where you cannot show working (e.g. putting values in a calculator to find Pearson's correlation coefficient), make sure you do these questions twice to avoid silly mistakes from incorrect calculator entries.

Never leave an answer blank, even if you have no idea how to do the question. In multi choice, if you have left answers blank, answer them all as B and you have a 1/4 chance of getting it right. In the writing section, even if you get just one step of working correct, you may gain a mark, and these marks really add up in Maths--no pun intended!

Once you've finished the exam, there's a number of steps you can take to maximise your marks:

1. Redo multiple choice
2. Double check your working and answers for the questions you found the most difficult (usually with the highest mark values)
3. If you still have time, begin double checking the rest of your answers

In Summation

That concludes my advice for how to survive and thrive in both Standard Maths and your HSC year more broadly.

Ultimately, the only thing a high ATAR reveals about you is a great work ethic and discipline. You get out what you put in. The more work you do, the better your results will be and the more worthwhile your schooling experience will feel. Don't forget to stay organized, but not so organized that you can't keep up. In my opinion, it is far more important to have uncompromisable values, to be erudite, generous and compassionate – four virtues not reflected by the number you receive on the 17th of December.

To finish, here is a poem by Leunig that I hung over my desk for motivation during the HSC.

> *'Go to the end of the path until you get to the gate.*
> *Go through the gate and head straight out towards the horizon.*
> *Keep going towards the horizon.*
> *Sit down and have a rest every now and again,*
> *But keep on going, just keep on with it.*
> *Keep on going as far as you can.*
> *That's how you get there.'*

Keep hustling, and always back yourself.

Finn's Standard Mathematics Cheat Sheet

- Choose courses you are passionate about
- Don't waste a second worrying about scaling
- Take a week off after exams to refresh
- Study in local libraries
- Make daily checklists
- Make time for your hobbies and social life
- Strongly consider getting private tuition
- Choose Standard Maths ;)
- Write concise notes using flash cards
- Get to know your calculator intimately
- Neatly show all steps you took to solve a problem
- Eliminate mistakes by sleeping well
- Take a highlighter into every exam

Tallulah's Standard Maths Cheat Sheet

- Find out the study and learning habits that suit you the best
- Always double check your answers – no more silly mistakes!
- Do multi choice twice without looking at your initial answers
- Show your working
- Make use of teachers, tutors and study guides – They're here to help!

Studies of religion: How to become a practising adherent

By Julia Lo Russo and Christopher Farag

> *"You are not the first person to do the HSC. If millions of students can get through it, so can you."*

Introduction - Julia Lo Russo

I'm Julia Lo Russo and I attended Bethany College, Hurstville. I graduated in 2019 with an ATAR of 99.70, receiving Band 6s in all of my units (English Advanced, Economics, Legal Studies, Mathematics, Mathematics Extension 1 and Studies of Religion II). I came 5th in NSW in Studies of Religion II and 4th in NSW in Legal Studies.

I surpassed all my expectations in achieving what I did, and having these opportunities now present themselves to me is a dream come true. I didn't make it into a selective school, and I didn't go to a flashy tutoring agency. I just worked hard using this one main philosophy:

This is one year of my life, so I am going to work hard for this one.

Introduction - Christopher Farag

"The only way to do great work is to love what you do. If you haven't found it yet, keep looking"- Steve Jobs

Passion is the key to success. If you love what you do, the HSC becomes a hurdle, not a mountain. My name is Christopher Farag, and I graduated from St Patrick's College, Strathfield as Dux of 2019, a Premier's All-Round Achiever and with an overall ATAR of 99.70. I received a mark of 97 in Studies of Religion II, placing me 6th in the state. If I can do it, you can too!

For me, my HSC experience was definitely a positive one. Of course, it was no easy feat, but looking back and seeing the fruits of my labour makes it all worth it. One of my closest friend's mother always told me that the world is my oyster, but I never really understood what she meant until now. I never wanted anyone to be able to tell me what I can or cannot achieve in life, and this is what motivated me. I always dreamt big, sought to open doors to opportunities and ultimately wanted to forge a successful path for myself. . I had a passion for the subjects I chose and it made all the difference. It made achieving these dreams not a chore, but something I enjoyed. Perseverance, passion and determination truly is key!

General Tips

1. Notes

Write notes after every class. This way you stay on top of your work and free up more time to study when exams come along. Colour coding your notes is a great aid for memorisation (e.g. yellow for definitions and blue for statistics). Notes do not have to be flashy. Indeed, simple phrasing is often better as it makes the notes far easier to recall. I recommend using a table format like below so you can tick off all the syllabus dot points.

Syllabus	Content
The Global Economy	**Global Economy:** Interconnected links b/w national economies developed through increasing trade, finance and other flows of resources and ides.
Gross World Product	**Gross World Product (GWP):** Agg value of all g/s produced in a year worldwide in global economy (output) • 35 Developed Countries: 16% world population but 45% GWP

2. Organisation

I wrote a checklist every day so I could tick off everything I needed to do. I would do some work for every subject each day (or thereabouts). Ticking off the tasks gave me a sense of satisfaction, and it also quantified the progress that I was making.

3. Procrastination

Contrary to popular opinion, you are allowed to procrastinate – just not too much! You need to take your brain away from the last formula that you learnt or the last quote that you memorized in order to allow your mind to concretize the information. I would always watch 4-5 minute videos on Facebook as a quick and mindless escape. However, after a break, I would put my phone down and get back to work.

4. Collaboration

Share your notes, teach each other and divide up the workload in order to improve your marks. Don't fall into the mentality that you must compete for the best rank. Starting a Facebook page and a shared Google drive folder with your classmates so that everyone can contribute are great ways to facilitate collaboration.

5. Practice

Get in the habit of looking at practise questions from past HSC papers after you finish a dot point or module. This way you can understand the style of questions asked and see if your notes correspond. I regret not doing this more because when I got to Trials and the HSC I realised I lacked some information necessary for certain questions - things such as statistics or an evaluation. Preparing for every eventuality and knowing how it will be asked of you is a sure fire way to succeed!

6. Don't Give Up

As clichéd as it may sound, I cannot stress enough that the HSC really isn't over until it's over. In fact, after we graduated from school, the Director of Curriculum gave us a **half-time** pep talk. He reminded us that even after graduating, the HSC is only half completed. It truly is a marathon, not a sprint.

After a series of average marks, I remember feeling like everything just came crashing down for me during Term 1 of Year 12, and that I had already lost all chance of doing well. Little did I understand that no HSC path is smooth. It took me a while to realise that everyone meets bumps on the road, and a couple occasional hurdles really is just normal. In the grand scheme of things, one 20% assessment task is only 10% of your mark for that subject. In turn, this is only 2% of your ATAR, or even only 1% if it is a 1-unit subject! Although it's hard, sometimes we just need to step back and see the bigger picture. One bad mark is not the end of the world. Keep on working hard, and don't be too disheartened by one poor result.

7. Make sacrifices....but not too many!

As much as we want to do everything, we simply can't. During the HSC, be prepared to make cutbacks. Whether that's not going out as often, limiting phone usage or reducing co-curricular hours, sometimes it becomes a bit too much to balance with the pile of HSC work. Although it may seem hard at first, I promise it's worth it. Unfortunately, study is very time-consuming and these cutbacks are necessary to focus on school and reach your academic potential.

However, don't get me wrong, to do well in your HSC, you definitely don't need to quit everything! Balance is essential. Although that Golden Mean is incredibly hard to find, a sweet compromise between academic and personal life is key. For me, during my two senior years I participated in Duke of Edinburgh, mock trial, social justice action group, debating, a PNG immersion and St Vincent De Paul's volunteer work. Alongside meeting up with my mates, these activities served as a form of respite. They gave me a break from the books and allowed me to find this crucial balance. However, I did decide to drop piano, soccer, my job and public speaking. I also limited the times I went out and left the house. This decision to make sacrifices, but not too many, is definitely something I'd advise to future students.

TIPS FOR STUDIES OF RELIGION (SOR)

SOR is notorious for being a simple subject, but there is a lot of unavoidable memorisation and formation of arguments that require both brainpower and time. Nevertheless, SOR is a highly rewarding subject. There is so much nuance to a religion that even a practising adherent may not understand. For that reason, there is so much flexibility. SOR improved my writing skills and made me appreciate religion in our world.

In many ways, good study practice in this subject can be ironically allegorized to a religion:

BELIEFS AND BELIEVERS - Believe in yourself and your potential. Believe in your class and always work with them. These are the fundamentals of success.

SACRED TEXTS AND WRITINGS

1. Your syllabus. Structure your notes using the syllabus, write practise responses to the syllabus and try to use the terminology of the syllabus to give clarity in your responses. The syllabus is your Holy HSC Bible!

2. Your textbook. This has the baseline content and quotes that set you up for success.
3. Google and books. These have the detailed information to give you depth and clarity in your responses. This is what sets you apart from other students.

ETHICS - Find what governs your study behaviour and motivates you. Time management, organisation and a good sleep schedule are imperative.

RITUALS AND CEREMONIES - Give yourself 1-2 weeks to prepare for tasks and ease yourself in. Create alternate ways of study such as flowcharts, timelines and mind maps to see your religion and content as a whole and not individual syllabus dot points. Reflect on your tasks to pinpoint your weaknesses. This is how you turn a Band 4 or 5 into a Band 6.

I honestly could not think of a better way to sum up success in this subject than by quoting Albert Einstein; *"You have to learn the rules of the game, and then you have to play better than anyone else!"*

There is no textbook out there that explains these *"rules"* to doing well, but SOR is absolutely full of them. There are so many criteria for the course that can only really be learnt by doing the subject. So, over the next few sections I'll try to explain each of these unofficial *rules*, how they work, what to do, and ultimately how to use them to impress your marker.

Rule # 1: Use Evidence

The first necessity for success in this subject is that you must learn and memorise lots and lots of evidence! For SOR, evidence can take the form of sacred texts, traditional sources, scholars, religious leaders, adherents, statistics or examples from the lived tradition. In every single response I ever wrote, I included at least one quote. Whilst it may not be obligatory for a 3-mark short answer question, it definitely shows the marker that you know your content and have an in-depth understanding. For a 5 marker, I'd aim for 2-3 bits of evidence, and for a 7-8 marker I aimed to use at least 4. Whilst evidence use does not appear in every marking criterion, you never know when it will, so always use it. Especially in a short answer question, this is definitely one way to show off and impress your marker. As for essays, quite simply, no evidence equals a mediocre mark. Evidence shows your marker that what you are saying is based on fact, is real, tangible, and ultimately isn't just a figment of your imagination. Aiming for at least three pieces of evidence per body paragraph is ideal.

As you will quickly learn, different syllabus dot points also require quite specific and specialised evidence types. Here are a few examples from the *Post 1945* topic:

Syllabus Dot Point	Evidence Required
Changing Religious Landscape	Census data and statistics. Trend language.
Ecumenism	Real world examples of Christian ecumenical movements e.g. the Uniting Church or the ecumenical work of individuals like Sam Clear. Also include specific action of different organisations e.g. the NSW Ecumenical Council's work in the 'House of Welcome' initiative.
Interfaith Dialogue	Real world interfaith activities and the specific work of organisations e.g. the Jewish Christian Muslim Association's annual 'friendship walk'.
Aboriginal Dispossession	Statistics on Aboriginal disadvantage or findings from the Bringing them Home Report.
Reconciliation	Real world Reconciliation examples of at least 2 religious traditions e.g. Pope John Paul's visit to Alice Springs in 1986 or the Jewish Board of Deputies' 'Statement on Reconciliation'.

The takeaway: use lots of evidence and know what evidence is required from different syllabus dot points. For the 2 Unit students, *Religion and Peace* requires many real-world examples too!

Rule # 2: Ensure evidence is well-chosen

Now, it isn't enough to just throw in your evidence all over the place. There are several unofficial *rules* that must be followed to make sure this evidence takes your response to a top-level band.

First of all, make sure a quote is well-chosen. Let's look at two examples from scholars to understand what this means.

   a. By codifying the Talmud into clear, concise Hebrew, Maimonides made Halachic law *"authoritative, comprehensive, and accessible to the entire Jewish people"* (Bernie Steinberg).

   b. Maimonides *"systematised all the commandments of the Torah"* (Kenneth Seeskin).

Now, both of these sentences tell us the exact same thing. However, a) uses judicious choice of evidence, whilst b) does not. When I chose a piece of evidence, I always thought to myself, *what does this piece of evidence add?* There is absolutely no value in using evidence for factual recount. The whole idea is to use the evidence to elevate your response and the judgement that you are making. For example, I looked for quotes that may testify to the importance, significance or impact of the given content area. Example a) does this perfectly - it provides a scholar's verification that Maimonides' literature is highly significant and lists why this is so. In contrast, b) adds no such value - it shows the marker no evidence of higher order thinking. Instead, it simply regurgitates a fact that didn't need to be quoted.

The take-away: to elevate your response, choose your evidence carefully, and don't just settle for any quote. Pick those that add value and meaning to your response and help prove the point you are trying to make.

Rule # 3: Ensure evidence is integrated

When you use evidence in your responses, you must integrate them into your sentences. This adds to the flow of responses. I admit this is a lot harder to do in exam conditions, but you should try and aim to embed them into the main clause of your paragraph. It allows the evidence to add to your overall argument and shows a higher level of sophistication.

Here's an example:

- Emulating Christ's own descent into baptismal waters, as the Orthodox neophyte is immersed into the Baptismal font, the infant too becomes a *"member of Christ"* and is called to become a *"sharer in the mission"* (Catechism no. 1213) of Christian vocation. This has implications for the adherent as they then become responsible for sharing the good news of Christ and becoming witnesses of the Gospel.

A quick check for this is to block out the quotes. If the sentence still makes sense, then the evidence has not been integrated appropriately.

By integrating the evidence, rather than 'chucking' in a quote, a student can explain its meaning and ultimately draw out its implications. It very effectively elevates the strength of a student's analysis as it demonstrates higher-order thinking. Afterall, you are critically analysing the quote, not just throwing it in.

This is an example where this has **NOT** been done correctly:

- During baptism, an infant dies a spiritual death and is risen again with Christ. This is seen when St Augustine said, *"Do you wish to rise? Begin by descending as Christ did."*

The take-away: aim to integrate your evidence into your sentences to add to the flow of your response.

Rule # 4: Ensure evidence is referenced

For every piece of evidence, make sure you reference where it came from. This can take a number of forms. For example:

- (Genesis 8:1)
- (Rabbi Sacks)
- (Bob Brown, 2019)
- (Surah 3:28)
- According to ABC consulting,….
- Made apparent by….
- As …. said….

Rule # 5: Ensure evidence is diverse

As I wrote before, evidence can take a range of different forms. It can be from sacred text, a religious leader, an adherent, a traditional source, an official religious document, a scholar, the lived tradition, statistics and many more. To really produce a sophisticated and comprehensive response, you should aim to include evidence from a few different sources, not just the same one every time. When writing my notes, I was conscious of this and ensured I had quotes from many different sources.

Rule # 6: Reference variants

Another SOR *rule* is the need to make reference to variants. Whilst doctrinal creeds may be common to most religious denominations, the lived tradition often varies. Given that the study of Christianity is not the study of just Catholicism or any other one religious sect, you must speak about Christianity holistically. Same applies to all other traditions - it is not right to speak, for example, of only Shi'a or Sunni Islam.

For example, ensure you make claims such as *Baptism is the rite by which* **most** *Christian variants believe an adherent is given the prospect of salvation.* It is an SOR cardinal sin to make a blanket statement such as the one above but omitting 'most'. For in fact, Salvation Army does not actually follow this belief. Just avoid speaking in absolutes. Make reference to the variation within a religious tradition. This is particularly easy when writing about the ethics section of the syllabus.

Let's look at how I would do this in a response about Christian baptism:

Baptism is a fundamental Christian ritual that expresses the principal belief in the nature of God and the Trinity and the belief in the forgiveness of sins. As a Maronite Catholic priest exclaims, "To you we pray, O Lord, that the purifying action of the Trinity may descend upon the baptismal waters and give them the grace of redemption," the Catholic community immediately witnesses the baptismal expression of credence in the Trinity. Further echoing the belief in the sacramental grace that it affords, it is believed to liberate the infant catechumen of Original Sin (Catholic) or Sin of Adam (Anglican), and initiates them into a life dedicated to faith and good works. Whilst some religious variants, such as the Pentecostal or Jehovah's Witness Churches may not recognise it as a sacrament, for most Christians adherents, the prevalence of the Trinitarian formula, "I baptise you in the name of the father and of the son and of the Holy Spirit", does still profess this belief. For an Orthodox community, anointing a neophyte three times with the Oil of Chrism also forges a parallel between baptism as a practice and this belief in the Triune nature of God.

Have a read of my response, you will see my use of certain words such as *"may"*, *"some"* and *"most."* This ensures I am not speaking in non-factual absolutes and that I mention religious variation. This is one very specific and important rule in SOR.

Rule # 7: Use the correct terminology

One more definite way to strengthen your response is to use relevant terminology. Using words in other languages is often necessary to achieve this and is an important part of any high-level response. Integrating this terminology into your sentences not only shows a comprehensive understanding of your content but it also shows the marker that you have gone that extra mile to remember words in another language. It also adds a layer of authenticity to your response. Here is a list of sample Arabic words I memorised for my Islam depth study.

Person: Al-Ghazali		Ethics: Bioethics		Practice: Hajj	
Ihya	Batin	Taqwa	Nutfah	Tawaf	Ihram
Tassawuf	Kimiya	Ihsan	Tughyan	Jamrah	Ka'ba
Falsifa	Zahir	Halal	Jahannam	Sai	Wukuf
Asharite	Mantiq	Haram	Shariah	Yawm ad-Din	Hajji
Tahafut	Kalam	Fatwa	Sabr	Rakat	Eid al-Ad-ha
Is'mailite	Avicenna	Fard	Mustahabb	Talbiyah	Dhul-Hijja
Fiqh	Nafs	Wajib	Makrooh	Niyyah	Muzdalifa

As you write more and more practice responses, using the terminology will become second nature. I promise it's not as daunting as it might seem. Rather than specifically memorising these words, it should come naturally with proper written preparation and revision of the course content.

Rule # 8: Link back to principal beliefs

Do you remember having to learn the principal beliefs back in the preliminary course? Well, linking your depth study material back to a principal belief is a sure way to elevate the strength of your response. By doing so, you immediately show your marker that you are thinking comprehensively and critically about your course material and are drawing out links between it - a higher order skill. Just integrating a reference to the belief is enough for this rule - there is no need to go into too much depth. Here's an example:

As adherents remark, "The living God we praise, exalt, adore! He was, He is, He will be evermore! No unity like unto His can be: Eternal, inconceivable is He," it becomes clear that the Yigdal Elohim Chai serves as a profound declaration of the Jewish faith. By professing credence and rejoice over their living G-d, the practice establishes a means by which Jews can express their principal belief in G-d and His "eternal", "inconceivable", incorporeal and transcendental attributes.

EXAM ADVICE

Multiple Choice

This can be the hardest part of the paper. Questions are getting harder as the syllabus gets older and the easy, straight-forward questions are being exhausted. Remember to read ALL the answers even if you think you know the correct one. Crossing out the obvious wrong ones and using a process of elimination if you do not know the answers is a great way to succeed.

I also wouldn't do these first in the exam. Doing the MC later in the exam after an essay or short answer response gave my hand a bit of a break and my brain was free of the other content to fully concentrate.

5 Mark Questions

Your notes per syllabus dot point should not exceed more than 8 key features. The questions are derived from the syllabus dot points, so having succinct notes means you can recall and apply your notes to the question.

> **Example: Analyse the importance of the Dreaming to the Land Rights Movement.**
> - Gained momentum as Mabo and Wik understood the importance of the Dreaming for Aboriginal communities and spirituality.
> - Dreaming is inextricably connected to the land ⇒ reinforce that regaining the land results in the continuation.
> - Dreaming, stories and knowledge cannot be shared without the land.
> - Re-establish links to the land could provide a greater sense of identity and safety.
> - Land and the LRM would empower and restore the community.
> - Public recognition of its importance.

A 5-mark question should take 8 minutes. Practise individual questions with a timer. This is a good way to work up stamina for the full 3-hour exam whilst also not exhausting yourself by consistently sitting full-length papers.

Another great tip is to link EVERY statement you make in your response to the question and stimulus if provided. There is no room for throw-away statements in a 5-mark question, as you have limited space to write and should not be giving the marker the impression that you are simply filling the pages with unnecessary information.

Lastly, remember the terminology of the syllabus. For example, the *"rise in New Age religions"* should not be called "new religions" or "recent spiritualities." Using the syllabus terminology enhances your response.

Short Answer Questions

For all questions that are above three marks, it is imperative that you include a quote from a sacred text (as above). This strengthens your response and will maximise your marks

> **Try:** Since adherents are "created in the image and likeness of G-d" (Beresheith 1:27), they are a manifestation of G-d attaining the highest ethical imperative.
>
> **Not:** Humans have the highest ethical imperative as they are a manifestation of G-d. "Humankind was created in the image and likeness of G-d." (Beresheith 1:27)

There is no set amount to write per mark. In general, however, I would recommend writing ¾ of a page for a 3-mark question. For an 8-marker, I would suggest writing 2+ pages. Obviously, this depends on the style and size of your writing. Look at past marking criteria on the NESA website and work out how you can best write responses. Then, get them marked by your teacher, or even a peer. You'll know where you've gone wrong and how to improve.

SIGNIFICANT PERSON OR SCHOOL OF THOUGHT

To maximise marks in this section, **provide social, religious and historical context** of the person/school of thought. This shows the marker the reasons **WHY** the person/school of thought contributed to the development and/or expression of the religion.

> **Example**
>
> "In reinforcing the authority of the authenticated Hadith, Al Shafi successfully improved access to reliable sources of information for greater submission to the will of Allah. *As a Salafi (a successor of a successor of Muhammad's companions), Al Shafi had an acute awareness to the need for reliable and authentic documentation of Muhammad's actions and words.* This extensive work promoted the perfect actions of the Hadith to a pivotal source of authoritative meaning in Islam."
>
> **Explanation**
>
> The italicised sentence provides reason for why Al Shafi needed to change the way Muslims approach submission and practise and the the next sentence flows into the contribution made.

ETHICS

You need to explain the ethical TEACHING, not the ethical ISSUE. For reference, in bioethics you need to talk about the *"sanctity of human life"* rather than the issue of *abortion*. To achieve this, explain the importance of the teaching and how that teaching influences an adherent. Try to do some research on how ethical teachings are being used in the modern world to maximise your marks.

> **Example:**
>
> "For the pertinent issue of abortion, the sanctity of human life guides adherents to make ethical decisions regarding the call of

> God. The sanctity of human life is derived from the belief that "humankind was made in the image and likeness of God" (Genesis 1:27). In recognition of this, Christians understand all decisions must respect human life as this reflects honour to a transcendent God who the person in a manifestation of. This strict adherence to biblical ethics is centralised for traditional Churches such as Catholicism and Greek Orthodoxy that affirm this teaching as intrinsic and vital to any decision of abortion. Due to the NSW Parliamentary debate on abortion, many recent statements including one from Catholic Archbishop Fisher highlighted that the sanctity of life must be priortised in taking a strong stance against abortion. This lends itself to reflect the Christian belief that human life begins at conception. As a result, abortion is prohibited and tantamount to evil as it challenges an understanding that all human life is sacred for these particular denominations."

Notice how I explain the application of the ethical teaching to abortion rather than explaining what abortion is. Always:

1. Find an ethical teaching and apply it to an issue.
2. Back it up with at least one sacred text quote.
3. Reference variant differences or features - not all will view an ethical issue with the same lens.

SIGNIFICANT PRACTICE

You don't need to memorise the entire practise to receive good marks. Instead, find 3-4 main events or features within the practise that you can describe, link to the principal beliefs and analyse the significance for both the individual and community. I recommend creating a table like the one below to cover all aspects of the syllabus.

Describe	Principal Belief	Individual	Community
Ketubah Marriage Contract	1. Mirrors the Covenant – outlines obligations of the Chatan to the Kallah like God and the Chosen 2. Affirmation that the mitzvah are fulfilled	1. Physical indication of a union that forms a whole under the guidance of God 2. **Genesis 2:20**: man should cherish woman 3. Security + drawn closer to God 4. Assigns new roles and responsibilities 5. *When husband is worthy, the Devine Presence abides with them" – Talmud*	1. Links generations – all united by divinely inspired law 2. Minyan: requisite 10 people to have a marriage – relationship with the community to support and guide the relationship alongside God

Question deconstruction

To finish off, let's just look at a sample question and how to approach it.

> *"I am the light of the world. He who follows me shall not walk in darkness, but have the light of life."- John 8:12*
>
> Explain how ONE *significant person* OR *school of thought, other than Jesus, has guided adherents to live a life that imitates Christ?*

Straight away, your immediate reaction should be to look at the directive term, the stimulus and what the question is actually asking. The task really is only found in the last clause of the question- it's about adherents emulating Christ and how they have been influenced by the significant person.

The given directive term is *explain,* which, according to NESA, means to *"relate cause and effect."* Therefore, you must provide clear examples and evidence of not only what the significant person has done, but also its implications for real world people, movements or organisations today. Simply recounting their contribution is not enough here as it does not answer the directive verb.

The stimulus is a quote from the Gospel of John which outlines the significance that following Christ has for an adherent; i.e. they *"have the light of life."* Think critically what this means, define it and explain it. Think, what does a Christian adherent do that demonstrates they possess this *"light"*?

Ensure that when a stimulus is provided, you also continually integrate it throughout your response.

Another unofficial rule is to always begin a response with a thesis statement. That is, a sentence or two that directly answers the given question. For this question, I would write something along the lines of:

> *Through their writings, theology and actions, many significant people have guided Christian adherents to live a life in emulation of Christ. St Paul of Tarsus is one example of an individual who has utilised Christian epistles and missionary journeys to instil this guidance, and in turn directed adherents to "not walk in darkness, but have the light of life."*

In my opening two sentences, I have directly answered the question, addressed the directive, introduced my significant person and integrated the stimulus. This is what you should also aim to do in your responses. I personally believe that the thesis statement is the most important section in the whole response. This informs the marker of your position on the topic and must be sustained throughout the rest of the response.

Depth Study Essays

A way to cut down study time is to choose a religion to write in Section III (the essay) prior to the exam. This is not advised by many teachers as you can be caught out by a difficult question on the day.

However, in saying that, if you know your chosen religion back to front and prepare for all possible questions you increase your chance of formulating a succinct and creative essay.

Do not forget your Year 11 Preliminary Content. SOR is one of the few subjects where knowledge of the preliminary syllabus is a must. Refresh yourself on **sacred texts, principal beliefs and ethical teachings** before starting your depth studies. These MUST be referenced both implicitly and explicitly in your responses, as a religion cannot function without these cornerstones.

Something I learnt the hard way is that there is NO one way to structure a SOR essay. In some of my essays I would have three long body paragraphs and in others I would have eight small ones. It's about finding what works well and what is logical to you. It can be structured chronologically, by central ideas or by main features. If it is logical and flows, any way that you can argue well will receive good marks. Find what works for you and be flexible!

A thing I want to share which is too often left out of HSC guides and articles is the emergence of INTEGRATED QUESTIONS, requiring all parts of the syllabus to be referenced. Since the 2013 HSC, there has been a rise in essay questions with generic wording.

> **Q: How does Christianity guide its adherents to follow in the footsteps of Jesus Christ and respond to the call of the Bible?**
>
> Firstly, the question above does not reference a main dot point in the Depth Study syllabus, so you NEED to reference ALL parts of the syllabus (significant person + ethics + practise).
>
> You can write three independent paragraphs (one on each part of the syllabus), but you cannot access the highest marks this way as you cannot capture enough detail in a single paragraph. In recognition that religion is holistic and integrated, the greatest success is finding links between the syllabus

The main way I did this was through a central idea. Create a mind map like the one below to see the links. Get creative and trust your instincts. If you can prove your reasoning with sacred texts, you maximise your marks. For Judaism below, the central idea was the covenant, as this is central in practise and belief.

An example of this in writing:

"Through Baptism, Christians derive the power of the Holy Spirit to aid the uncertainty inherent to modern bioethical issues. In reflecting a Christian's belief in the Triune God, Baptism bestows the Holy Spirit to dwell within each Christian and provide spiritual direction from the outset of initiation. In witnessing the power of the Holy Spirit, Christians derive the ethical teaching that human beings are temples of the Holy Spirit as "you are a temple of God with the Spirit of God living in you" (1 Corinthians 3:16). In this manner, Christians recognise that the bioethical issue of euthanasia is prohibited as it exhausts the strength of the Holy Spirit to strengthen and guide a Christian throughout life's challenges and uncertainty."

In the extract, I have linked a practise with ethics. This is not a complete paragraph, but it includes:

1. Baptism - a significant practise in Christianity
2. Principal Belief - the Triune God as a foundational belief
3. Ethical Teaching - human beings are temples of the Holy Spirit
4. Ethical Issue - euthanasia

Another way to attack these integrated questions is through the principal beliefs. In some way, shape or form, every practise or person is motivated by the core beliefs of the religion. So, each paragraph can revolve around a belief.

Also remember that your response does not have to be an exhaustive description. Finding a quote by your school of thought/significant person on ethics or the practise shows to the marker that you have gone above and beyond. While fleshing it out further will maximise your marks, simple links enhance your writing immensely.

Remember, no way is the correct way, and some ways are harder than others. While it might be stressful and tiring, practise your own way and read your classmates. Finding new and improved ways to answer these questions is at the heart of a really good essay.

Religion and Peace Essay (SOR2)

This part of the syllabus defines a 2-unit student. Peace is NOT just the absence of war. It is a holistic and extensive experience of tranquility, balance and freedom. If you just write an essay on how religions guide adherents to not start or enter a war, you will receive a maximum mark of 12/20 (if that!). It is capturing the removal of resentment, the outlook to betterment and service to another person that truly encompasses how religions guide peace.

You are only required to write an essay for Peace. Therefore, you should not be preparing for short answers. You should develop a system (e.g. flowcharts, mind maps, tables) to capture how sacred texts inform an understanding of peace and then how that filters into inner and outer world contributions.

I used a flow-chart system to capture this and then moved onto paragraph planning to be concise. I found preparing paragraph plans to be the best and most comforting option. It gave me an idea of what I was going to write, whilst still affording me flexibility and adaptability.

For structure, I would have a central idea and then include quotes, examples, reports and scholar opinions to back up my response. This is where memorisation is key. Your marks come from using this information to show that your religion is a sustainer and promoter of peace. In an essay, I would aim for 4 paragraphs.

Principle Teaching	**Agape** → a sacrificial, unconditional love which is at the core of Christianity
Understanding	→ Human support/dignity can culminate in greater peace than the individual
Scared Texts	→ *"Love one another as I loved you"* – *John 13:34* love in tantamount to Jesus w/o constraint or external pressure
	→ *"The fruit of the spirit is love, joy, peace"* (Galatians 5:22) – intrinsic value of peace is within Christians as humanity are temples of the Holy Spirit
Inner	→ Love of self alleviates stress and resentment that can lead to an imbalance
World	→ Palm Sunday Marches across the world embody love – focus on refugees and asylum seekers to share in love.
	→ Largest religion in the world currently → imperative for Christianity to spread the notion of agape and strengthen the contribution to world peace.

Conclusion

The last thing I want is for students to think that SOR is a subject far too complicated and that high marks are unattainable. In fact, I truly believe it's the opposite. From everything I have written, it may seem like there are so many criteria to fulfil. However, I promise you that if you start practicing these skills early they will become second nature. Many things in SOR are 'tick-a-box' (such needing to reference variants or integrate a stimulus). These are things that you must do to get a high-level response.

I wish you the best of luck over the coming year. It only takes a few weeks to build a habit, so start a routine. Never forget to give yourself time to relax, but also find what motivates you and set some goals. You will do great!

Julia's Studies of Religions Cheat Sheet

QUOTATIONS - Use sacred texts and writings as often as possible. While this takes extra memorisation, they do boost your writing and validate your argument.

TOPIC SENTENCES - Always introduce your argument with a topic sentence. Don't get stressed over the typical English-style paragraph, just let your writing flow after a strong topic sentence.

VARIANT DIFFERENCE – This provides so much depth to your response. To access a Band 6, you need to show how different variants of a religion approach a belief or practise.

EXPLAIN EVERYTHING - SOR markers WANT you to explain the features and details. Writing one more sentence explaining the influence of religion on the adherent will create a better response.

PRELIM CONTENT - is a must. Referencing a principal belief or ethic is expected by the syllabus and will maximise your marks instantly.

READ THE QUESTION - Questions no longer look exactly like the syllabus dot points. You need to take a minute to read the question and work out what it is asking of you. It is far better to lose one minute reading the question rather than five minutes and five marks for writing the wrong thing.

STIMULUS - If there is stimulus, you MUST reference and explain it. If you do not, you will not be able to access the highest marks. Often, the stimulus will guide your response. Further, if there are two stimuli, both need to be referenced.

Most importantly, please remember throughout this year that:

- It is one year of your life, so give it your all. (The holidays at the end of the HSC are worth it!)

- You are not the first person to sit the HSC. If millions of kids can get through it, so can you.

Chris' Studies of Religions Cheat Sheet

- Integrate evidence into your responses.
- Be selective and judicious in your evidence choices. Don't just settle.
- Don't toss in evidence. Integrate the quote into your sentence and ensure it flows.
- Never provide a quote without referencing where it comes from.
- Use different forms of evidence.. For example, use sacred text, scholars, statistics and religious leaders.
- Don't be vague in your writing. Use specific terminology relevant to your depth study - even if it is in another language.
- Make sophisticated links back to the principal beliefs of the faith where possible.
- Integrate a stimulus when one is provided.
- Always start your response with a detailed, specific and relevant thesis statement.
- Sustain your thesis throughout your response.

Good luck!!!

Bonus International Baccalaureate Chapter:
Keep it interesting

By Sarah Kanuk

"Stay interesting." —*My Year 12 English Teacher*

Introduction

The 'High School Experience' can be daunting or exciting, stressful or inspiring, soul-sucking or enriching. My name is Sarah Kanuk and I attended Kambala School for Girls. Throughout my final years, I undertook the ACTs (American College Testing), the SATs (American Scholastic Aptitude Test), four SAT subject tests, and the International Baccalaureate (IB) Diploma Program (DP). On top of this, I tackled a TEFL course to qualify me to teach English as a foreign language, competed internationally as part of the Australia Shotokan Karate Team, played in several musical ensembles, performed in the school musical, and held a casual job. I graduated in 2019 with the aim of pursuing tertiary education in the United States. I hope that I can provide some advice on approaching formal education in general, as well as finding opportunities outside of the classroom.

My motivation over Year 12 and beyond came from my English teacher. She was my mentor for my IB Extended Essay, and we formed a strong friendship over our discussions of literature, life, and politics.

She told me how she had seen students spend all of their energy worrying about the final high school exams. Despite these students gaining incredible marks, they lost their personality. From her, I found my new motto: "Stay interesting."

General Advice

1. Motivation and Memory

Many people I've spoken to have told me that their mindset throughout Year 12 was something along the lines of: "I'm on the home stretch. I just need to push through. It will be over soon, and then I will feel so much better."

While I believe that there is a time for this, I don't think that this source of motivation is sustainable, nor do I think it's a good way to approach education. This source relies on the assumption that learning is a chore, whereas I prefer to approach education as a privilege and as a way to both make myself more interesting and to discover things about the world . I've found that convincing myself to be excited about learning, and even excited about studying, is a more sustainable and more effective approach to Year 12.

How do you do this? You chose your subjects, so remind yourself why. What about your subject is exciting to you? How can you incorporate it into your life? Manufacture passion if you must; our brain is powerful enough to convince ourselves of anything. This will help with both your motivation and your memory. Attention and rehearsal of information is required to convert short term memory into the long term store (Atkinson & Shiffrin, 1968). By choosing courses you are interested in, you are more likely to pay attention to and acquire the information by incorporating it into your life, you are promoting its casual rehearsal. Thus, you are more likely to remember information relevant to your course, and this is before we've even approached formal study.

I'll break down this method by applying it to some of the IB subjects that I took:

Politics

I started bringing up the essay topics at the dinner table, and I set up monthly dinners with politically-minded friends where we discussed our opinions on the coursework. By discussing the topic so frequently and in a fun way, I was better able to write my essays and remember the subject.

Moreover, I found a TV show (Hasan Minhaj's *The Patriot Act*) that explored political issues in a fun, engaging, and well-researched way to study for this subject. This meant that I would remember an impressive amount of information, allowing me to justify watching 5 hours of a TV show on a Monday night! My essays demonstrated great depth and breadth of knowledge, even though I was mostly quoting a TV show and linking it back to the topic in question.

Chemistry

The kindest, most unassuming girl in my class had an incredible method for remembering Chemistry: she would try and find a way that she could use each topic to kill someone. It should be noted that this is the very same girl who releases cockroaches into the garden instead of crushing them. While she would never kill someone, this is how she kept the subject matter fresh, exciting, and memorable. Find your method of murder!

Psychology

I could apply most of these lessons to myself and my self-improvement, and understanding the world around me. By approaching a lesson with the mindset of "How can I use this to better my life?", you pay a lot more attention.

French

I found a reason to love the French culture: almost every French person I've met is ready to talk politics at any given time. By starting political debates with my newfound French friends, my French improved dramatically. I also started reading my favourite books and watching my favourite movies in French. Suddenly things that were "procrastination" were justified and helpful.

Literature

I'm particularly interested in politics and philosophy, and so I would try and find how the text I was reading linked back to my interests. What was Shakespeare's opinion on objective versus subjective morality? What was he trying to tell us about the political tensions of his time?

Moreover, my literature teacher once told me that everything is about sex or death. While this was probably a joke, I took it to heart and it helped me greatly in the initial analysis of any text.

Mathematics

Also known as advanced Sudoku. This topic needs so much practice, so slip it into anywhere you would do Candy Crush: on the bus, in front of the tv, procrastinating Chemistry, etc.

2. Maintaining Balance

Don't lose yourself to studying. I did this briefly in Year 11. I started wondering if I was anything more than a regurgitating store of information, all of which could be found in a textbook. I started to become the guy in the bar from *Good Will Hunting* who Matt Damon eviscerates for both his lack of personality and individual thought. Interestingly, while I was doing very well in my subjects, I was becoming less happy, less excited about life, and less motivated to study.

Everyone needs an escape from study. I found that my life needed every area to be balanced in order for my sanity to survive the hectic combination of academics, exercise, social life, creative expression and the rest. I also included a scheduled work shift every week.

Below is my weekly schedule* in Year 12:

Monday:

- 5:45-7:45: exercise (gym)
- 8:30-15:20: academic (school)
- 15:30-16:30: creative (orchestra)
- 17:00-19:15: academic (study)
- 19:30-21:00: exercise (karate)

Tuesday:

- 5:45-7:45: exercise (gym)
- 8:30-15:20: academic (school)
- 15:30-17:00: creative (orchestra)
- 17:30-18:30: academic (study)
- 19:30-20:30: academic (study)

Wednesday:

- 5:45-6:45: exercise (gym)
- 7:20-8:30: creative (jazz orchestra)
- 8:30-15:20: academic (school)
- 15:50-17:00: rest
- 17:00-18:30: academic (study)
- 19:30-20:30: academic (study)

Thursday:

- 5:45-7:45: exercise (gym)
- 8:30-15:20: academic (school)

- 15:50-16:30: rest
- 16:30-19:15: academic (study)
- 19:30-21:00: exercise (karate)

Friday:

- 5:45-7:45: exercise (gym)
- 8:30-15:20: academic (school)
- 15:50+: rest/socialising

Saturday:

- 7:00-8:30: exercise (karate)
- 8:30-9:30: socialising (karate breakfast)
- 10:00-14:00: academic (study)
- 18:00+: socialising

Sunday:

- 8:00-18:30: work (part time job)
- 19:00+: rest (homework if necessary)

*My online TEFL course was done in sporadic 5-hour chunks, often in the middle of the night. Additionally, I was often open to spontaneous socializing, and would adjust my schedule for that week accordingly. For example, my friends and I had a habit of meeting at a 24-hour café after a particularly stressful day. On the morning after these nights I would sleep instead of exercise. Tune in to your body to make sure that you don't overwork yourself.

This schedule worked well for me through Year 12. In the final two months before my exams, I stopped all extracurriculars except Tuesday orchestra and morning exercise. My weekends were full of study, and the nights' socialising events were tamer so I could study the next morning.

3. Exercise

I found exercise to be my most important asset in Year 12. I exercised for several reasons:

- **To escape from a loud mind.** It's very hard to think about your chemistry homework when you're in a fight. Karate required concentration that took me away from my academic world so that my mind could rest and rejuvenate.
- **To have a stress output.** Year 12 can be stressful and throughout it adrenaline runs high, especially around exam season. Exercising kept me calm throughout the year because it released my high-stress energy and adrenaline.
- **To create an energy source.** Due to my commitment to several extracurriculars, the studying I squeezed into the gaps and the socializing I did by night, I was exhausted. I was falling asleep in class, tuning out of almost every conversation and failing to efficiently complete tasks. While quitting some extracurricular activities or socializing less in order to get more sleep was an option, I wanted an alternative. I found that exercising before my day, taking a cold shower and then drinking a double shot coffee was giving me more energy than that extra 2 hours of sleep. Counterintuitively, I cut some sleep to replace with exercises, and I was more awake throughout the day.
- **To put my brain into "memory mode".** I would take textbooks and flashcards onto the elliptical and read them as I worked out. I found that my recall of this information improved dramatically when I did this. I looked like an idiot, but at least I was an educated idiot!

Study Advice

1. Note-taking

Step 1: Get down important information you find during class in any way that you can. I did this on a computer using Google Drive, because I loved sharing notes with my friends/peers. I was also very afraid of my computer crashing, and I wanted to be able to access my notes from any device.

Step 2: I used the Cornell Note Taking system. A template can be found both below and online. I both handwrote and typed these notes. I wrote because this helped my recollection of content, and I typed because I tend to lose everything. The process also allowed me to reinforce the information in my memory.

These notes would be written at home or during a free period after a lesson. I first typed and then wrote so I could edit the concise sentences easily. These would be made considering the information I learned in class, information from my friends' notes, the wording of the relevant syllabus point, the textbook and online sources. I needed to completely understand the topic, know how much information I needed and how to use it before I wrote these notes.

Cue side includes:	Note side:
• key words • headings • main ideas • possible exam questions	• the content • concise sentences • diagrams
	Summary of the content

Step 3: I would summarize the content extremely carefully so that I could fit each syllabus point on one flashcard. This is not supposed to be easy. The act of summarising forces you to both understand the content and simultaneously revise it. The flashcard does not need to be legible to anyone else (you can use abbreviations and symbols as long as you can translate it back into exam language when you need to).

2. Study Blocks:

I go insane if I study for two hours straight. My concentration decreases, I get fidgety and I stop processing information.

I developed a system** of studying for a long time, while working efficiently:

1. 45-60 mins studying
2. Make a cup of tea
3. 50 sit ups
4. 45-60 mins studying
5. 15 mins break
6. Repeat

**This being said, practice papers should be completed under exam conditions and therefore without break. This system and my weekly study schedule which was outlined previously are guidelines for studying. I worked more efficiently when I had task-based goals instead of home-based ones. That is to say, my mindset was "I will finish this syllabus point before my break," instead of "I'll study for 45 minutes." However, if the syllabus point took 2 hours, I would take a brief break during this period whenever I started to feel drowsy.

3. Past papers

1. Complete under exam conditions.
2. Use a different colour pen and go over the exam with an open book to fill in missing information and mark your work.
3. Use the marking rubric to mark your work from Step 1, then again for Step 2.
4. Write down the things you need to work on.
5. If you can, hand this in to your teacher. Otherwise, give it to a peer whose opinion you trust.

4. Exam day

Night before

I knew my course by this point. I was comfortable with the paper's formats. Just to make myself comfortable and assure myself that I knew the content, I would skim read the entire textbook with a highlighter. I picked a fictional character who was a genius with a good memory (Mike Ross from *Suits*) and I pretended I was him. The information was fresh in my mind for the next day.

Prioritise sleep over finishing the textbook if you can't finish it by 21:00. You know the content, whether or not you read it again.

Morning of the exam

Develop an exam routine throughout the year that you use before any school-administered exam, and even before some self-administered practice tests. Using this same routine before your final exams will assure you that you are simply going through the same motions that you have been over the last year. The final exam is just another past paper, except one that nobody has ever sat before.

My pre-exam routine involved the following:

1. Fruit smoothie
2. Half an hour of light weight/body weight exercises at the gym.
3. An hour on the elliptical machine. I would read my flashcards for the first half hour, then I would increase the resistance and listen to music to eliminate all stressful energy for the second half hour.
4. Forty five minutes to shower, change, and walk up to school.
5. An hour before the exam I would be at school, eating my comfort food and chatting with friends.

If I had an exam early in the morning, I would skip the smoothie, and the second part of the cardio would be 15 minutes of sprinting on the treadmill.

If I had multiple exams in a day with sufficient break between them, I would go for a 15 minute run around school between them. I would then read the flashcards and eat my food in the common room at school.

If there wasn't a sufficient break, I would eat a couple bites of my food (it was super comforting for me) and focus on relaxing.

At the exam room

I finished my routine. I went to the bathroom. I checked to make sure that I had all the materials I needed for the exam.

I avoided people that seemed stressed. I found my friends. We smiled reassuringly. We didn't talk about the content.

Advice for Inside the Exam

- Relax
- Highlight key words
- Use subject-specific vocabulary
- Assume the markers are idiots. Explain everything. Point out painfully obvious steps, implications and conclusions.
- Use short sentences to ensure clarity.
- Show off what you know, so long as this information relates to the question.
- Link everything back to the question.
- I had difficulty writing quickly. To help, I bounced my knee inaudibly to a beat. This helped me to keep pace.

- For short answer questions and math tests, divide the time by the number of marks of which the test is comprised. This should guide how you manage your time.

Outside of school

School has opportunities for challenge and diversity in intellectual pursuit. It also allows you to build a network in your cohort, and you can use school to set yourself up for a successful life after. For many people, this is enough to satiate their interests over the course of Year 12. However, I, personally, wanted to expand my interests, my network and my intellectual pursuits outside of school. This is how I did that.

1. Mindset: Say 'Yes'

In Year 9, I was bored with my routine so I made this commitment to myself which has lasted to this day. *Say "yes" to everything* (within reason). This led to a few incredibly embarrassing attempts at theatre, my attendance of an underground bunker rave, a meal of bile and rat stew in a small village in Laos, as well as many more strange events too long to list here. This challenge also led to me receiving a scholarship I didn't imagine I could ever receive, meeting people I thought were unreachable, and becoming passionate about topics I thought I would hate. Most of the time, the path I tried was a dead end, but the experiences were always worthwhile, and the incredible opportunities I took were worth a few embarrassing moments.

Everything will be okay, no matter what (so long as it isn't life-threatening). It's clichéd, but for a reason. I used to fear rejection, which limited the opportunities that I could chase. To remedy this, I gave myself exposure therapy. I'd go to stores and ask for unreasonable things. For example, "May I please have a free cup of coffee?" Obviously, they'd reject me. It was a ridiculous task, but upon each repetition, I didn't care so much. Rejection became normal and expected. So, when a scholarship to some space camp was advertised at my school, I figured that it was another opportunity to practice getting rejected. Amazingly, I wasn't.

This same method works for the fear of social rejection. I started talking to strangers everywhere: on public transport, at the coffee shop, in the uber. Not everyone responded well, and I became comfortable with being rejected in this way. However, I also learned how to meet people, find out what they're interested in, and learn something from there. An unexpected bonus was that, after a while, there was rarely a week that went by without some person approaching me on the street asking, "Don't I know you from somewhere?"

I was also afraid of being ridiculed for trying something and failing. This fear was alleviated as I used my plethora of embarrassing stories as icebreakers, or ways to make my friends laugh. If something goes wrong, think: "This is going to be a good story."

2. Talk to people
Casually

You don't know who is around you. Smile at the barista, chat to your customers at work, talk to the person sitting next to you. From this alone, I was offered an internship at an aerospace engineering company in California. I learned how to travel for six months for under $5000, found part time work after school and made friends all over the world. By talking to people, you are making your own opportunities.

(this section is more 'life advice', not sure how relevant it is in the context of CUTWA but still go advice :)

Question Time

Say you're attending a lecture/presentation and you want to form a connection with the speaker. I did this through asking questions.

Principles of a good question:

- Relevant to the presentation/lecture.
- Has not already been answered in the presentation.
- Cannot be Googled (why are you asking *them* in particular?).
- Demonstrates that you have understood the concepts already addressed.
- Makes the presenter think.

Some types of questions include:

- Demonstrated interest/advice: "As a successful diplomat, what advice would you give someone interested in pursuing diplomacy?"
- ***Respectful counterarguments: "How powerful can diplomacy be when it can be destroyed so easily, as in the case of the photo of US soldiers abusing Vietnamese citizens during the Vietnam War, and takes years to build?"
- Comparison questions: "Do you think soft power is more or less effective than hard power for the US?"
- Application questions: "How does [this concept] apply to [this situation]?"
- Clarification question on their particular area of expertise (this works better if it's a difficult concept, there aren't many questions being asked, and there is no assumed knowledge).

*** This is the best.

When to ask question:

- After the lecture, walk up to the lecturer and say, "Hi. My name is __ and I'm from [your school]. I loved your presentation. I have a question I didn't get a chance to ask before. I was wondering…"

- If they're unavailable, email them. Be sure to include the name and date of the presentation.

- If there are not many people asking questions during question time and there are awkward pauses when no one has a question, ask then.

- Always email a follow up question. If you don't have a good one, send a gratitude email.

3. Reaching out

Adults generally love the prospect of inspiring aspiring teenagers. They've all seen *Good Will Hunting* and *The Dead Poets Society*. I am yet to meet an adult who doesn't want to be a Robin Williams character. If you make them believe that they are, you have yourself a mentor. Similarly, if you make someone feel like they're your hero, and that you're bright enough to blossom under them, they will want to help you.

So send an email to the person you want to reach. Tell them who you are, give them a reason to respect you, convey that you're the type of person they want to grab lunch with, and show genuine interest in them and their work. Have fun.

Final words

Year 12 is really what you want it to be. If you're expecting stress, you'll get it. If you want to have a good time, you will. If you can make your goals fun and exciting for yourself, as well as the inevitable low points less daunting and less impactful, you're more likely to have a successful Year 12 IB experience.

Small Worlds: A Conclusion

High school is what I like to call a 'small world.' In many ways, it is an all-consuming experience, particularly in the lead up to final exams. It becomes the only thing that you can think about, the only thing that matters – that little number which so defines and shapes your future reality. By the time of my final exam, my memorised essays had begun to invade my dreams!

Now you can wage the argument that everyone has outlets away from school, and I tend to agree. Things like friends, sport, Netflix, video games and other activities you tell your parents are 'co-curricular' all provide an escape from this scholastic reality. However, the fact is, that your life in these years is mostly defined by your schooling experience. You attend for five days every week, and, when you include the recommended hours of study, almost two thirds of your waking life are consumed by this process of learning.

What I have painted so far is a very bleak picture of a high school quotidian. Indeed, I would not feel maligned if your response was 'you mustn't have been invited to many parties.' The point that I am so verbosely trying to make returns me to my first line--that high school is a 'small world.' An existence consumed primarily by learning, not experience.

I read Orwell, Ishiguro and Yeats, learnt about Hindenburg, Lenin and MacArthur. War crimes, human rights and indigenous issues dominated my Legal Studies class, and Mathematics taught me the basic language of the universe. In Drama, my re-imagining of Shakespeare leant me a deeper understanding of the importance of art in shaping our perspectives within the real world, a way of elucidating and criticising the 'dream' of existence.

These lessons ranged in my limited perspective from fickle, abstract and arbitrary to intriguing, informative and downright inspiring. Yet it is only now, after a year out of school, that the content of these messages take the shape of their enduring relevance. Not in the form of essays, dates or equations, but in the very lens through which I view the world.

Einstein wrote that "education is what remains after one forgets what they have learnt in school." Your schooling experience teaches you how to see society, how to treat people, and, perhaps most importantly, how to learn.

As I sit here now, on an aeroplane over a vacuum black ocean transporting me from Austria to Iceland, the perspective that I gathered in my education is what has allowed me to navigate this experience with passion, awe, interest and care. The Australian education system values free thinking above all else, and I have taken this with me on my gap year with an open mind and an open heart. It is easy for us to take this for granted. However, when backpacking through the Balkan State of Bosnia and Herzegovina, I saw how fortunate we are firsthand.

To have grown up in a society that values your individualism, that wants to prepare you best for this rapidly changing world and gives you unprecedented social and economic opportunities, you have already won the lottery. You owe it to both yourself and everyone else who does not have the same opportunities to learn to the best of your ability, to apply yourself and open doors with such dedication.

From my ATAR mark, I managed to procure both a scholarship to university and a position as a private tutor in Austria. These are the tangible results, but they are far outweighed by their social benefits that have been informed by the lessons taken from this 'small world' into the far bigger one that we all live in. Tattooed to my passport have been the philosophies and facts alike discussed in the academic forum of High School, the diatribe spilled onto my essay pages shaping conversation at 5am deep in the Albanian mountains.

Now, I am more aware than anyone that not everything that you learn at school is directly relevant. The facts and figures will fade, but the lessons of how to learn, how to apply yourself and how to express your vision of the world lucidly can never be forgotten.

As such, I hope that, at the end of this book and its highly specific advice, that you do not forget to keep in mind the bigger picture. Realise that what you are doing this for is not arbitrary. Instead, it is the doorway to the rest of your life. The mark you receive becomes less and less important as time goes on, but the lessons learnt will always endure.

Good luck!

End Note

If you are in an emergency situation or need immediate assistance, contact mental health services or emergency services on 000.

- **Lifeline**
  13 11 14 (24 hour crisis hotline)
  www.lifeline.org.au

- **Kids Help Line**
  1800 55 1800
  Online counselling available at www.kidshelpline.com.au

- **Mensline**
  1300 78 99 78
  www.mensline.org.au

- **Suicide Call Back Service**
  Free nationwide counselling 1300 659 467
  www.suicidecallbackservice.org.au

Also by Catch Up With Top Achievers:

Catch Up With Top Achievers: 2019 HSC Edition

Purchase *Catch Up With Top Achievers: 2019 HSC Edition* directly from our website Top-Achievers.com.au with a 10% discount using the coupon code 'TA2020'